T0185227

Cloud Debugging and Profiling in Microsoft Azure

Application Performance Management in the Cloud

Jeffrey Chilberto
Sjoukje Zaal
Gaurav Aroraa
Ed Price

Apress®

Cloud Debugging and Profiling in Microsoft Azure: Application Performance Management in the Cloud

Jeffrey Chilberto
Auckland, New Zealand

Sjoukje Zaal
Lisse, The Netherlands

Gaurav Aroraa
Ghaziabad, India

Ed Price
Redmond, WA, USA

ISBN-13 (pbk): 978-1-4842-5436-3
https://doi.org/10.1007/978-1-4842-5437-0

ISBN-13 (electronic): 978-1-4842-5437-0

Copyright © 2020 by Jeffrey Chilberto, Sjoukje Zaal, Gaurav Aroraa and Ed Price

This work is subject to copyright. All rights are reserved by the Publisher, whether the whole or part of the material is concerned, specifically the rights of translation, reprinting, reuse of illustrations, recitation, broadcasting, reproduction on microfilms or in any other physical way, and transmission or information storage and retrieval, electronic adaptation, computer software, or by similar or dissimilar methodology now known or hereafter developed.

Trademarked names, logos, and images may appear in this book. Rather than use a trademark symbol with every occurrence of a trademarked name, logo, or image, we use the names, logos, and images only in an editorial fashion and to the benefit of the trademark owner, with no intention of infringement of the trademark.

The use in this publication of trade names, trademarks, service marks, and similar terms, even if they are not identified as such, is not to be taken as an expression of opinion as to whether or not they are subject to proprietary rights.

While the advice and information in this book are believed to be true and accurate at the date of publication, neither the authors nor the editors nor the publisher can accept any legal responsibility for any errors or omissions that may be made. The publisher makes no warranty, express or implied, with respect to the material contained herein.

Managing Director, Apress Media LLC: Welmoed Spahr
Acquisitions Editor: Smriti Srivastava
Development Editor: Laura Berendson
Coordinating Editor: Shrikant Vishwakarma

Cover designed by eStudioCalamar

Cover image designed by Freepik (www.freepik.com)

Distributed to the book trade worldwide by Springer Science+Business Media New York, 233 Spring Street, 6th Floor, New York, NY 10013. Phone 1-800-SPRINGER, fax (201) 348-4505, e-mail orders-ny@springer-sbm.com, or visit www.springeronline.com. Apress Media, LLC is a California LLC and the sole member (owner) is Springer Science+Business Media Finance Inc (SSBM Finance Inc). SSBM Finance Inc is a Delaware corporation.

For information on translations, please e-mail rights@apress.com, or visit www.apress.com/rights-permissions.

Apress titles may be purchased in bulk for academic, corporate, or promotional use. eBook versions and licenses are also available for most titles. For more information, reference our Print and eBook Bulk Sales web page at www.apress.com/bulk-sales.

Any source code or other supplementary material referenced by the author in this book is available to readers on GitHub via the book's product page, located at www.apress.com/9781484254363. For more detailed information, please visit www.apress.com/source-code.

Printed on acid-free paper

To my family, whose love and support give me strength and purpose.

—Jeffrey Chilberto

To my younger brother, Amit Kumar, who taught me to remain hopeful, even in situations that are not favorable.

—Gaurav Aroraa

To the Azure development community: Thank you for your dedication, passion, and innovation, as we seek to build a collaborative ecosystem of tools and resources.

—Ed Price

Table of Contents

About the Authors

Jeffrey Chilberto is a software consultant specializing in the Microsoft technical stack, including Azure, BizTalk, MVC, WCF, and SQL Server. He has enterprise development experience in a wide range of industries, including banking, telecommunications, and health care, in the United States, Europe, Australia, and New Zealand.

Sjoukje Zaal is a managing consultant, Microsoft Cloud architect, and Microsoft Azure MVP, with more than 15 years' experience providing architecture, development, consultancy, and design expertise. She works at Capgemini, a global leader in consulting, technology services, and digital transformation.

Gaurav Aroraa is a serial entrepreneur and startup mentor. He holds an MPhil in computer science and is a Microsoft MVP award recipient. He is a lifetime member of the Computer Society of India (CSI), an advisory member and senior mentor of IndiaMentor, certified as a Scrum trainer/coach, ITIL-F certified, and PRINCE-F & PRINCE-P certified. He is an open source developer and contributor to the Microsoft TechNet community. Gaurav was named "Icon of the year—excellence in mentoring technology startups" for 2018–19 by Radio City—a Jagran Initiative, for his extraordinary work spanning a 22-year career in the field of technology mentoring.

ABOUT THE AUTHORS

Ed Price, a senior program manager in engineering at Microsoft, holds an MBA in technology management. He ran Microsoft customer feedback programs for Azure Development and Visual Studio. He also was a technical writer at Microsoft for six years and helped lead TechNet Wiki. He now leads efforts to publish key guidance from AzureCAT (Customer Advisory Team).

About the Technical Reviewer

Samuel Rowe is a technologist specializing in application innovation and problem-solving. An agile advocate with extensive experience in DevOps and cloud practices, he is currently employed at Microsoft as a solution architect, having worked previously for IBM and CodeWeavers.

Acknowledgments

Life teaches each of us in its own way. Sometimes its lessons are difficult to understand, and sometimes you don't find support. I am among the lucky ones who is blessed with a lovely and supportive family, which always inspires and supports me. My wife, Shuby Arora, and my little angel daughter, Aarchi Arora, permitted me to steal time for this book, which I should have spent with them. Thanks to the entire Apress team, especially Shrikant, whose coordination and communication during the period of writing this book was tremendous. Special thanks to our technical reviewer, Samuel Rowe, for all of his valuable suggestions, which improved and polished the contents. Thanks also to my fellow coauthors, Ed Price, Jeffrey Chilberto, and Sjoukje Zaal, for their support in completing the book.

—Gaurav Aroraa

Introduction

Cloud Debugging and Profiling in Microsoft Azure is both a primer and handbook for working in Azure. Every organization's and individual's adoption and experience of cloud-based software development is unique, so this book aims to strike a balance between providing content relevant to introductory users as well as more experienced ones. As the many services and features of Azure are constantly evolving, it is not possible to provide a manual addressing all aspects of Azure, so this book highlights some of the more common features, including samples of services from the major categories: Functions as a Service (FaaS), Software as a Service (SaaS), Platform as a Service (PaaS), Infrastructure as a Service (IaaS), and Database as a Service (DaaS).

To aid in the discussion of the many topics, a fictitious company's journey through Azure is used to illustrate how cloud adoption can benefit many enterprises. The journey involves moving many on-premises components to similar Azure services, as well as highlighting some of the benefits and advanced tooling offered as part of the Azure ecosystem.

This book is for developers and DevOps engineers looking for insight into the complexities of distributed systems and the features available, to enable a better understanding of how to profile and debug cloud-based solutions in Azure.

CHAPTER 1

Building Solutions in the Azure Cloud

There are many different facets and considerations for developing on Microsoft Azure. This chapter discusses why and how building for the cloud differs from on-premises development. It introduces you to different terms that will be explored further as we explain their blades in the Azure portal, including Function as a Service (FaaS), Software as a Service (SaaS), Platform as a Service (PaaS), and Infrastructure as a Service (IaaS). Then we will explain why you need a comprehensive strategy for debugging and profiling in Azure, as well as the basics of what that entails. Throughout the chapters, we will use a fictitious company to illustrate different scenarios, and in this chapter, we will introduce the company, its business objectives, and how we will use Azure to achieve them. The goal of this chapter is to provide a high-level view of development on Azure, as well as to set the tone of the book, in explaining an introductory perspective on debugging and profiling.

When considering how to profile and debug on Microsoft Azure, you should first explore all your options for building solutions in this cloud platform. This chapter discusses why and how building for the cloud differs from on-premises development. We'll progress through different terms that will be explained further in later chapters, including FaaS, SaaS, PaaS, and IaaS. Then we will show you why you'll require a comprehensive strategy for debugging and profiling in Azure, and we'll cover the general structure of that strategy.

© Jeffrey Chilberto, Sjoukje Zaal, Gaurav Aroraa and Ed Price 2020
J. Chilberto et al., *Cloud Debugging and Profiling in Microsoft Azure*,
https://doi.org/10.1007/978-1-4842-5437-0_1

Introduction to Microsoft Azure

Microsoft Azure is a collection of cloud services that is constantly improving and expanding to cover additional development and platform requirements, integrations, and deployments. Using the Azure cloud-computing infrastructure and platform, you can build, deploy, and manage your applications, services, and IT solutions in the cloud, using Microsoft's worldwide network of data centers. Microsoft manages more data centers (directly and with partners) than any other cloud service provider, which includes 54 regions worldwide, making Azure available in 140 countries (as of the writing of this book). More data centers results in an increasing scale, preserving data residency, compliance, resiliency, and global consistency.

With on-premises software development and deployment, enterprise companies hold the responsibility for building, maintaining, and upgrading all the layers and levels in their software and its underlying infrastructure. Microsoft Azure provides a massive library of services that gives you more options and control of your solution and software architecture, without the infrastructure maintenance.

Azure utilizes virtualization, which entails creating an emulation layer to map the software instructions to the hardware instructions. Through this process, the virtualized hardware executes in software as if it was the physical hardware. And then the user can run this virtualized hardware on the physical servers.

Services

As of this writing, Microsoft Azure is composed of more than 180 services and products. Those products are typically and currently broken down into 22 categories: AI + Machine Learning, Analytics, Blockchain, Compute, Containers, Databases, Developer Tools, DevOps, Hybrid, Identity, Integration, Internet of Things (IoT), Management and Governance, Media, Migration, Mixed Reality, Mobile, Networking, Security, Storage, Web, and Windows Virtual Desktop.

The following provides a summary of the different categories.

AI + Machine Learning

With machine learning, computers use data to forecast future events, including behaviors, outcomes, and trends. Computers can learn without being directly programmed for that learning outcome. For example, when you purchase an item at a store, machine learning can compare your purchase to all your previous purchases and all the similar purchases made by other customers, thus determining which coupons to give you, knowing which ones you're most likely to use.

Another example is predictive maintenance. You can use AI to predict future failures and then prevent them, to maximize the life and uptime of your product, service, app, or web site. You can minimize unscheduled equipment downtime and detect anomalies (such as when devices will fail). You can prevent expensive failures and outages.

Azure Machine Learning Services provides a scalable platform of model management. Azure Databricks leverages the Apache Spark analytics platform. Cognitive Services provides a library of API capabilities for contextual interactions (such as image-processing algorithms to identify, alter, and moderate photos). And Azure Bot Service allows you to build intelligent bots that interact naturally with users on web sites or in apps. There are 35 services in this category.

Analytics

Now that you have some data options, you must explore solutions that will transform that data into actionable insights. SQL Data Warehouse, Azure Databricks, and Machine Learning all provide analytics. There are 15 services in this category.

HDInsight is a managed Hadoop and Spark service. Data Factory is an integration service that orchestrates and automates your data movement. Stream Analytics provides real-time data stream processing, which can be from millions of IoT devices. Data Lake Analytics is on-demand and pay-per-job. Azure Analytics Services is an enterprise grade analytics engine.

Blockchain

Blockchain solutions provide a trusted means for organizations to collaborate without requiring a central authority. Azure Blockchain Service, Azure Blockchain Workbench, and Azure Blockchain Tokens are services to build and manage blockchain-based applications.

Compute

The services offered in Compute range across FaaS, IaaS, and PaaS services. As a FaaS service, Azure Functions provide serverless application development. Offering more control over the environment but letting the developer concentrate more on the application instead of the hardware, cloud services provide a scalable PaaS offering. IaaS services offer a wide range of virtual machines across Windows and Linux operating systems, with an assortment of base images. Later in this chapter, we will explore each category of cloud-based solutions.

Containers

Using containers is an effective way of bundling and managing applications that use OS-level virtualization to support efficient application isolation. Azure offers a range of services for managing and hosting containers, including the Azure Kubernetes Service, Container Instances, Service Fabric, Azure Container Registry, and Web App for Containers.

Databases

Azure has more than 10 fully managed database services that free you from managing a database. You can scale quickly and distribute globally, without experiencing downtime. SQL Database is a fully managed relational database that provisions and scales very quickly. You can find similar high-availability and security in Azure Database for MySQL, as well as Azure Database for PostgreSQL.

Cosmos DB is multi-model and supports NoSQL. Or you can use virtual machines to host enterprise SQL Server apps. SQL Data Warehouse is an elastic data warehouse with security built into every level of scale. For an exhaustive architectural tour of Azure data options, see the Azure Data Architecture Guide on the Azure Architecture Center web site (`http://aka.ms/DataArchitecture`).

Developer Tools

Azure provides many developer tools for exploring, building, managing, and monitoring Azure services, including Visual Studio, Azure Lab Services, Azure DevTest Labs, software development kits (SDKs), and command-line interfaces (CLIs).

DevOps

Azure DevOps is Microsoft's suite of tools for managing an application Software Development Lifecycle (SDLC), including Azure Boards for planning and tracking tasks across teams, Azure Repos for secure and reliable source control repositories, Azure Pipelines for managing the build and release process, and Azure Test Plans for managing and monitoring automated tests, load tests, and test scripts.

Hybrid

Azure supports many services that allow for solutions to span both on-premises data centers and cloud data centers. These services vary greatly and include, but are not limited to, Storage, Identity, DevOps, AI + Machine Learning, Networking, Security, and Storage. Additionally, Azure provides the ability to host many cloud services in private data centers by using Azure Stack.

Identity

Azure Active Directory (AD), Azure Active Directory Domain Services, and Azure Active Directory B2C are examples of services Azure provides for managing user identity and securing applications and data.

Integration

Azure supports integration in the cloud and on-premises, and some services allow the integration to span across both. Logic Apps allow complex business processes and workflows to be developed in an intuitive cloud service. Azure Service Bus and Event Grid are powerful services that provide reliable cloud messaging and event-based solutions.

Internet of Things

Azure offers many services that support Internet of Things (IoT) devices, and it provides both a flexible and comprehensive platform for building scalable IoT solutions. Azure IoT Hub, Azure IoT Central, and Windows 10 IoT Core Services provide support for connecting and managing billions of IoT assets in a secure and reliable manner. Azure Sphere and Azure IoT Edge allow you to extend the cloud out to the smallest of devices. When these IoT services are combined with other Azure services, Azure has excellent and leading-edge support for building IoT solutions.

Management and Governance

Many Azure services are provided to simplify and automate the management, compliance, and monitoring of cloud resources. These include services for protecting data, such as Azure Backup and Azure Site Recovery, as well as services for monitoring applications and infrastructure, such as Azure Monitor, Azure Service Health, Network Watcher, and the Azure portal. Services for automating many tasks include Scheduler,

Cloud Shell, and Automation. Traffic Manager and Azure Lighthouse provide control to allow a customer to protect, manage, and scale a cloud network. Cost Management + Billing has many views and features to support how costs are managed, including detailed interactive views, alerts, and integration support to monitor cloud spending.

Media

Azure provides several services for delivering high-quality video content globally. These include Content Delivery Network and Media Services for delivering content, as well as services for encoding and streaming. Content Protection, Video Indexer, and the Encoding service allow for scalable services for handling media content. The Azure Media Player simplifies playback by providing a single player for a wide range of media formats.

Migration

Migrating solutions to the cloud, disaster recovery, and data transfer are supported by many services, including Azure Site Recovery, Azure Database Migration Service, Data Box, and Azure Migration.

Mixed Reality

Immersive interaction is supported in Azure, using cutting-edge technologies, including Azure Digital Twins and Spatial Anchors, for building mixed-reality experiences. Remote Rendering allows for rendering high-quality 3D content, and the Kinect Development Kit provides building solutions with advanced AI sensors.

Mobile

Building and deploying cross-platform and native mobile applications is supported in Azure. Services for building mobile applications include Xamarin, which supports cross-platform development, while Mobile Apps simplify building back-end services for mobile applications. Visual Studio App Center allows you to continuously build, test, release, and monitor mobile applications.

Networking

Services are provided to support connecting cloud and on-premises infrastructure and services. Services for managing network security include Azure Firewall Manager and

Traffic Manager, while Azure Firewall, Azure DDoS Protection, and Web Application Firewall provide powerful and scalable protection. Azure ExpressRoute, VPN Gateway, Virtual WAN, and Azure Bastion provide secure connectivity options to data centers, virtual machines, and cloud services.

Security

Security is a primary concern for Azure, and many services are available to monitor, detect threats, and keep customer data safe. Security Center and Azure Sentinel are examples of security management services provided to protect enterprise data. Key Vault provides a best-practice approach to maintaining secure control of sensitive keys and other secrets.

Storage

Azure Storage has a range of solutions to fit any size enterprise's requirements. Supporting both SMB 3.0 and HTTPS, Azure File storage provides an inexpensive and simple storage solution designed for lifting and shifting migrations of on-premises data to the cloud. Designed as a cost-effective solution for massive volumes of data, Azure Blob storage provides a scalable storage solution for unstructured data. Also, part of the storage suite of services is Azure Table storage, which provides a simple, low-cost service for schemaless storage of data. Optimized for Apache Spark and Hadoop analytics engines, Azure Data Lake Storage provides secure data lake storage. These are just highlights of some of the storage-related services provided by both Microsoft and other vendors, including massively scalable cloud repositories, archiving services, as well as storage designed for high-performance computing.

Web

Azure has many services for building scalable web applications. Azure App Service and Web Apps allow for hosting scalable, global cloud web applications. Azure SignalR Service, Notification Hubs, and API Apps provide specialized services for web application development.

Windows Virtual Desktop

Windows Virtual Desktop provides a comprehensive desktop virtualization service that runs in the cloud, allowing for a highly scalable, always up-to-date experience that is available on any device.

Categories of Cloud-Based Solutions

This section uses five general categories to discuss cloud-based solutions, in order to provide more background context.

FaaS—Function as a Service

Function as a Service (FaaS), also known as Serverless, is an offering of services that provides a platform for running and managing functionality (i.e., code) in the cloud, without any of the complexity of the infrastructure required to run the functionality. This is where the term *serverless* comes in, as the detail of the servers that run the functionality have been abstracted away, thus no longer making it the concern of the application developer.

Serverless has many benefits for cloud-based solutions. In general, serverless applications are easier and faster to deploy. They tend to support modern architectures, such as microservice architecture, very well. As their scope is limited to the functionality required, they tend to be quicker and less costly to develop than traditional applications. With built-in scalability, serverless applications are a cost-effective way of hosting reliable and resilient functionality.

Azure FaaS offerings are under Azure Functions. They will be covered in more detail in Chapter 3.

SaaS—Software as a Service

Software as a Service (SaaS) consists of products that are consumed directly where the building and hosting of the service are not handled by the consumer. This includes services such as Dynamics 365, SharePoint Online, and Office 365. The Azure portal and Azure DevOps themselves can be viewed as SaaS offerings, as they function to provide a view of the Azure services customers have access to. The details of hosting the two portals are completely managed by Microsoft.

The Azure portal is primarily covered in Chapter 2, although it is referenced throughout the chapters. Azure DevOps is covered in Chapter 8. Application Insights, an SaaS for recording and viewing application telemetry, is covered in Chapter 4.

PaaS—Platform as a Service

Customers can build upon a Platform as a Service (PaaS) without being concerned about the infrastructure used to support the service. This includes Cloud Services and App Service, wherein the customer is responsible for building the service but does not have to be concerned about the infrastructure that hosts the solution.

Azure App Service is covered in Chapter 6.

IaaS—Infrastructure as a Service

Infrastructure as a Service (IaaS) provides essential infrastructure to cloud-based solutions. From networking to storage, IaaS powers many of the other Azure services and provides secure and reliable communication to on-premises solutions. Many of the cloud-based infrastructures mirror on-premises components and allow for cloud-based networks to be defined, linking virtual machines, storage repositories, and other services running in and external to the Azure data center.

Azure Storage is covered in Chapters 3 and 5.

DBaaS—Database as a Service

Database as a Service (DBaaS) provides repositories that run in the cloud and include RDBMS and schemaless databases. Azure SQL provides a managed cloud-based SQL Server repository that includes many features tailored to running in the cloud, including encryption, auditing, and automated backup support using Azure Blob storage. Azure Cosmos DB provides a multi-model database service that has been designed to support globally distributed applications.

Azure SQL and Azure Cosmos DB are covered in Chapter 5.

Building for the Cloud

Previously, monolithic, single-tiered applications formed one program on a dedicated platform. This design made it easier to be predictably scalable and consistent. Now, with a cloud-based architecture, your application can be built as small independent services, which leverage APIs to send messages and events. This is a new microservices approach to application development.

9

Your application can grow as much as necessary, by adding new instances. Your application can now scale elastically, as required. Rather than fewer large updates, you have the agility to regularly make smaller updates. Rather than a manually managed system, you're now looking to design automated self-management.

Knowing how to profile and debug cloud-based solutions is essential to gaining the most value from running solutions in Azure. We will explain these topics in the subsequent chapters, but the following sections cover another aspect of gaining the benefits of the cloud: architecture.

Architectural Solutions

A successful cloud-based solution must take into consideration the cost vs. the value gained, the application's resiliency, disaster recovery, scalability, and security. In addition, you want to build a DevOps process to ensure predic table and reliable automated deployments. In order to achieve this, you'll need a system of monitoring, diagnostics, and testing.

In general terms, architecting cloud-based solutions does require a shift in designing and developing solutions to take advantage of the cloud's many benefits, including elastic infrastructure, improved accessibility, more resilient availability, improved security, and more rapid application development. For some organizations, the initial move to the cloud will include moving applications from on-premises infrastructure with little or no modification. This is referred to as lifting and shifting. Though this approach is cost-effective and reduces the risk of potential regression, in many situations, it will require additional effort to gain the benefits of running in the cloud.

Solutions architected with the cloud in mind, known as cloud-native solutions, tend to be made up of smaller, distributed services and applications. There are many architectural patterns that fit this profile, and we will cover event-driven architecture and microservice architecture as examples.

Event-Driven Architecture

A solution made up of applications and services that responds to changes in state can be termed as event-driven architecture (EDA). As an example of EDA, let's consider the scenario of a customer's address changing. In this example, the system will take three actions: send an acknowledgment e-mail, update the customer's address in the database, and create a log of the address change. In a more monolithic application, this might be comprised of a single web page that performs these three steps in a single method, as illustrated in Figure 1-1.

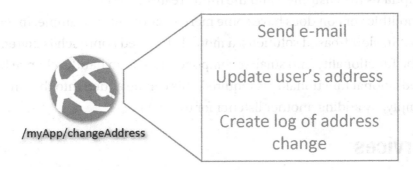

Figure 1-1. *Monolithic architecture*

In EDA, this might be changed to use the publish-subscribe pattern, or pub-sub. In this pattern, an event is published to a shared service, known as a service bus. Applications interested in events subscribe to the service bus to be notified when events of a certain type are published. In our example, this is the change address event. Figure 1-2 illustrates how this might look in Azure.

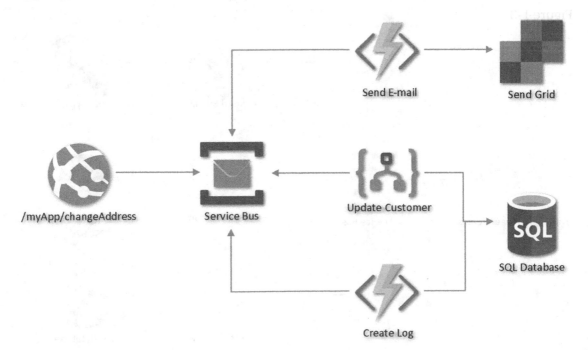

Figure 1-2. *Event-driven architecture*

In this diagram, a request is still made to the `changeAddress` web method, but instead of handling the functionality in the web application, an event is published to the service bus. Three subscribers are then triggered by this event. The first sends an e-mail; the second updates the customer; and the third creates a log entry.

The monolithic version does have some merit over the EDA example, in its simplicity, but in cloud-based solutions, a more distributed approach is better. First, by separating the functionality into smaller components, we can handle change better. For example, if additional functionality is required, this can be added into this architecture relatively simply, by adding another listener for the event.

Microservices

The microservice architecture is a popular architecture for cloud development. You can build apps that are scalable and resilient and that you can easily automate and deploy. This is achieved by designing smaller services that are autonomous and independent. Each of your services is given a singular purpose. Rather than rebuilding and then redeploying your application, you can update the services individually and independently. And rather than creating a data layer to persist the data, each service persists its own data.

If we revisit the EDA sample, we can illustrate microservice architecture, as shown in Figure 1-3.

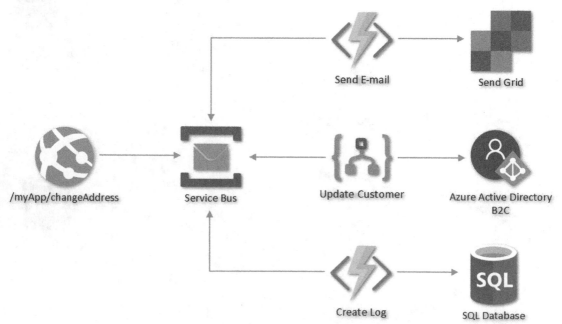

Figure 1-3. *Microservice architecture*

In the diagram, each service becomes independent, including its persistence layer. As you will have noticed, the difference between the diagram for EDA and microservices is not significant. This is intentional, as the two architectures complement each other.

Architecture Summary

EDA and microservice architecture lend themselves to cloud-based solutions in many ways. As the coupling between areas of the solution is reduced, multiple teams contributing to the same solution are less likely to run into conflicts as the solution evolves. Also, as the solution is made up of independent and isolated components, different areas of the solution can be scaled independently, allowing for both improved reliability as well as improved cost-effectiveness, as only the areas of the system requiring additional resources are increased. Another important consideration: in general, multiple smaller components are less costly in cloud-based solutions than a single larger component.

There are other architectures that are relevant, and the following are provided as additional resources to explore:

- *Azure Customer Advisory Team*: http://aka.ms/CAT

- *Azure Architecture Center*: https://docs.microsoft.com/en-us/azure/architecture/

- *Azure solution architectures*: https://azure.microsoft.com/en-us/solutions/architecture/

Profiling and Debugging Strategies

As cloud-based solutions benefit from different architectures rather than traditional solutions, the profiling and debugging strategies used for cloud-based solutions also change. The following chapters will progress through different categories of cloud-based development, and for each one, different profiling and debugging strategies will be discussed. Because cloud-based solution development is vast, so is the range of strategies that could be shown. We strove to provide a collection of the most effective and helpful strategies for a wide range of teams.

To aid in the discussion of the different strategies, a fictitious organization will be used to illustrate one company's journey into the cloud, from an on-premises solution. Our focus is to provide context for the different categories of cloud-based solutions and not how to develop a solution. Because of this, we have made the samples as simple as possible but complex enough to provide useful scenarios.

The following section will introduce the fictitious company, followed by a summary of the chapters and how they relate to the company's journey into the cloud.

CoffeeFix

Throughout the chapters we will use a fictitious company, CoffeeFix, to illustrate different profiling and debugging aspects of Azure. CoffeeFix is a manufacturer of high-quality coffeemakers (machines and pots that brew coffee), used in the most prestigious coffeehouses in the world. Its signature feature is a sensor-controlled brewing process that is designed to produce consistently full-flavored coffee. Because of the competitiveness of the coffeemaker market, CoffeeFix coffeemakers send information back to a central system, to be analyzed, in case the coffeemakers are showing signs of requiring maintenance.

For our purposes, the company has been very successful and now has coffeemakers installed across the globe. Unfortunately, the current solution has not been able to scale as smoothly as the business, and CoffeeFix is looking to invest in scaling their current solution.

Current Solution

The current CoffeeFix solution consists of an application that runs on the coffeemakers, a central web site, and a database. Both the web site and the database are currently hosted in a server at CoffeeFix headquarters. Figure 1-4 illustrates the current solution.

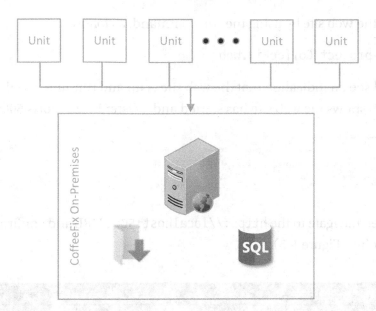

Figure 1-4. *CoffeeFix architecture*

We will point out some key elements of the diagram. First, there are many coffeemakers, and CoffeeFix refers to each coffeeemaker as a *unit*. As the units are running in coffeeshops across the globe, they are deployed externally to the CoffeeFix headquarters. Periodically, each unit will submit information back to a web site hosted on the CoffeeFix premises. The information submitted contains data about running the unit and whether there have been any issues detected. The information received from the units is stored in SQL Server and the file system. Both SQL Server and the file system are located at the CoffeeFix headquarters.

Source

Included in this chapter's source material is a starting solution that represents the CoffeeFix solution. It includes a .NET Core console application and a .NET Core web site. The console application represents the application used by a unit to submit information to a web API that is hosted by the web site. The web site API saves the submitted information, or telemetry, to a file in a folder called *telemetry*.

Please take a moment to become familiar with the solution, as we will be modifying it in subsequent chapters. First, using a shell of your choice (for example, PowerShell or Bash), navigate to the root directory of the Chapter 1 source. The following command should be issued to build the solution:

```
dotnet build .
```

Next, start the web site by using the run command, as follows:

```
dotnet run --project CoffeeFix.Web
```

You should see an indication that the web site is up and running. See the following example, which shows the web site has started and is listening on ports 5000 and 5001:

In a browser, navigate to the `https://localhost:5001` URL and confirm that the web site is running (Figure 1-5).

![CoffeeFix.Web Home Privacy — Welcome — Learn about building Web apps with ASP.NET Core.]

Figure 1-5. *CoffeeFix web site*

With the web site still running, we will run a console application to submit data to a web API hosted on the web site. This represents a unit that is submitting data back to headquarters. In a new shell, navigate to the root of the solution again. Run the following command to launch the console application that represents the unit:

```
dotnet run --project CoffeeFix.Console https://localhost:5001 CCC791E1-
C95A-4253-AA2B-C95240D2E430
```

The preceding run command uses two parameters. The first is the URL of the web site to submit telemetry to, and the second parameter is an ID that uniquely identifies the unit. Any unique ID or GUID will work.

If the telemetry is successfully submitted, a success message is shown. See the following example:

```
PS J:\git\Cloud-Debugging-and-Profiling\Chapter1> dotnet run --project CoffeeFix.Console https://localhost:5001 CCC791E1-C95A-4253-AA2B-C95240D2E430
CoffeeFix Console successfully submitted telemetry.
CoffeeFix Console completed.
```

As an additional step to validate that everything worked, look at the telemetry folder inside the web site folder. You should see a folder created with the ID that was submitted (Figure 1-6).

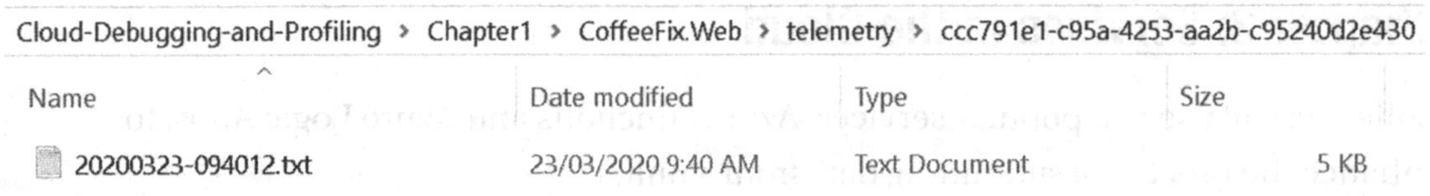

Cloud-Debugging-and-Profiling › Chapter1 › CoffeeFix.Web › telemetry › ccc791e1-c95a-4253-aa2b-c95240d2e430

Name	Date modified	Type	Size
20200323-094012.txt	23/03/2020 9:40 AM	Text Document	5 KB

Figure 1-6. *CoffeeFix telemetry*

Take a moment to review the solution, to get a general idea of how the sample solution was constructed. The purpose of the solution is to provide an illustration that many developers will be familiar with, while including enough complexity to make the migration to the cloud performed in subsequent chapters meaningful. Both the application and web site were created using the templates provided by Visual Studio.

Business Requirements

The CoffeeFix business has recognized that the current solution requires some investment. As the business has been growing, the solution has not been able to keep up, and certain activities that were fine with a small number of units have not scaled well. For example, the upgrade of the application on the individual units is a costly and sometimes faulty process. Currently, a representative is required to manually update the software when a release is required. As more units have been deployed, the process of manually updating the units has become impractical.

CoffeeFix in Chapters

In the different chapters, we will go into more detail on the required enhancements to the solution. The chapters have been designed to provide both an example of how an on-premises solution might move to being cloud-based, as well as practical debugging and profiling examples.

Following is an overview of the enhancements, by chapter.

Chapter 2: Azure Portal Overview

Chapter 2 provides an overview of the Azure portal and many of its features, including creating a new subscription, menus, and some important settings to tailor the portal to a user's requirements. The chapter is intended as an overview and does not cover the CoffeeFix scenario specifically.

Chapter 3: Services in the Cloud

CoffeeFix will use two popular services, Azure Functions and Azure Logic Apps, to enhance the process of submitting data from a unit.

Chapter 4: Application Insights

The current method of sending telemetry back to the main web site will be replaced with Application Insights. The CoffeeFix business is looking to use Application Insights to improve how the telemetry is recorded, viewed, and analyzed, by leveraging the capability of a performance-monitoring solution.

Chapter 5: Databases and Storage

The current database and file storage runs on an on-premises infrastructure. In this chapter, we will use Azure SQL Database and Azure Cosmos DB to provide cloud-based repositories.

Chapter 6: Web Apps

The main web application is currently running at the CoffeeFix headquarters. In this chapter, we will move the application to Azure App Service.

Chapter 7: Identity Security with Azure AD

Currently, user authentication to the main web application is done using local identity management. In this chapter, we will move the identity management to Azure AD.

Chapter 8: Azure Build and Release Automation

The business is looking to improve the current method of upgrading units, by running the application in a container and using Azure DevOps to automate and control the process of building new versions of the application reliably.

Chapter 9: External Tooling

This chapter will show how external tooling can be used to enhance a customer's Azure experience, by using services external to Azure.

Chapter 10: Monitoring the Solution

The final chapter will illustrate how an organization can achieve a high-level view of a cloud-based solution, using the CoffeeFix services now running in Azure.

Summary

Many of the strengths of the cloud encourage solutions that are more distributed in nature. Of course, it is possible to build a monolithic solution in the cloud or a solution composed of microservices in a single on-premises data center. The point made in this chapter is because of the cloud's elasticity, the cost-effectiveness of smaller, independent services, and the cloud's globally distributed nature, cloud-based solutions are better suited to a solution with a more distributed architecture.

Because of this, there are challenges in how to profile and debug distributed solutions. Many tools exist in the Azure portal and Azure DevOps, among others, that allow for individuals, ranging from operations to management, to get visibility of the different aspects of a solution. From server status to application telemetry to cost, this book aims to provide an understanding of where to look and how to configure comprehensive profiling and debugging in Azure.

Chapter 2 provides a first look at the Azure portal and its main features. Many of these features are relevant for all services in all categories, including FaaS, SaaS, PaaS, IaaS, and DBaaS.

CHAPTER 2

Exploring the Azure Portal

Opening the Azure portal for the first time can be a daunting experience! The goal of this chapter is to help both individuals new to Azure and more experienced users navigate and get more from the Azure portal experience.

Azure Portal

The Azure portal is an extensive single-page application with two purposes. First, it provides a means of viewing the details of your Azure subscriptions. Second, it supports most actions that can be applied to your Azure subscription and its many different blades. This chapter explores the Azure portal and some of its common features. We will explain the dashboard and how you can create different views for different scenarios. The Favorites section also is covered, as is using the Cost Management + Billing blade. Also, we will explore the portal's support features and introduce the Cloud Shell.

Subscriptions

There are several types of subscriptions, ranging from pay-as-you-go to enterprise agreements. Everything covered in this book is applicable to all subscriptions, and all the examples are built using a pay-as-you-go subscription. However, it is worthwhile to provide an overview of the different subscription types.

> *Pay-as-you-go*: This provides a flexible payment plan that offers no minimums or commitments.

> *Enterprise agreements*: Large organizations can have a tailored enterprise agreement, which offers flexible billing options and best prices.

© Jeffrey Chilberto, Sjoukje Zaal, Gaurav Aroraa and Ed Price 2020
J. Chilberto et al., *Cloud Debugging and Profiling in Microsoft Azure*,
https://doi.org/10.1007/978-1-4842-5437-0_2

Dev/Test: This provides discounted rates on Azure, to support development and testing.

It is also worth noting that Azure has many programs that provide free monthly credit to Visual Studio subscribers and verified student accounts.

Getting Started—Creating a Subscription

This section covers creating a new Azure subscription and walks through the steps for getting set up. Getting started with Azure is easy, by using the wizard provided at `https://azure.microsoft.com/en-us/free/`. After navigating to the page, you will be greeted by a banner with the Start free button (Figure 2-1).

Figure 2-1. *Starting a free subscription*

The Start free button opens a wizard that walks you through the setup process. If you have not yet logged in with a Microsoft account, you will be asked to do so. This can be a work or school account used to access Office 365 or a Microsoft account used for Outlook.com, Hotmail, Office, OneDrive, Skype, Xbox, and Windows. The first step is to set up some background information about the owner of the subscription (Figure 2-2).

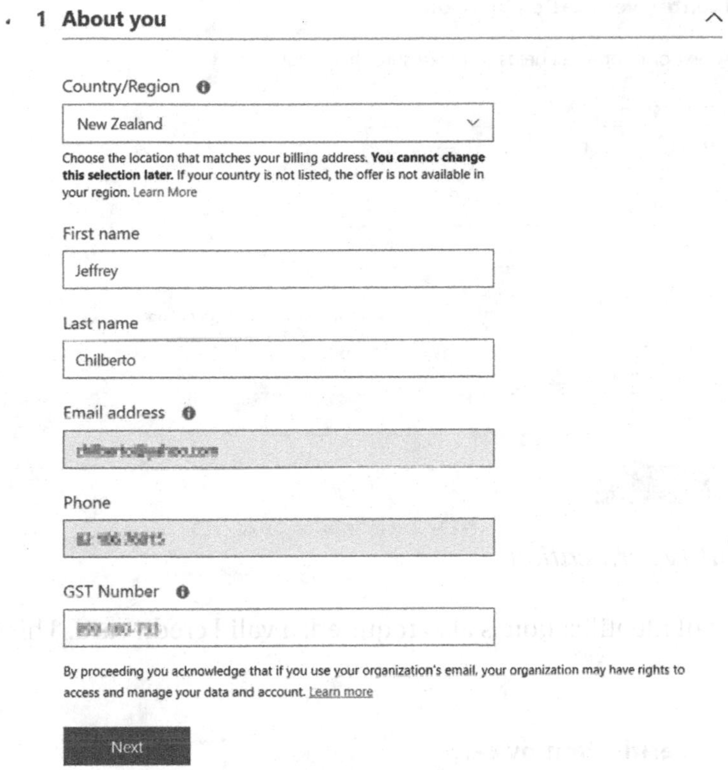

Figure 2-2. *About you*

This is especially useful for countries that support a goods and services tax or value added tax (for example, New Zealand and the United Kingdom). This simplifies the billing process, if the subscription progresses beyond a free status. Also, this information can be supplied later, if required.

Next, a simple phone verification step is required, either by text or phone. The following example (Figure 2-3) shows the verification by text, with a sent verification code entered.

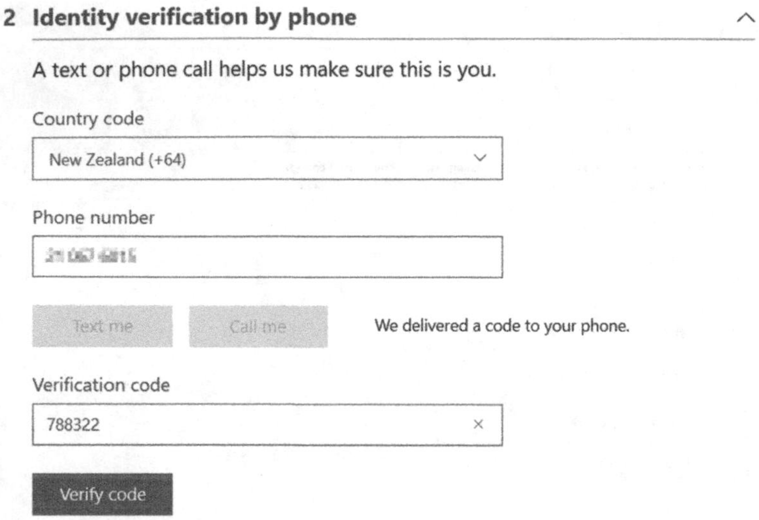

2 Identity verification by phone   ∧

A text or phone call helps us make sure this is you.

Country code

New Zealand (+64)   ∨

Phone number

（　）

| Text me | | Call me | We delivered a code to your phone.

Verification code

788322   ×

| Verify code |

Figure 2-3. Identity verification

A second form of identification is also required: a valid credit card. This is shown in
Figure 2-4.

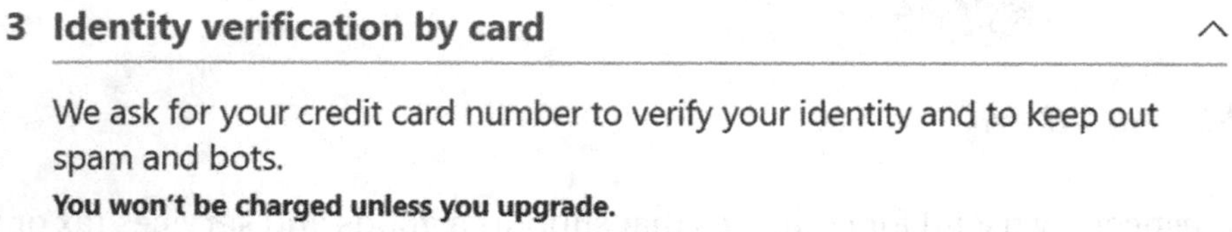

3 Identity verification by card   ∧

We ask for your credit card number to verify your identity and to keep out
spam and bots.
You won't be charged unless you upgrade.

Figure 2-4. Identity verification by credit card

The last step is to accept the subscription agreement and offer details and
acknowledge the private statement and communications policy (Figure 2-5).

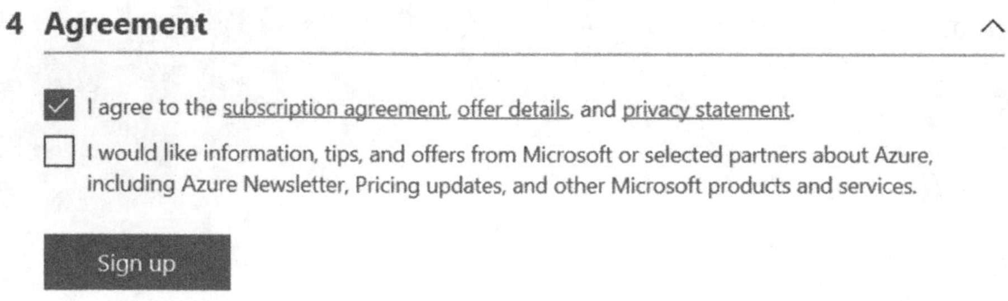

4 Agreement   ∧

☑ I agree to the subscription agreement, offer details, and privacy statement.

☐ I would like information, tips, and offers from Microsoft or selected partners about Azure,
including Azure Newsletter, Pricing updates, and other Microsoft products and services.

| Sign up |

Figure 2-5. Agreement

It will take some time to provision the subscription. Once the subscription is ready, a link is provided for accessing the portal (Figure 2-6).

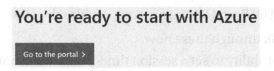

Figure 2-6. *Ready to start*

By clicking the *Go to the portal* link, the browser navigates to the Azure portal. Even in an empty subscription, this can be somewhat overwhelming, as illustrated in Figure 2-7.

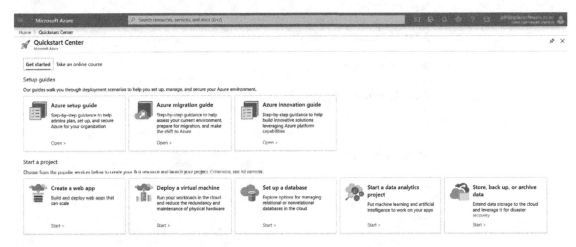

Figure 2-7. *Portal dashboard*

We will point out the major sections now and expand upon them later in this chapter. First, the main section is the dashboard. The dashboard is primarily used to get a quick view of a subscription and its resources. There can be multiple dashboards per subscription, and each can be customized in both layout and content. To the left of the dashboard is a dynamic menu of blades, as well as services that are marked as favorites. At the top of the portal is a header menu bar containing a search function, settings, the current user and directory, and some other useful features.

Portal Settings

One of the first features to visit in the portal is Portal Settings. This is at the upper right, displayed as a cog (⚙). The Portal Settings menu provides the ability to apply general changes, and we will walk through these now.

The first option is the ability to set a session time-out, which controls when the user should be logged out when inactive. Figure 2-8 shows the different options available.

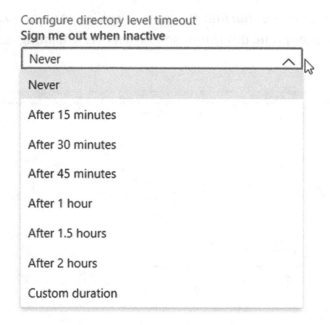

Figure 2-8. *Portal Settings: Log me out*

It is great to allow the users to set this, depending on their environment and requirements. For example, administrators might want to have a shorter time-out window, in case they want to make sure that if they forget to lock their workstation, their session will time out after 15 minutes of idle time. Someone in operations, however, might use the dashboard to monitor activity and use an idle workstation to present the dashboard on a shared monitor.

There are two default views: Dashboard and Home. This helps personalize the experience, as some prefer a dashboard-type view, as shown in Figure 2-9.

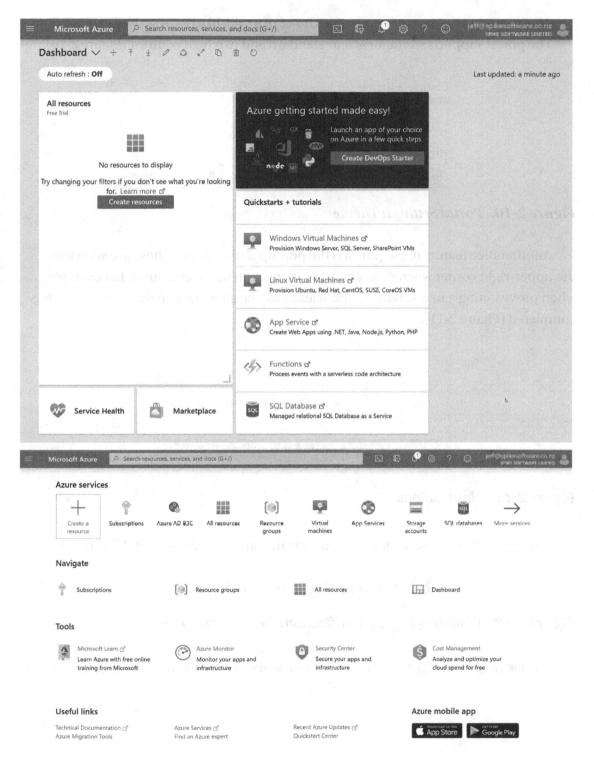

Figure 2-9. *Dashboard and Home views*

Alternatively, the Home view provides more of a grid-like list of services and options. The portal supports six themes: four standard and two high contrast (Figure 2-10).

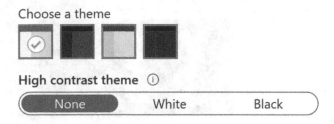

Figure 2-10. *Portal Settings: Themes*

Another nice feature of the portal is the pop-up notifications. These are shown in the upper-right corner when different activity occurs in the background. For example, when provisioning a new service, a notification will be shown when the deployment has completed (Figure 2-11).

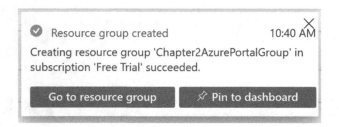

Figure 2-11. *Notifications*

These can also be disabled, by unchecking the option in the settings (Figure 2-12).

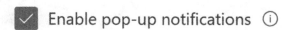

Figure 2-12. *Disabling pop-up notifications (uncheck the box)*

The language and regional settings can also be specified in Portal Settings (Figure 2-13).

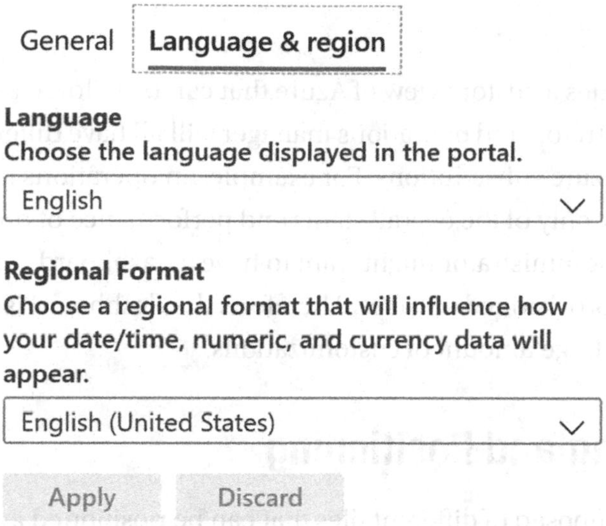

General   **Language & region**

Language
Choose the language displayed in the portal.

| English   ⌄ |

Regional Format
Choose a regional format that will influence how
your date/time, numeric, and currency data will
appear.

| English (United States)   ⌄ |

Apply   Discard

Figure 2-13. *Portal Settings: Language*

Also, Portal Settings allows you to export your settings, and you can reset to the
default settings (Figure 2-14).

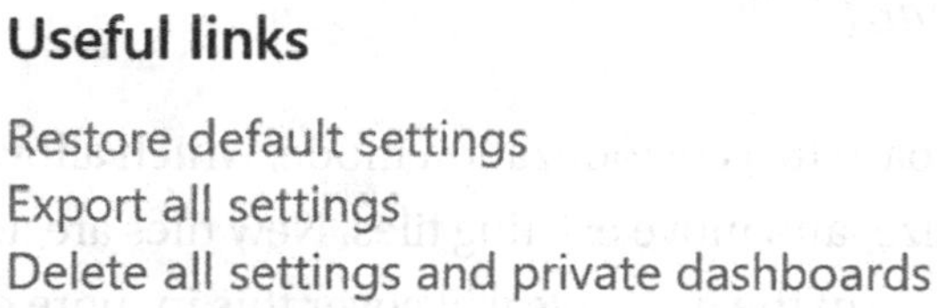

Useful links

Restore default settings
Export all settings
Delete all settings and private dashboards

Figure 2-14. *Portal Settings: Restore and Export*

What Is an Azure Blade?

The main portion of the Azure portal displays the currently selected blade. When you
first log on to the portal, the dashboard blade is presented by default. Other blades exist
for different resources or services in the portal. For example, the SQL databases blade
displays the provisioned databases in the current subscription. It provides the ability to
view details about each database and to provision a new database. Most of the blades
have a similar structure or template, which allows for a more consistent experience, even
though the content might differ greatly.

Dashboard

The dashboard provides a custom view of Azure that can be tailored as needed. A developer, administrator, and operations manager will all have different requirements when viewing their Azure subscriptions. For example, an operations manager might want to have visibility only of the overall status and performance of provisioned resources, while the administrator might want to have a dashboard summarizing the cost across different provisioned services. Therefore, the dashboard is very flexible and allows you to make a large amount of customizations.

Tiles—Resizing and Positioning

The dashboard is composed of different tiles that can be positioned and resized. We will illustrate this by changing some of the tiles. First, start by selecting the Edit action at the top of the dashboard (Figure 2-15).

Figure 2-15. *Dashboard Edit*

This sets the dashboard to a customization mode, which allows you to add new tiles, and you can delete, resize, and move existing tiles. New tiles are added by using the Tile Gallery at the left side of the page. We will cover this in more detail in the following "Creating a New Dashboard" section. To adjust the existing tiles, you hover over a tile (Figure 2-16).

Figure 2-16. *Dashboard adjusting an existing tile*

As shown in the following image (Figure 2-17), the cursor changes to reflect the tile, and it can be dragged to a new location. Also, a delete icon and a context menu are shown.

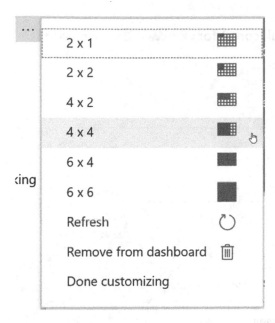

Figure 2-17. *Dashboard tile context menu Edit*

The context menu allows you to reshape the tile to certain available sizes. Not all tiles support all sizes. For example, the Marketplace tile only supports the three sizes shown in Figure 2-18.

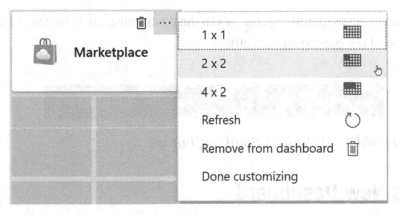

Figure 2-18. *Dashboard Marketplace tile*

The size is written in columns by rows. For example, 4 × 2 indicates four columns by two rows. It is possible for tiles to support shapes not covered in the drop-down menu. These tiles support the ability to resize the tile by dragging a handle in the bottom-right corner.

For example, the handle is shown in the following tile, which is used to display metrics collected about a running application (Figure 2-19).

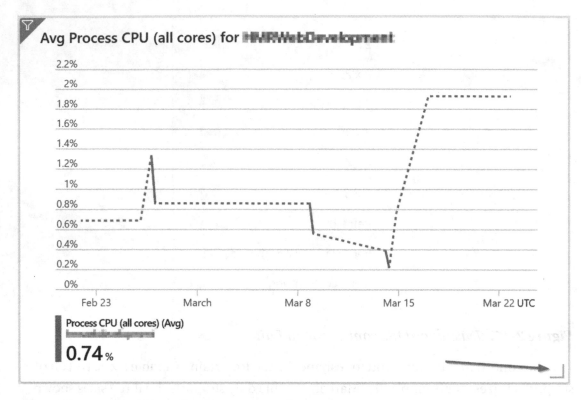

Figure 2-19. *Dashboard metrics example*

When you have finished making changes to the dashboard, click the *Done customizing* button at the top of the page (Figure 2-20).

Figure 2-20. *Dashboard Done customizing button*

Creating a New Dashboard

The portal supports having multiple dashboards, which allows you to have different views of the Azure resources. For example, you might want a view of only the production services, or a view that provides a summary of the activity of all the databases.

To create a new dashboard, use the New dashboard action at the top of the current dashboard (Figure 2-21).

Dashboard ∨ ⊞ New dashboard   ⬆ Upload   ⬇ Download   ✎ Edit   ⌂ Share   ⬀ Full screen   ⧉ Clone   🗑 Delete   ↻ Refresh

Figure 2-21. *New dashboard*

This creates a new dashboard and sets your view to editing the new dashboard. At the top of the view, you can specify a new name, as illustrated in Figure 2-22, with the name *Production Database Dashboard*.

Production Database Dashboard

Figure 2-22. *Dashboard name*

On the left side, the Tile Gallery is shown (Figure 2-23), which allows you to add tiles to the dashboard.

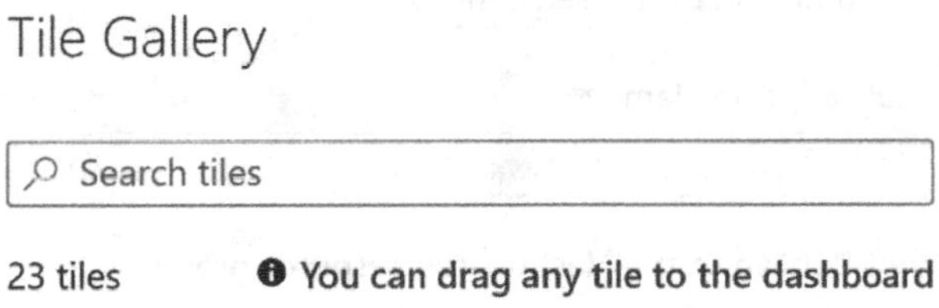

Tile Gallery

🔍 Search tiles

23 tiles   ❶ **You can drag any tile to the dashboard**

Figure 2-23. *Dashboard Tile Gallery*

Spend some time looking at the different types of tiles. As you progress through the chapters, we will provide examples of different tiles that might be of interest. The list of tiles grows significantly once you have provisioned services.

Sharing Dashboards

Another feature of dashboards is the ability to share a dashboard with other users. The other users must be within the same subscription. Access is controlled by using role-based access (RBAC). This is done by publishing a dashboard, which creates the dashboard as a resource within the subscription. The dashboard resource can then be managed in a similar manner to the other resources within the subscription.

To share a dashboard, select the Share link at the top of the view (Figure 2-24).

Dashboard ∨   ⊞ New dashboard   ⬆ Upload   ⬇ Download   ✎ Edit   ⌂ Share   ⬀ Full screen   ⧉ Clone   🗑 Delete   ↻ Refresh

Figure 2-24. *Dashboard sharing*

You will then be prompted to enter some information about sharing the dashboard (Figure 2-25).

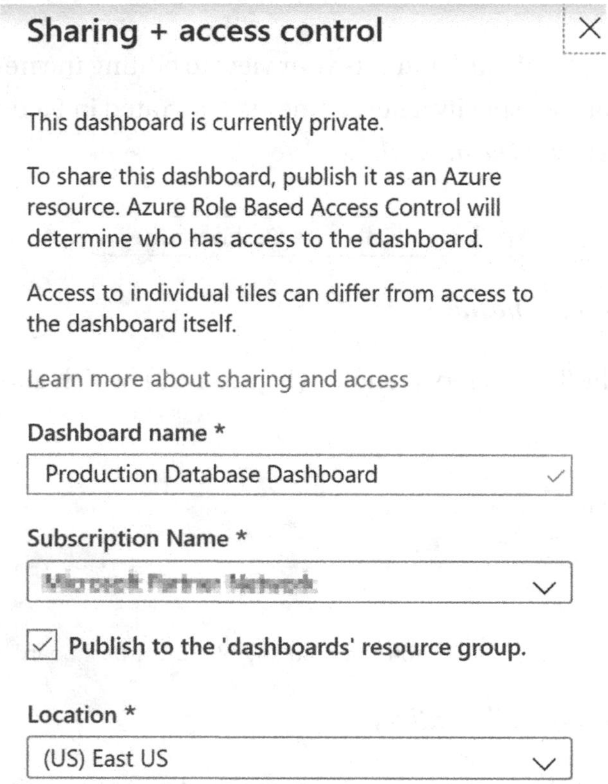

Figure 2-25. *Dashboard sharing using RBAC*

The Dashboard name is what other users will use to identify the shared dashboard, as shown in Figure 2-26.

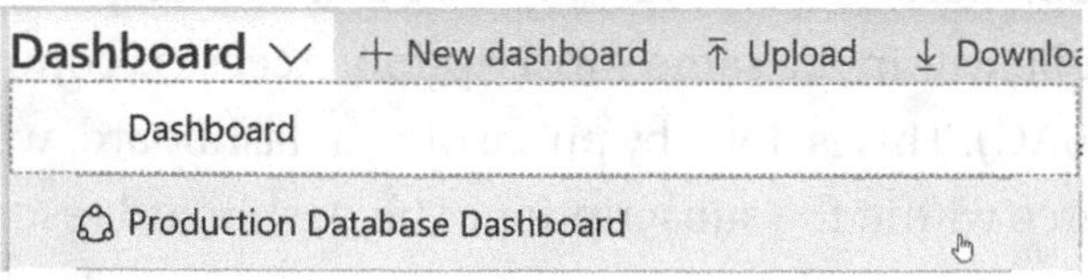

Figure 2-26. *Shared dashboard*

Navigation

Being able to quickly navigate the Azure portal is essential. This section includes some useful tips and explains the features of the portal that are designed to assist with navigating the site.

Setting Favorites

On the left side of the portal is the Favorites bar, which provides a convenient way for accessing blades that you often view. This is set to some common blades by default. One of the first things you should do is set this to the blades that are the most relevant to you. Located above Favorites is All services (Figure 2-27). Select this option to show all the blades.

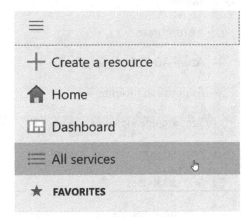

Figure 2-27. *Service favorites*

To the right of each blade is a star, which indicates whether you want it to be shown as a favorite. The blades are organized into categories, and some are shown in more than one category. Because this list can become overwhelming, a handy tip is to use the Filter located at the top (Figure 2-28).

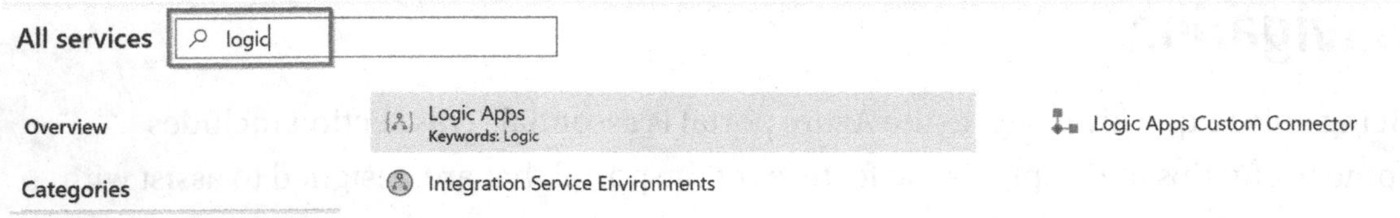

All services
logic
Overview
Categories
Logic Apps
Keywords: Logic
Integration Service Environments
Logic Apps Custom Connector

Figure 2-28. *Favorites filtering*

The above image shows how the filter can be used to show only those blades relating to *logic*.

In the Favorites menu, the items can be reordered. To reorder a favorite, first mouse over the item to be moved. Three dots will then appear toward the right side of the item (Figure 2-29).

FAVORITES
All resources
Azure AD B2C
Application Insights
Resource groups
App Services
SQL databases
Storage accounts
Azure Active Directory
Monitor
Advisor
Security Center

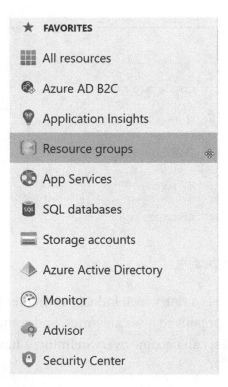

Figure 2-29. *Reordering favorites menu*

By clicking the dots, the item can be moved to a new location within the Favorites menu. This way, you can quickly reorder your list alphabetically or put your more frequently used items at the top.

Searching for a Resource, Service, and Docs

Navigating through Azure resources and services can be a challenge when there are multiple subscriptions or when the number of services provisioned grows. The Favorites menu helps you organize the blades into what logically makes sense to you. This next section shows you how to quickly jump across the subscriptions and other areas of the portal. At the top of the Azure portal is the ability to search resources, services, and docs, and it provides an efficient way for you to navigate across the different elements of Azure (Figure 2-30).

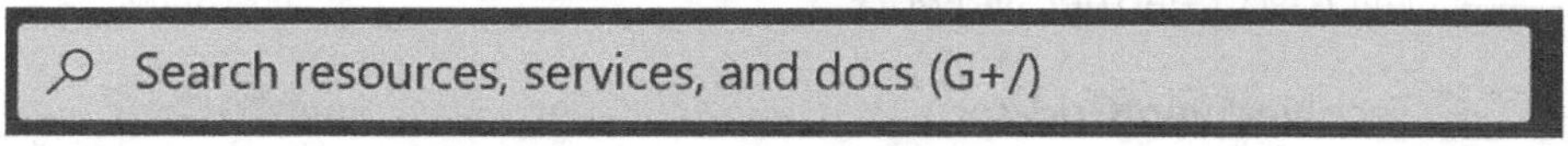

   🔍   Search resources, services, and docs (G+/)

Figure 2-30. *Search bar*

This capability has some great features that are worth highlighting. First, when you click the search bar, it displays a list of recent blades (Figure 2-31).

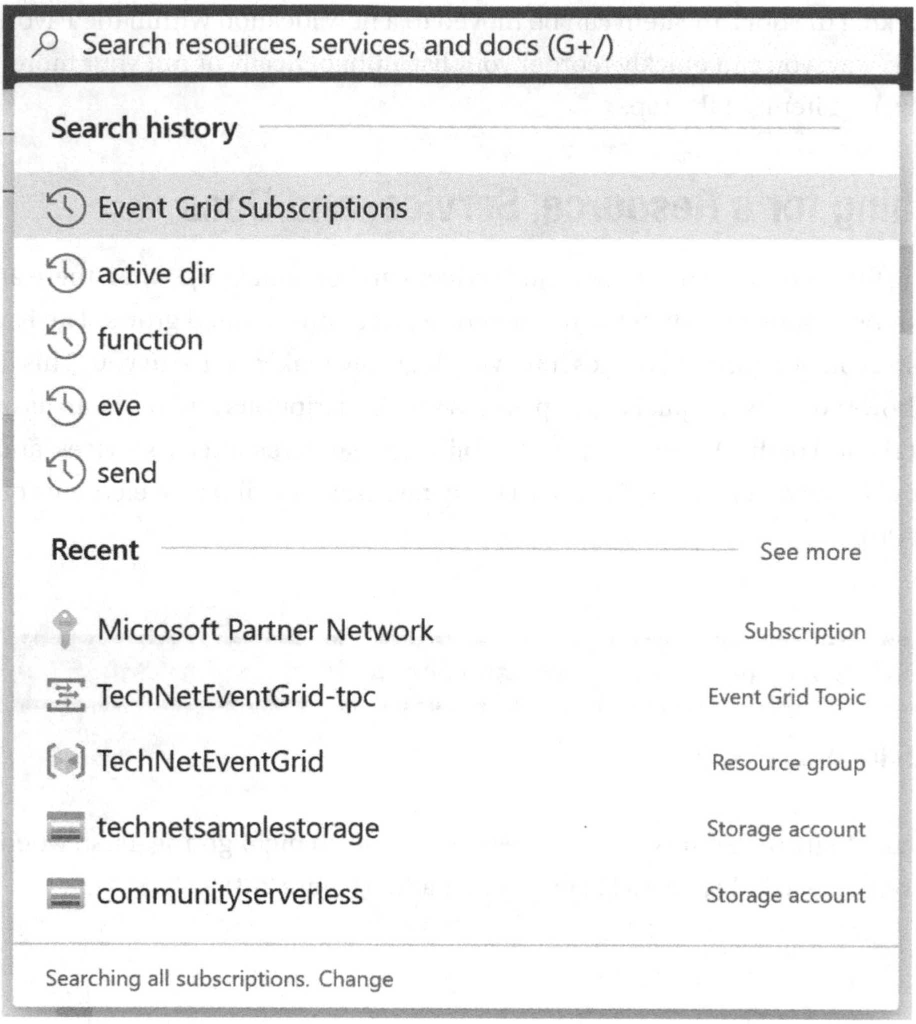

Figure 2-31. *Recent search history*

There are two subtle points to this: a See all link (on the right, under the search box) and the ability to change the filtering when there are multiple subscriptions.

Once you enter some text, the list is changed to display the matching items (Figure 2-32).

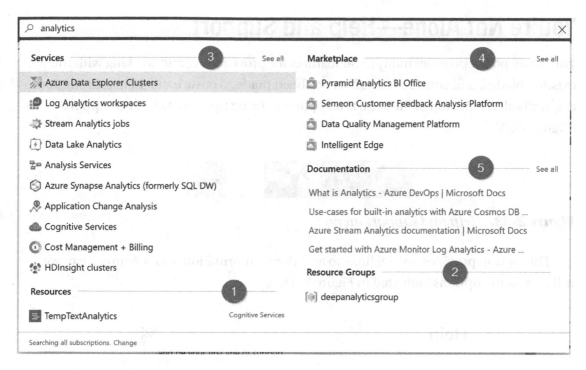

Figure 2-32. *Broad search*

The preceding screenshot illustrates this feature well, as it shows the search spans across multiple types of resources. In this example, we entered the word *analytics* into the search bar. The first section (1 in the preceding image) shows resources matching the text. In this example, the match was TempTextAnalytics, a Cognitive Services resource containing *Analytics* in the name. Similarly, the second section (2) shows the resource groups that match our search. The third section (3) shows the services that either match the name or the keywords associated with the service. The fourth section (4) indicates entries from the Marketplace, while the fifth section (5) provides links to the documentation, with our search text in the title. Note that only the first two sections are provisioned components, while the other sections provide a means of either jumping to provisioning a new resource or viewing the documentation.

You're Not Alone—Help and Support

The Azure portal provides many great features for provisioning and working with the existing blades, and considerable effort has been made to ensure that help and support are available. At the top of the page is an option to bring up more help and support (Figure 2-33).

Figure 2-33. *Help and support menu*

This option provides several links to additional information about Azure. Next, we will look at the options indicated in Figure 2-34.

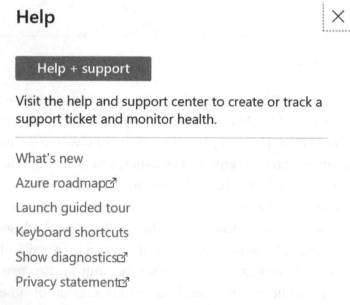

Figure 2-34. *Help + support*

Help + Support

Azure is complex, and being able to receive help and support is essential. The Help
+ support section provides access to documentation, including tutorials and how-to
articles, community resources (such as the MSDN Forums and Stack Overflow), as well
as the ability to create support requests (Figure 2-35).

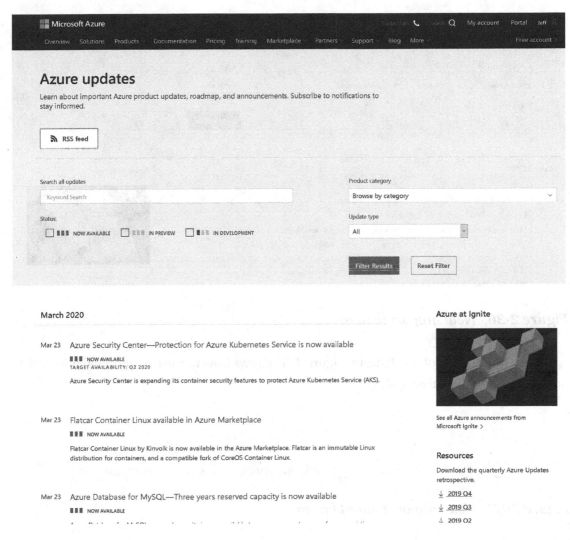

Figure 2-35. *Help + support options*

Before contacting support, you should explore the documentation and community resources, but it is valuable to have support available. Select the support plan that fits your subscription. The plans range from a free Basic plan to the Premier plan for critical systems that require a high level of service to minimize the business impact.

A new support request can be created by using the New support request option, which guides you through raising a support ticket (Figure 2-36).

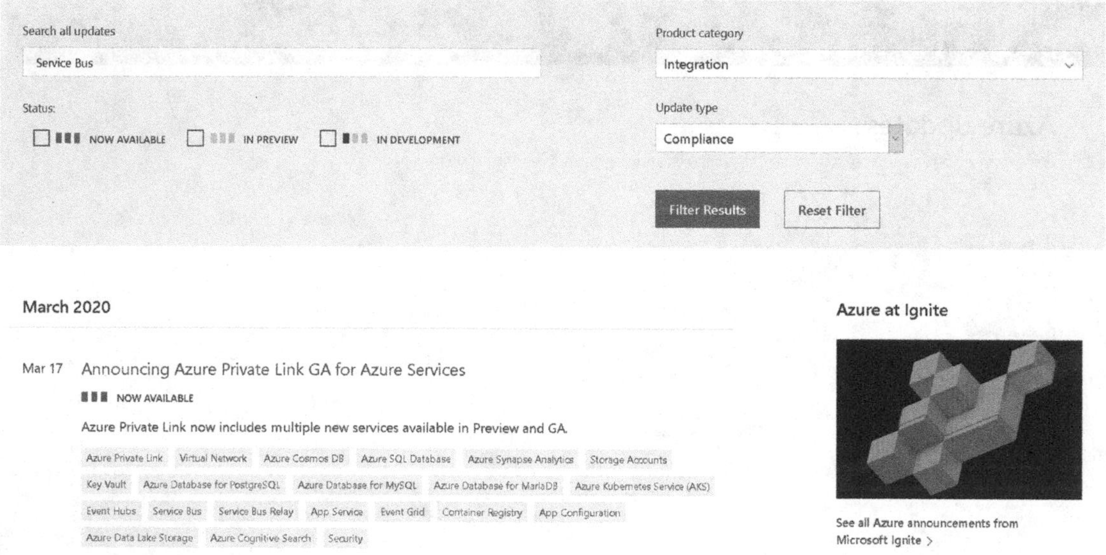

Figure 2-36. *New support request*

As an illustration of this feature, Figure 2-37 shows how to raise a technical issue on a function app in the subscription.

Figure 2-37. *New support request basics*

Describe the specific problem and upload any supporting files, as shown in Figure 2-38.

Figure 2-38. *New support request problem*

The last step is to provide your contact information, including your preferred contact method (Figure 2-39).

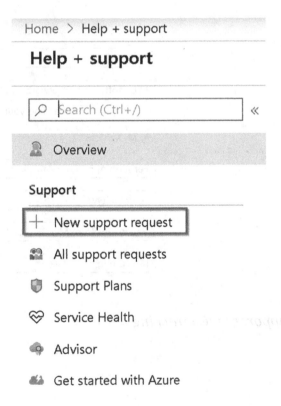

Figure 2-39. *New support request contact*

Depending on the support plan, Microsoft support will investigate and resolve the support request. Submitted support requests can be viewed in the All support requests link, as shown in Figure 2-40.

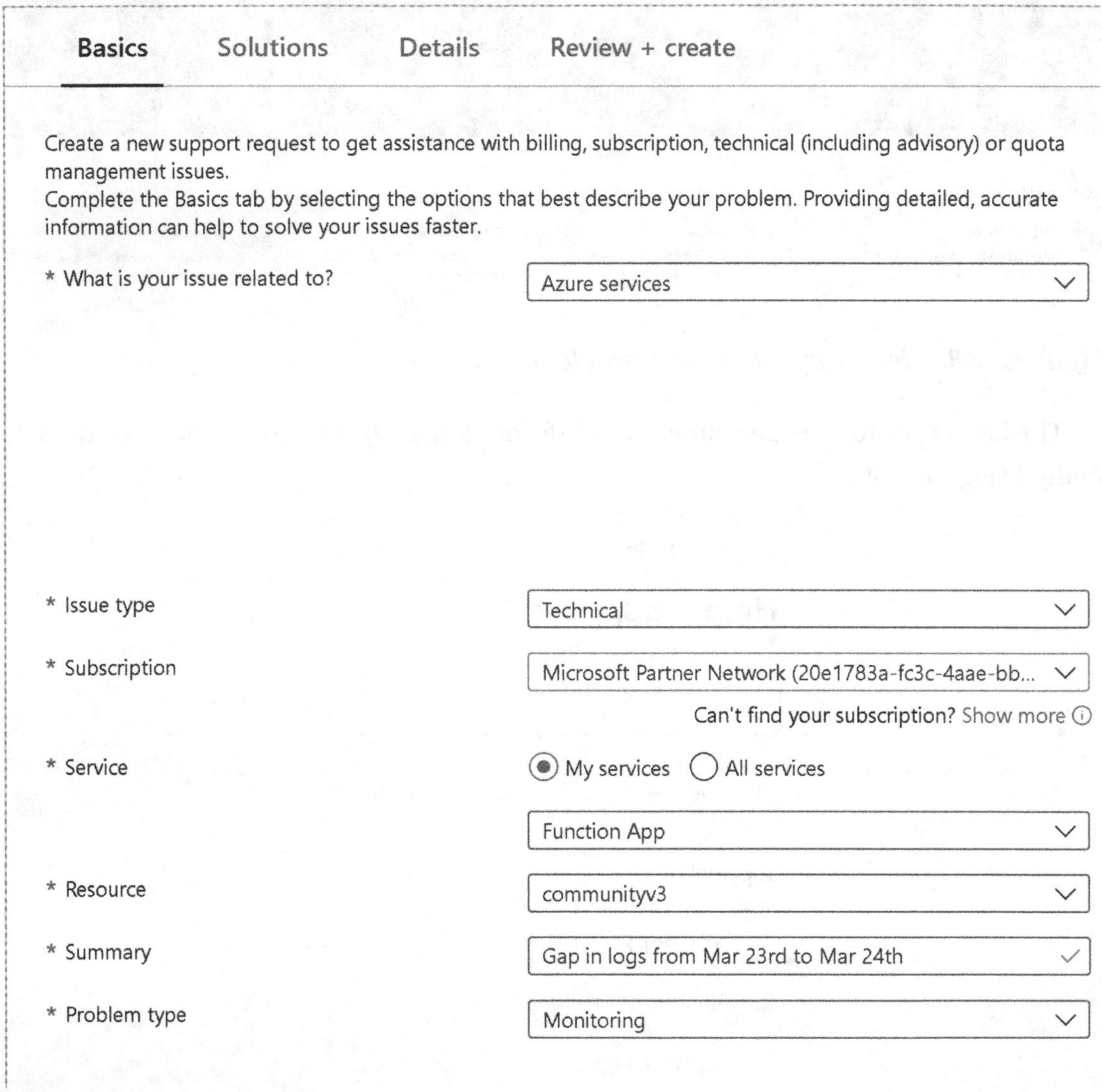

Basics	Solutions	Details	Review + create

Create a new support request to get assistance with billing, subscription, technical (including advisory) or quota management issues.
Complete the Basics tab by selecting the options that best describe your problem. Providing detailed, accurate information can help to solve your issues faster.

* What is your issue related to?   Azure services ⌄

* Issue type   Technical ⌄

* Subscription   Microsoft Partner Network (20e1783a-fc3c-4aae-bb... ⌄
                                               Can't find your subscription? Show more ⓘ

* Service   ⦿ My services ○ All services
                                               Function App ⌄

* Resource   communityv3 ⌄

* Summary   Gap in logs from Mar 23rd to Mar 24th ✓

* Problem type   Monitoring ⌄

Figure 2-40. *New support request tracking*

Azure Roadmap

Azure is continuously being updated with new features and improvements to existing functionality. A great way to keep up to date with changes is by using Azure roadmap. The Azure roadmap link directs you to a feed of the latest Azure updates and news (Figure 2-41).

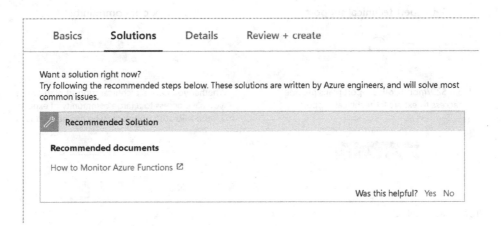

Figure 2-41. *Azure roadmap*

The Azure updates page gives you the ability to filter by product and type of update. For example, Figure 2-42 shows a filter of the Service Bus product for news related to compliance.

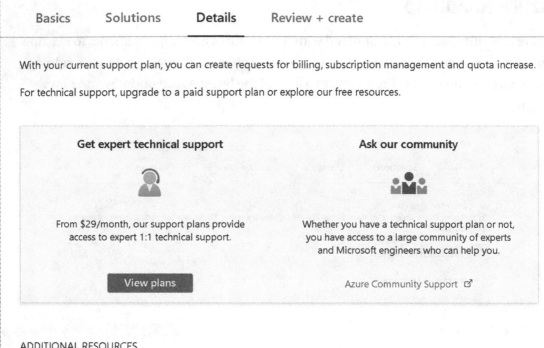

Figure 2-42. *Azure updates filtering*

As well as news about existing products, this is a great way of understanding what changes are being worked on by using either the In preview or In development tabs. For example, the following (Figure 2-43) indicates change currently in development.

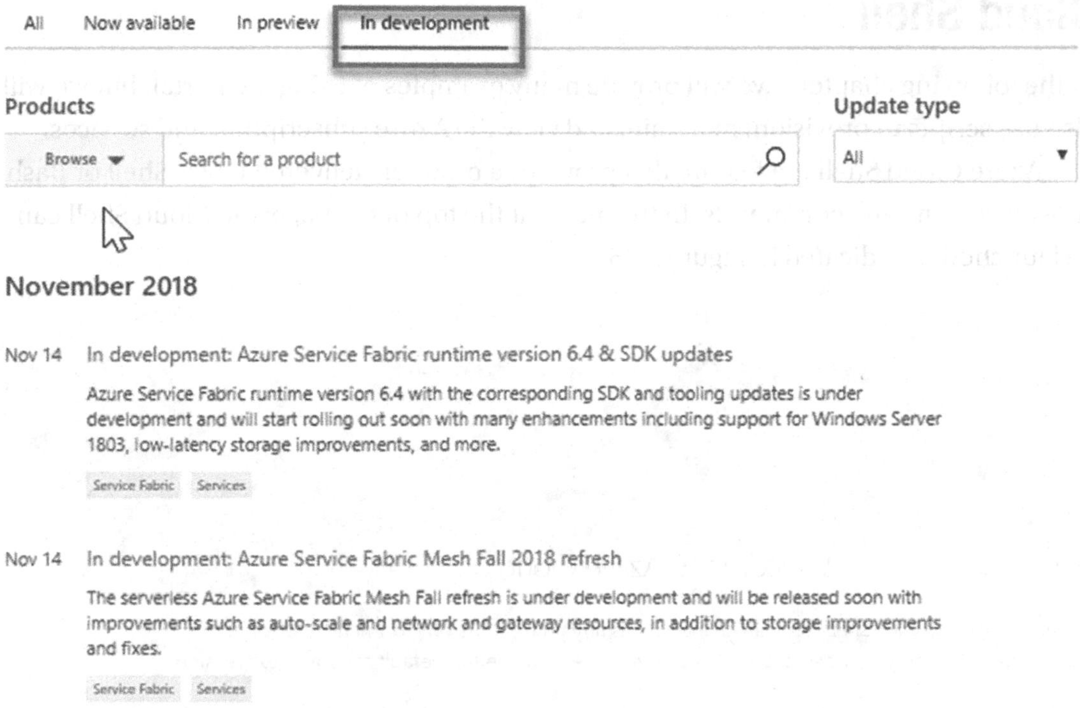

All	Now available	In preview	In development

Products

Browse ▼   Search for a product   🔍

Update type

All   ▼

November 2018

Nov 14   In development: Azure Service Fabric runtime version 6.4 & SDK updates

Azure Service Fabric runtime version 6.4 with the corresponding SDK and tooling updates is under development and will start rolling out soon with many enhancements including support for Windows Server 1803, low-latency storage improvements, and more.

Service Fabric   Services

Nov 14   In development: Azure Service Fabric Mesh Fall 2018 refresh

The serverless Azure Service Fabric Mesh Fall refresh is under development and will be released soon with improvements such as auto-scale and network and gateway resources, in addition to storage improvements and fixes.

Service Fabric   Services

Figure 2-43. *Change in development*

Launch Guided Tour

We recommend you take the guided tour, to become familiar with the Azure portal. By clicking the Launch guided tour link, a dialog is shown that enables the tour to begin (Figure 2-44).

Figure 2-44. *Launching the guided tour*

We will not repeat the tour here, but you should start it, to walk you through the major components of the portal.

Cloud Shell

In the following chapters, we will provide many examples of using the portal, but we will also use scripts to provision, maintain, and view the Azure subscription and services. The Azure Cloud Shell is a feature that provides a browser-delivered PowerShell or Bash console for running commands. In the menu at the top of the page, the Cloud Shell can be launched as indicated in Figure 2-45.

Welcome to Azure Cloud Shell
Select Bash or PowerShell. You can change shells any time via the environment selector in the Cloud Shell toolbar. The most recently used environment will be the default for your next session.
Bash
PowerShell

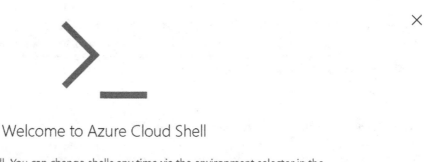

Figure 2-45. *Cloud Shell*

The shell launches and connects to the Azure subscription. If this is the first time the shell has been launched, storage will have to be mounted. We provide the steps to guide you through this process. First, you select the type of Cloud Shell: Bash or PowerShell (Figure 2-46).

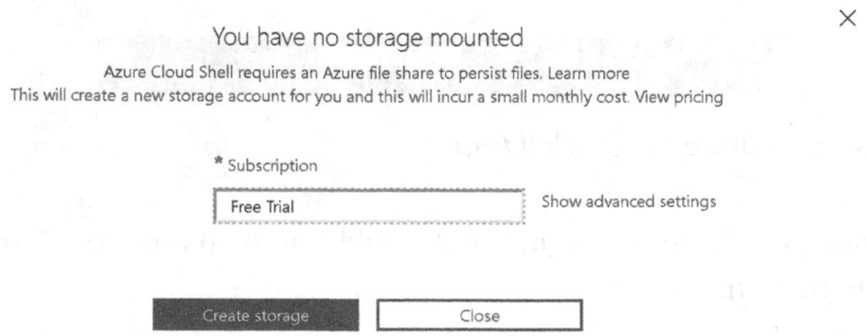

You have no storage mounted
Azure Cloud Shell requires an Azure file share to persist files. Learn more
This will create a new storage account for you and this will incur a small monthly cost. View pricing
* Subscription
Free Trial
Show advanced settings
Create storage
Close

Figure 2-46. *Welcome to Azure Cloud Shell*

The type is the default and can be easily changed later. The next step is to create storage in the subscription. This is shown in Figure 2-47.

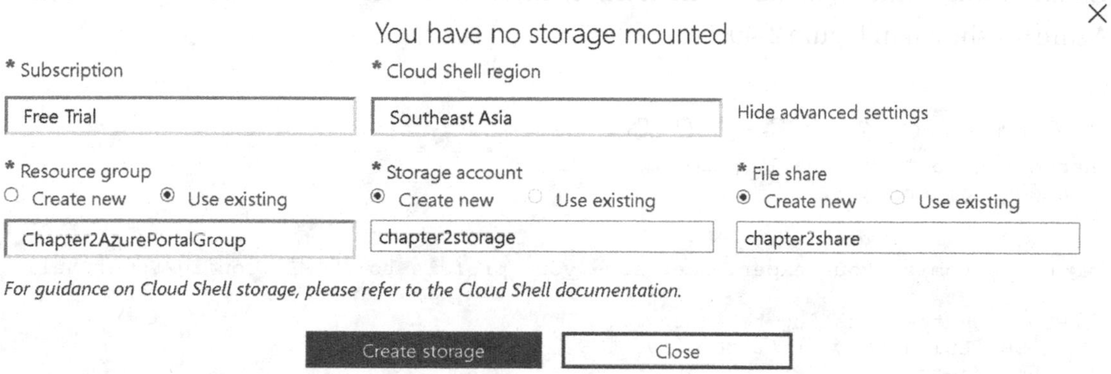

You have no storage mounted   ✕

* Subscription   * Cloud Shell region

| Free Trial | Southeast Asia | Hide advanced settings

* Resource group   * Storage account   * File share
○ Create new ● Use existing   ● Create new ○ Use existing   ● Create new ○ Use existing

| Chapter2AzurePortalGroup | | chapter2storage | | chapter2share |

For guidance on Cloud Shell storage, please refer to the Cloud Shell documentation.

Create storage   Close

Figure 2-47. *Cloud Shell setup*

For more control of the storage to be mounted, click Show advanced settings (Figure 2-48).

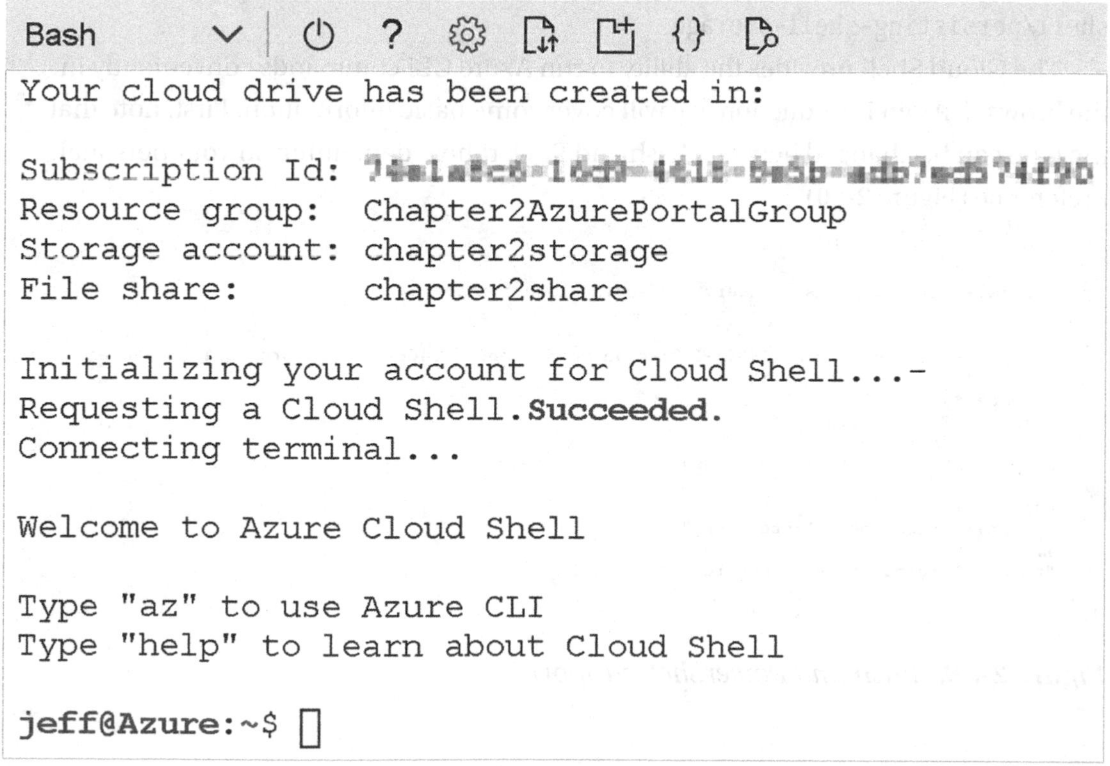

Bash   ∨ │ ⏻ ? ⚙ ⬓ ⬒ {} ⬓

```
Your cloud drive has been created in:

Subscription Id: ▓▓▓▓▓▓-▓▓▓▓-▓▓▓▓-▓▓▓▓-▓▓▓▓▓▓▓▓
Resource group:  Chapter2AzurePortalGroup
Storage account: chapter2storage
File share:      chapter2share

Initializing your account for Cloud Shell...-
Requesting a Cloud Shell.Succeeded.
Connecting terminal...

Welcome to Azure Cloud Shell

Type "az" to use Azure CLI
Type "help" to learn about Cloud Shell

jeff@Azure:~$ ▯
```

Figure 2-48. *Cloud Shell storage*

You can create a new resource group, storage account, and file share, or you can select existing components for each option. Once you select your settings, click the Create storage button, to mount the storage, initialize the terminal, and authenticate into Azure, as shown in Figure 2-49.

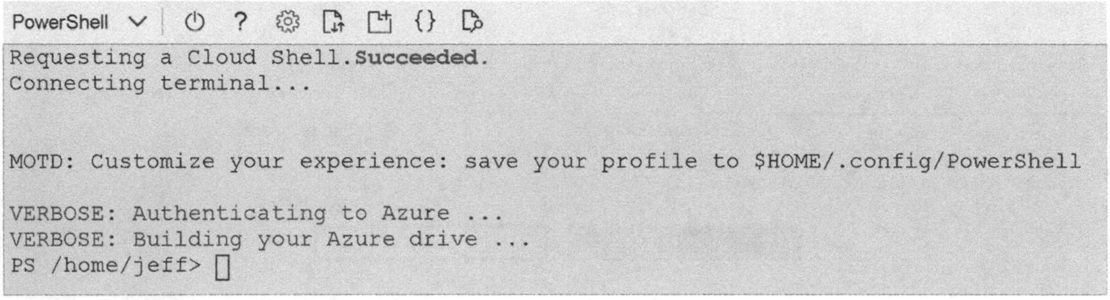

```
PowerShell  ∨    ⏻   ?   ⚙   ⤓   ⤒   {}   ⤵

Requesting a Cloud Shell.Succeeded.
Connecting terminal...


MOTD: Customize your experience: save your profile to $HOME/.config/PowerShell

VERBOSE: Authenticating to Azure ...
VERBOSE: Building your Azure drive ...
PS /home/jeff> []
```

Figure 2-49. *Cloud Shell authentication*

Additional information about persisting shell storage is located in the Azure Cloud Shell documentation, available at `https://docs.microsoft.com/en-us/azure/cloud-shell/persisting-shell-storage`.

The Cloud Shell provides the ability to run Azure CLI commands conveniently in the browser. As an introduction, we will cover some basic information. First, note that the type can be changed between Bash and PowerShell, depending on your personal preference (Figure 2-50).

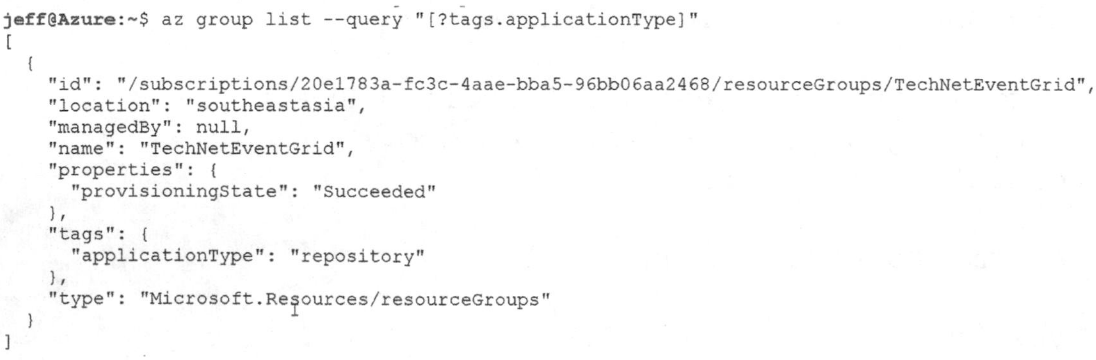

```
jeff@Azure:~$ az group list --query "[?tags.applicationType]"
[
  {
    "id": "/subscriptions/20e1783a-fc3c-4aae-bba5-96bb06aa2468/resourceGroups/TechNetEventGrid",
    "location": "southeastasia",
    "managedBy": null,
    "name": "TechNetEventGrid",
    "properties": {
      "provisioningState": "Succeeded"
    },
    "tags": {
      "applicationType": "repository"
    },
    "type": "Microsoft.Resources/resourceGroups"
  }
]
```

Figure 2-50. *Bash and PowerShell support*

Because the shell is authenticated with the current subscription, calls using the Azure CLI are immediately available. For example, if you wanted to list all the groups tagged with an application type of repository, you can use the command `az group list –tag "applicationType=repository"` (Figure 2-51).

```
jeffrey@Azure:~$ az group list --tag "applicationType=repository"
[
  {
    "id": "/subscriptions/                              /resourceGroups/PhotoBackupResourceGroup",
    "location": "southeastasia",
    "managedBy": null,
    "name": "PhotoBackupResourceGroup",
    "properties": {
      "provisioningState": "Succeeded"
    },
    "tags": {
      "applicationType": "repository"
    }
  }
]
```

Figure 2-51. *Cloud Shell group list*

More commands will be covered as we progress through the chapters.

The Cloud Shell is provided free of charge, but it requires local storage, which incurs a cost that depends on how much data you store, the volume and type of storage transactions, and which redundancy option you choose.

Summary

The Azure portal provides many features for managing, monitoring, and exploring Azure. Becoming familiar with Azure can be daunting, but the portal provides many resources, from help and support to flexible and powerful search, as well as navigation features to assist you in becoming comfortable with the features and components of Azure.

With Chapter 1 and Chapter 2, you have a basic understanding of Azure and the Azure portal. Now it is time to move the CoffeeFix organization into the cloud. Chapter 3 describes how to build services in the Azure cloud.

CHAPTER 3

Services in the Cloud

Working with various services in the cloud is fun. On the one hand, Azure allows you to add serverless components to the application, and on the other, you have app services and more. Organizations can keep their applications on-premises or in the cloud. Orchestration, however, can be a challenge. This chapter demonstrates the power of the cloud, using examples from Azure Functions and Logic Apps. We will add a serverless component to a solution that can be connected to application insights. An example of building an Azure function and calling it from a Logic App will be provided. Tags for billing also will be explored.

The chapter is broken into the following sections: "What Is Serverless," "Azure Functions," "Logic Apps," "An Overview of API Management Services," and "Using Tags for Billing."

Technical Requirements

This chapter uses sample code to explain the various topics under consideration. The following are prerequisites for working with these code samples:

- *Visual Studio 2019*: Visual Studio is available for both Windows and Mac. If you do not have Visual Studio 2019 installed on your machine, you can install it from here: `https://visualstudio.microsoft.com/ downloads/`. In this chapter, we used Visual Studio 2019 Community Edition for Windows, which is a free version. However, you can select any edition, per your choice, click Download, and follow the instructions on your screen to install Visual Studio. Do not forget to install Azure SDK. (Select Azure development from the Workloads tab; refer to Figure 3-1.)

© Jeffrey Chilberto, Sjoukje Zaal, Gaurav Aroraa and Ed Price 2020
J. Chilberto et al., *Cloud Debugging and Profiling in Microsoft Azure*,
https://doi.org/10.1007/978-1-4842-5437-0_3

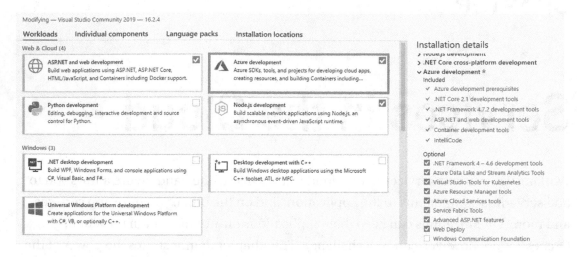

Figure 3-1. *Selecting Workloads*

- *A valid Azure account*: You will require login credentials for the Azure portal. If you don't have an Azure account, you can get a free account from here: `https://azure.microsoft.com/free/`.

Note   The source code for this chapter can be downloaded at `https://apress.com/9781484254363`.

What Is Serverless?

Before we begin to discuss serverless computing (in short, *serverless*), let's review web applications before the advent of serverless (let's call these traditional web applications). Traditional web applications are built and deployed on a server (most of the classic ASP. NET web applications are deployed on an IIS web server). The HTTP requests (via these web apps to the server) are managed to some extent.

To manage and provision resources for web applications, we must ensure the following:

1. Our server must be up and running, even if the web application is not serving a single request (also referred to as being in an idle state).

2. As an owner of the application, to better serve our users, we must make sure that our server is always up and running (known as server uptime).

3. We should make sure the server is secure and up to date (any new software updates should be applied).

4. Scaling is a salient factor for web applications. We should ensure that our server is scaled up or down, whenever scaling is required.

The preceding requirements vary from organization to organization. For example, if an organization is small or consists only of one individual, there may be a lot of overburden to handle. Owing to this overburden, important tasks, such as building and developing an application, might be overlooked. On the other hand, in big organizations, there are separate teams to handle infrastructure, and routine tasks could be performed by a team other than the development team. However, implementation and support of the process could slow down actual development tasks.

Note   Serverless computing is an adaptation that allows developers to worry less about resources, infrastructure, and operating systems.

If we think as a developer, our prime task is to handle all these glitches, so that we can concentrate on development tasks and not bother with extraneous issues. So, what are the possible solutions?

1. A server that has all the required software (operating system, required runtime, SDKs, etc.)

2. A server that is able to execute the code dynamically

3. A server that is infra-ready (such as sign-and-go)

The preceding solutions come with serverless computing. In serverless computing, we build serverless apps and do not have to provision and manage any servers. In this way, we work only on development tasks and can devote less attention to infrastructure concerns. The complete code runs on a cloud provider (in our case, Azure) and is triggered by such events as HTTP requests, database events, queueing services, monitoring alerts, file uploads, scheduled events, and so forth. The code that is sent to Azure for execution is usually sent as a function. That is why serverless computing is also referred to as Function as a Service (FaaS).

Note   In simple terms, Function as a Service (FaaS) is an arrangement of a platform that provides a facility to write/manage functionalities of the application, with no need to think about the infrastructure.

Why Develop Serverless Applications?

In the previous section, we identified the various issues with traditional web applications, and you saw how these can be resolved using serverless computing. Serverless computing has advantages over traditional web applications, and there are reasons (both technical and commercial) why serverless applications should be preferred over traditional server-hosted applications, such as the following:

- *Fully managed services*: With serverless applications, you need not worry about managing your servers, resources, etc. There is also no need to worry about the server's uptime. As a developer (organization or individual), you only need to concentrate on the development of your application.

- *Lower cost*: In a serverless application, we have lesser costs, as we will be paying only for the resources that are in use. No cost is accrued if the application is in an idle state (that is, if no request is being served).

- *Easy scalability*: Serverless computing can handle thousands of concurrent functions in less than a second.

An Overview of Azure for Serverless Applications

In this section, you will see the various services, provided by Azure, to work with serverless applications (Table 3-1).

Table 3-1. *Azure Services*

For	Services/Resource
Compute	Azure Functions
Storage	Azure Storage
Database	Azure Cosmos DB
Security	Azure Active Directory
Messaging	Event Grid and Service Bus
Workflow	Logic Apps
Managing API	API Management
Analytics	Event Hubs and Azure Stream Analytics

In the upcoming sections, we will expand our imaginary application, CoffeeFix. We will solve the problem of processing the report data, with the implementation of Azure Functions and Logic Apps.

Requirements

For our CoffeeFix application, we must implement the following, to solve the problems previously discussed:

- The application should collect the report and its data.

- Report data should be saved in a new file (Azure Blob Storage).

- The application must send an e-mail.

- The application must generate process report data and send a file (on-premises).

Figure 3-2 shows the implementation of our requirements.

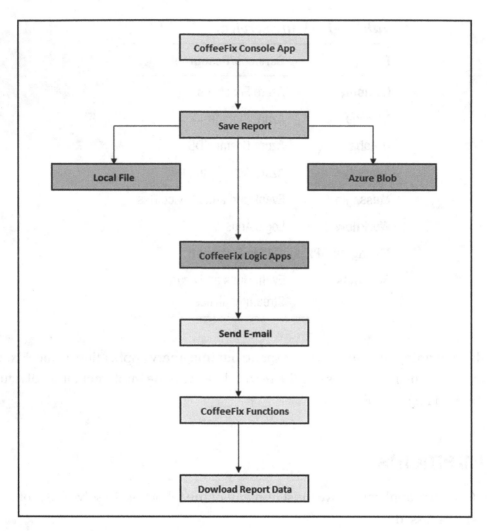

Figure 3-2. *Visualization of the app flow*

The preceding requirements can be fulfilled with a system containing a console application and a Logic App in the cloud. Our system will work like this: a console application will collect data and generate a report and add/update the report file to Azure Blob Storage. Any update in Blob will initiate an action by SendGrid and forward an e-mail. After this, it will also trigger an Azure function to generate a process report and send the file.

Azure Functions

In the previous section, we discussed serverless computing and serverless applications. Azure Functions helps us create serverless applications. With the use of Azure Functions, we can run a small piece of code on Microsoft Azure. As a developer, you should not have to worry about the infrastructure. With Azure Functions, you can concentrate on a specific problem. You can accelerate the development of an application by using these functions, because you do not first have to create a virtual machine (VM) or publish a web application on the server.

We can sum up Azure Functions by saying it consists of a piece of code executed on Microsoft Azure. It helps us run code on demand and does not require explicit provision or management infrastructure. So, we can conclude that Azure Functions does the following.

- *Provides ease of development*: We can choose the development language. (To check the complete list of languages for selection, please visit `https://docs.microsoft.com/en-us/azure/azure-functions/supported-languages`.) The choices can be any of the following:

  - C#

  - Java/Maven

  - JavaScript

  - PowerShell

  - Python

- *Is cost-effective*: Azure Functions are cost-effective because we pay only for the time our code runs. Refer to the complete pricing model at `https://azure.microsoft.com/en-us/pricing/details/functions/`.

- *Enables working with its own libraries*: We can add NuGet and NPM packages to use with our libraries or external libraries.

- *Is open source*: With an MIT License, the runtime of Azure Functions is open source, and you can make changes, if required. The complete source code can be found at `https://github.com/Azure/azure-functions-host`.

Note   Azure Functions' runtime has two major versions: 1.x and 2.x. 2.x is the current version, to which improvements are being made, although both versions support the production environment. Moreover, runtime 2.x runs on .NET Core 2. Therefore, a function built on this version runs on all platforms supported by .NET Core, including macOS and Linux.

Creating a Function App

As discussed in the preceding section, the CoffeeFix application needs to send e-mails. To implement this feature, we will create a function. Before you start this section, please make sure that you have fulfilled all the prerequisites, as outlined in the "Technical Requirements" section.

We must create a function app, so that we can group functions as a logic unit. We will create this app using the Azure portal. You can also create a function app with Visual Studio, Azure CLI, or PowerShell.

1. To start, log in to the Azure portal, via the URL `https://portal.azure.com`, by using your Azure portal credentials.

2. Click Create a resource from the left navigation bar of the Azure portal (Figure 3-3).

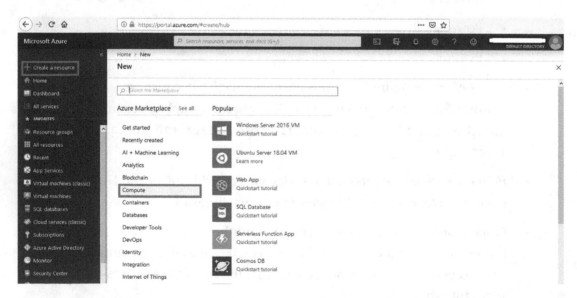

Figure 3-3. *Compute*

3. Click Compute and then Function App (Figure 3-4).

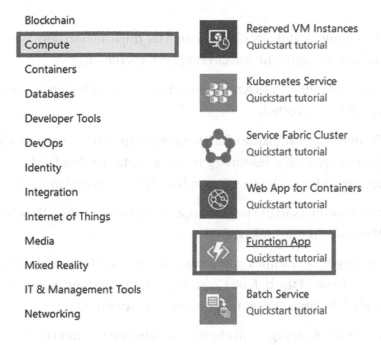

Figure 3-4. *Function App*

4. From Function App, the Create screen provides the app settings (Figure 3-5).

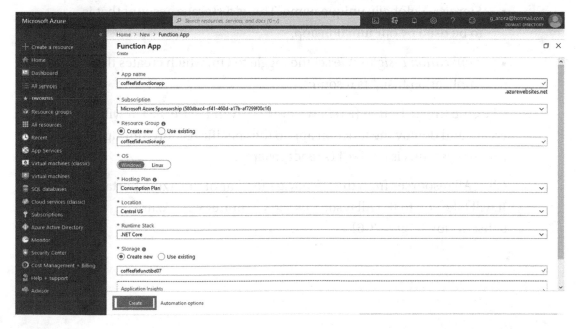

Figure 3-5. *Create screen*

The following are the required settings to create a function app, as shown in Figure 3-5:

- *App name*: A globally unique name for the function app. We have named our app function `coffeefixfunctionapp`.

- *Subscription*: A valid Azure subscription, under which our new app is to be created.

- *Resource Group*: Name of a resource group in which our new app is to be created. A resource group is a container that holds related resources for an Azure solution (in our case, Function App).

- *OS*: This refers to the targeted operating system (OS). We selected Windows as our preferred OS.

- *Hosting Plan*: Defines how resources are added to your function app. We used the default Consumption Plan, where resources are added dynamically, as required by our functions.

- *Location*: Your region of choice. We selected Central US.

- *Runtime Stack*: The preferred runtime stack. We selected .NET Core.

- *Storage*: A globally unique name. This is a storage account that is to be used by our function app.

- *Application Insights*: We set the toggle to On, which creates the Application Insights resource.

5. Click the Create button (as shown previously in Figure 3-5). It will create and deploy the function app to the specific resource group (in our case, this is `coffeefixfunctionapp`).

6. Click All resources from the left navigation bar of the Azure portal. It will take you to the All resources screen, under your Azure subscription (Figure 3-6).

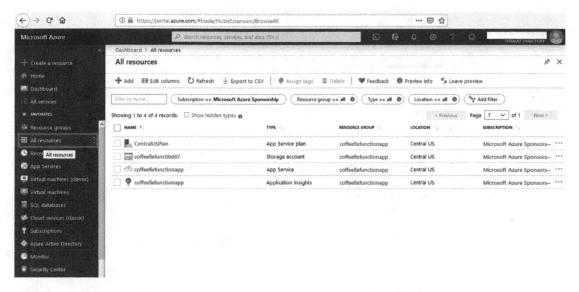

Figure 3-6. *Available resources*

7. From the All resources screen, you can filter or search a specific resource (as shown in Figure 3-7).

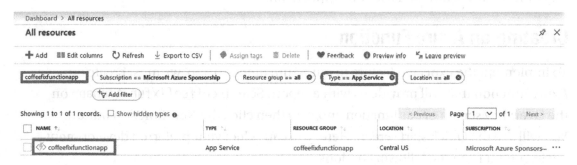

Figure 3-7. *Filter resources*

8. Click `coffeefixfunctionapp`, which has the type, App Service (as shown in Figure 3-7). It will take you to a new function app (Figure 3-8).

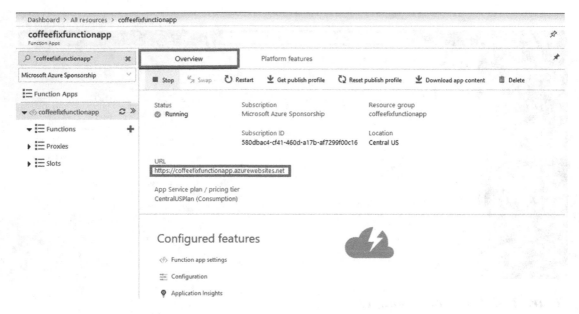

Figure 3-8. *Overview of the function app*

With the preceding steps, we have created our function app. Now we are ready to implement the requirements for our application.

Creating an Azure Function

To implement the expected feature to our Azure function app, we must create an Azure function that will provide us with a report. Search `coffeefixfunctionapp` on the Overview screen of our function app, and then click the New function button. You will see the Quick start screen. Here, you can select your preferred development environment from the following options:

- Visual Studio

- VS Code

- Any other editor (using Core Tools)

- In-portal

We are using the In-portal option to create our Azure function. Click the Continue button. From Create a Function, select Webhook + API and click Create (Figure 3-9).

Figure 3-9. *Webhook + API*

How Azure Functions Works

Azure Functions is made up of two important parts:

1. *Code* is the main part of Azure Functions. The previous step created an HTTP Trigger1 and code file with the name run.csx. We wrote this code in C#. Now we will amend this default code, so that we can download the report. The following is the amended code (Listing 3-1).

Listing 3-1. Amended code

```
using System.Net;
using System.Text;
using Microsoft.AspNetCore.Mvc;
using Microsoft.Extensions.Primitives;
using Newtonsoft.Json;

public static async Task<IActionResult> Run(HttpRequest req, ILogger log)
{
    log.LogInformation("Coffee report is being generated...");

    string name = req.Query["name"];
```

```
string requestBody = await new StreamReader(req.Body).ReadToEndAsync();
dynamic data = JsonConvert.DeserializeObject(requestBody);
name = name ?? data?.name;
string desc = name != null ? $"Fantastic Coffee made by {name}" : "Who
made this coffee?";
Guid reportId = Guid.NewGuid();
var report = new {
    ReportId = reportId,
    Maker = name !=null ? name:"no name",
    Desc = desc,
    Pass = name != null
};

byte[] filebytes = Encoding.UTF8.GetBytes(JsonConvert.
SerializeObject(report, Newtonsoft.Json.Formatting.None));
log.LogInformation("Coffee report is generated.");

return new FileContentResult(filebytes, "application/octet-stream")
{FileDownloadName = $"{reportId}.txt"};

}
```

2. *Config* is basically a JSON file, created with the name function.
   json. This config file defines the trigger, binding, and other
   configuration settings. The following (Listing 3-2) is the
   configuration code for the Azure function we created.

Listing 3-2. Configuration code

```json
{
  "bindings": [
    {
      "authLevel": "function",
      "name": "req",
      "type": "httpTrigger",
      "direction": "in",
      "methods": [
        "get",
```

```
      "post"
    ]
  },
  {
    "name": "$return",
    "type": "http",
    "direction": "out"
  }
 ]
}
```

The following are the properties of the `function.json` file:

- `authLevel` determines if a key is required to run the function. The authorization level has the following values:

  - `anonymous`: If this is selected, no API key is required.

  - `function`: The default value. For this, a function-specific API key is required.

  - `admin`: If this is selected, a master key is required.

- `name`: This is required. It is the variable name that is used in the function code for a request or request body.

- `type`: This is required and should be `httpTrigger`.

- `direction`: This is required and should be `in`.

- `methods`: In our case, we use the HTTP methods `get` and `post`.

Testing the Azure Function

Now that we have created an `httpTrigger` function, we can test it by calling a `get` or `post` resource. To do this, we require a function URL. Copy the function URL from the function screen (Figure 3-10).

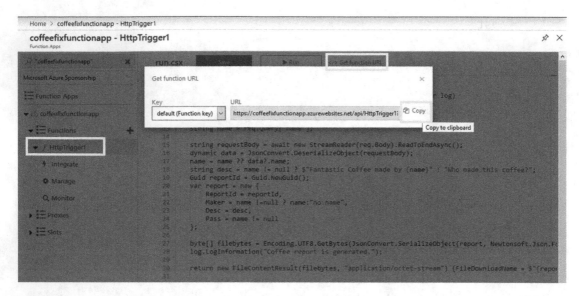

Figure 3-10. *Function URL*

Paste this URL in your browser, and you will receive a text file. Now, paste the URL in your browser again, by adding the query parameter name. This will again give you a text file. This text file is a randomly generated report file. (In the real world, you would implement business logic.) You will also see the logs from Logs (Figure 3-11).

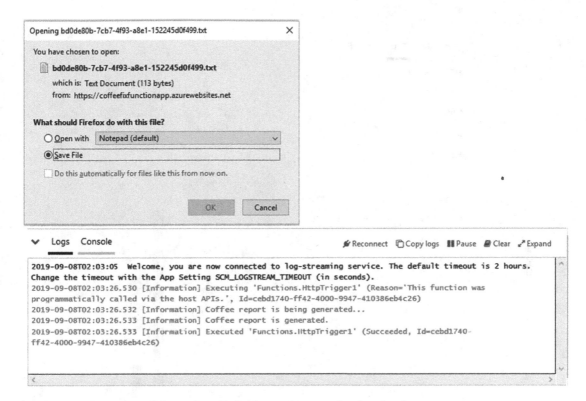

Figure 3-11. *Logs (downloaded file and Console display)*

We can also test our function, by clicking Test from the tab available at the right-hand side of the screen. Click the small icon ➤ to expand the Test section, provide the required values, and click Run at the bottom right (Figure 3-12).

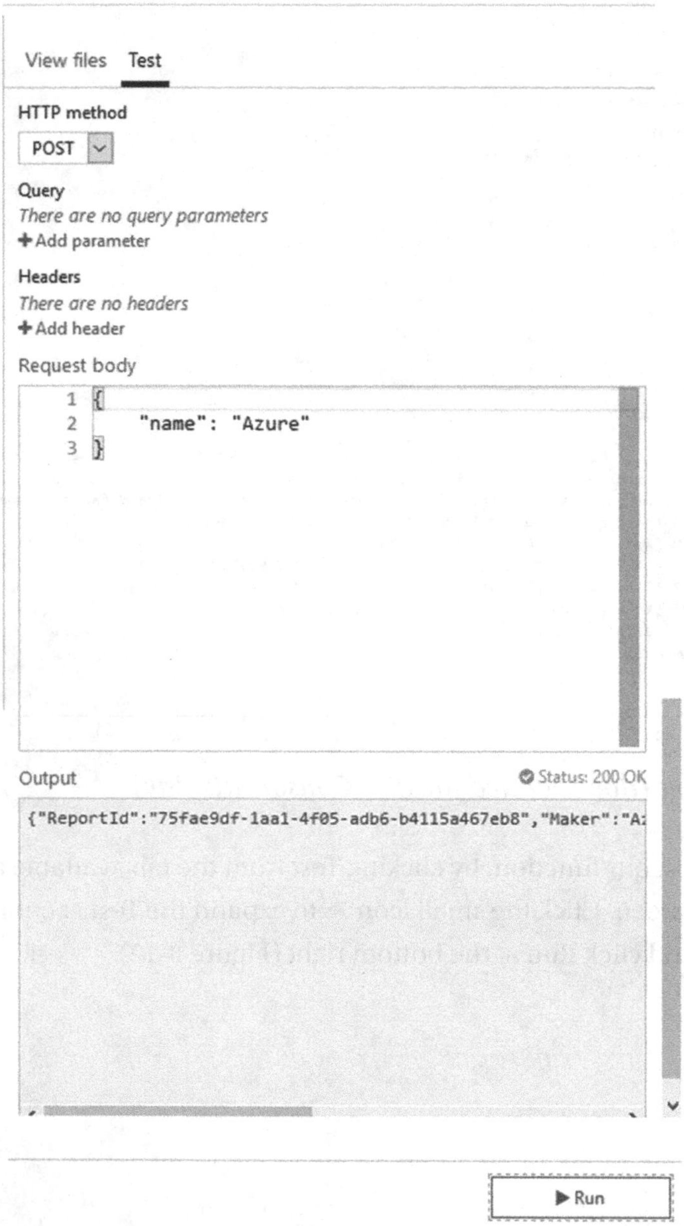

View files   **Test**

HTTP method

POST ⌄

Query
There are no query parameters
+ Add parameter

Headers
There are no headers
+ Add header

Request body

```
1  {
2      "name":  "Azure"
3  }
```

Output   ✓ Status: 200 OK

{"ReportId":"75fae9df-1aa1-4f05-adb6-b4115a467eb8","Maker":"A

▶ Run

Figure 3-12. *Testing*

Monitoring the Azure Function Apps

To begin, click Monitor on the Function App screen. The monitoring screen provides complete details of requests. It indicates the date and time in UTC, the success, the result code, the duration, and the operation ID of the request. This data reflects the previous 30 days. You can receive invocation details of specific operations by clicking Success/failure status. Figure 3-13 shows the data of our function apps (for the previous 30 days).

⟲ Refresh

| Application Insights Instance | Success count in last 30 days | Error count in last 30 days | Query returned 20 items | Troubleshoot your app |
| coffeefixfunctionapp | ✅ 14 | ❗ 10 | ▣ Run in Application Insights | ✖ Diagnose and solve problems |

DATE (UTC) ⌄	SUCCESS ⌄	RESULT CODE ⌄	DURATION (MS) ⌄	OPERATION ID ⌄
2019-09-08 02:03:26.522	✅	200	12.9269	01c3da6a0222dd4793fad6fea72e718b
2019-09-08 02:01:01.365	✅	200	10.7228	5ca8ca266726ef4194bab609a497c731
2019-09-08 02:00:47.339	✅	200	16.991	a6474d9af9f707439b4a59a283a0776d
2019-09-08 01:59:48.831	✅	200	6.0421	a6ab23a800be3540a4f2ca9cff6330c9
2019-09-08 01:59:36.503	✅	200	119.647	b15ed0f29fd92047acb1f5b486d159bf
2019-09-08 01:59:19.574	✅	200	176.1536	1e357365f8c8ec46b8f7a26de44a6a5c
2019-09-08 01:52:19.501	✅	200	254.2937	5e87f5f33a095f498044ba25fdb955a1
2019-09-08 00:35:03.508	✅	200	8.1854	5a74c16c06d3c145b123e407fe8c5d87
2019-09-08 00:35:02.976	✅	200	25.2979	cdd2dad96cd50842ba386de0d6765643
2019-09-08 00:33:45.125	✅	200	8.6025	0feae7d82b68b746b889b26936ac7b26
2019-09-08 00:33:43.356	✅	200	26.0753	2d5a255039fe4f419c47ce1434f2903e

Figure 3-13. Logs

Logic Apps

Workflows and processes are important mechanisms for running any organization or business smoothly. These workflows and processes could include drafting and sending e-mails to clients, extracting data from Excel spreadsheets, etc. For example, how much time and cost is incurred to send 100 e-mails? There should be some mechanism that automates such processes and workflows, to save time and reduce costs (from manual intervention). It would be more efficient to integrate these automated processes with multiple applications. We can achieve this with the help of the Microsoft Azure Logic Apps service.

Note   Azure Logic Apps is an iPaaS (Integration Platform as a Service) with in-built scalability.

Azure Logic Apps is serverless. It provides a mechanism for integrating workflows and processes with multiple applications on Azure. With the help of a visual designer, we can configure the workflows. Built-in standard connectors and enterprise integration connectors help us to do this and define a workflow.

The following are the various components of Azure Logic Apps:

- Workflow

- Managed connectors

- Triggers

- Actions

- Enterprise Integration Pack (EIP)

Creating a Logic App

In this section, we will create our logic app. Our logic app will make a workflow to send e-mail and return a workable file.

1. On the Azure portal, click Create a resource ➤ Integration ➤ Logic App (Figure 3-14).

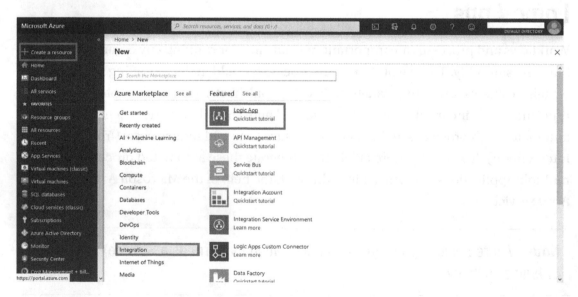

Figure 3-14. *Create a resource—Logic App*

2. The next screen provides all the information related to Logic App
    (Figure 3-15).

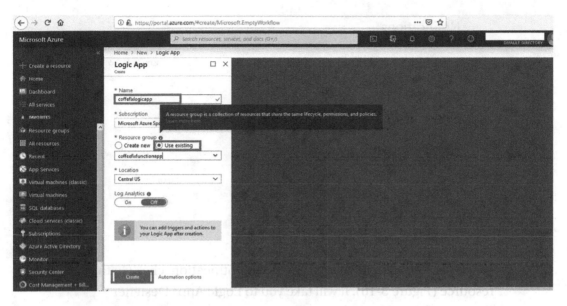

Figure 3-15. *Logic App details*

The preceding figure shows the following information to create
our logic app:

- *Name*: A globally unique name for the logic app. We have named
  our logic app `coffeefixlogicapp`. (You can provide any name of
  your choice.)

- *Subscription*: The Azure subscription. You could have more than
  one Azure subscription.

- *Resource group*: A resource group in which the app is to
  be deployed. We selected our existing resource group:
  `coffeefixfunctionapp`. You can create a new resource group.

- *Location*: The region where information related to our logic app is
  stored. We have chosen Central US.

- *Log Analytics*: On/off. We selected off, so that we can do
  diagnostic logging.

3. Click Notifications to follow the progress of the deployment of the logic app (Figure 3-16).

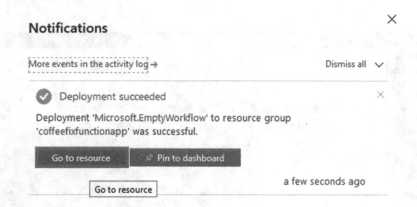

Figure 3-16. *Deployment notifications*

4. When you see a Deployment succeeded notification, click Go to resource (Figure 3-16). It will take you to Logic Apps Designer (Figure 3-17).

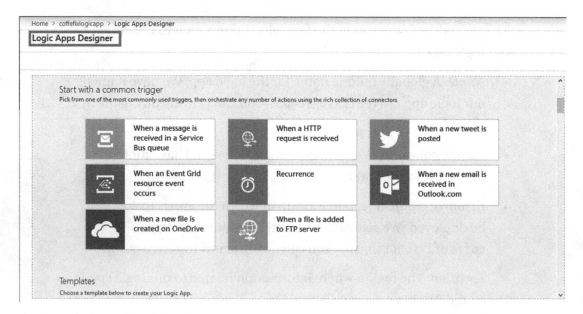

Figure 3-17. *Logic Apps Designer*

5.   From the available templates, click Blank Logic App (Figure 3-18).

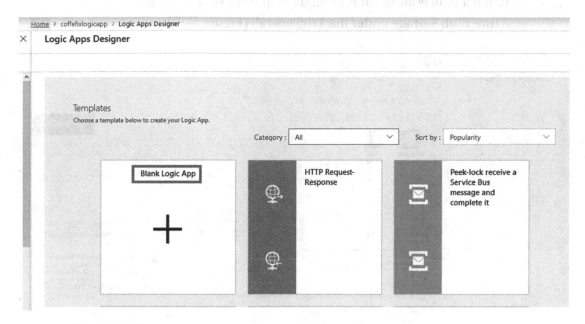

Figure 3-18. *Blank Logic App*

Per our requirements, we need to save a file in Azure Storage (we already created Azure Storage; refer to the "Creating a Function App" section), send an e-mail, and, finally, generate a report file. To complete this workflow, we must add triggers and actions to our logic apps.

Adding Triggers

In Logic Apps, triggers fire whenever a specific condition is met. Triggers are core components of Logic Apps, and every logic app must start with a trigger. By adding a trigger, we are setting up a workflow to implement our new requirements (discussed under "Section Requirements").

1. From Logic Apps Designer, search for Blob Storage and select
    When a blob is added or modified (properties only) (preview)
    Azure Blob Storage under the Triggers tab (Figure 3-19).

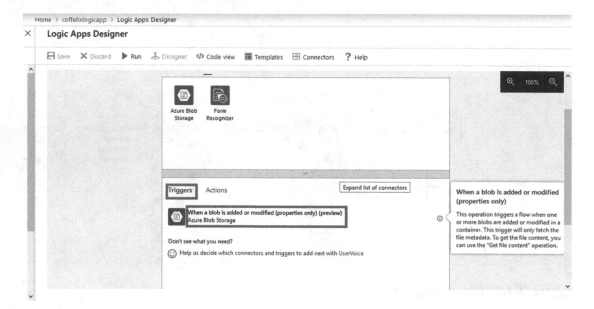

Figure 3-19. *Triggers*

By adding a trigger in the preceding step, we are telling our app to
begin a flow whenever at least one blob is added or modified in
the Azure Blob Storage container.

2. Select our storage, `coffeefixfunctibd07`, and click Manually
    enter connection information. If you do not see a list of available
    storage accounts, refer to Figure 3-20.

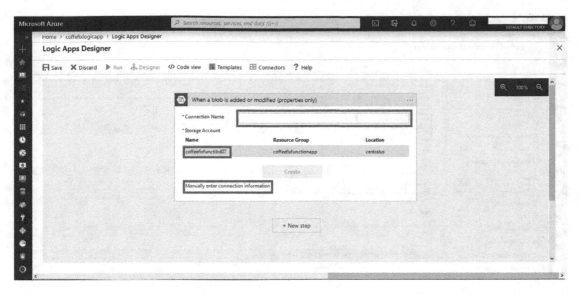

Figure 3-20. *Storage accounts*

Note   The system will require complete information for Azure Blob Storage (for Manually enter connection information), including such details as the connection name, Azure storage account, and a valid access key. You can provide all these details from the Storage Account screen. To reach this screen, search your storage account name from the Home screen of the Azure portal (our storage account is coffeefixfuncibd07). See Figure 3-21.

Figure 3-21. *Storage keys*

Click the Create button after adding `coffeefixblobcname` (Figure 3-21) as the connection name and select the storage account from the list (refer to Figure 3-22).

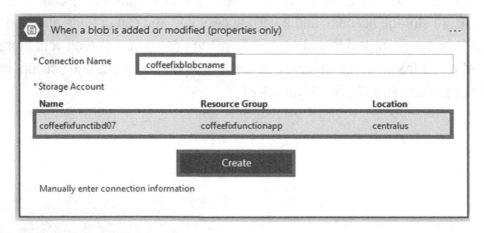

Figure 3-22. *Connection information*

We picked our existing Blob Storage account, and this account has the following existing containers:

- Azure-webjobs-hosts

- Azure-webjobs-secrets

We need a container that contains only our report files. So, we can add it from our Azure Blob Storage screen. From the Azure Blob Storage screen, search for Blob service and select Blobs. Now click Container, to add our new container, as shown in Figure 3-23. Let's name it "container-reports."

Figure 3-23. *Container name*

We must also set the Public access level, to specify how the container can be accessed. These levels are:

- *Private (no anonymous access)*: This is the default access level. With this access level, container data is not available publicly and is only accessible for the account owner. To demonstrate the access levels, we keep the default access level.

- *Blob (anonymous read access for blobs only)*: This allows read access of blobs to all.

- *Container (anonymous read access for containers and blobs)*: This allows read and list access to the container.

Complete your container selection and provide all the required information, and then click Save from Logic Apps Designer, to complete the trigger (Figure 3-24).

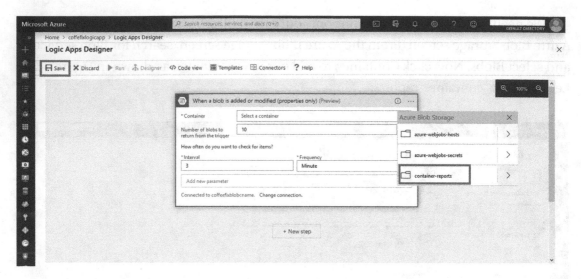

Figure 3-24. *Container selection*

Add Action

We completed the first step when we added a Blob trigger to our logic apps. To achieve the expected features for our logic apps, we must add an action that will send an e-mail.

To demonstrate this feature, we will use SendGrid to send e-mails. For this, you will require a valid SendGrid account. If you do not have a SendGrid account, you can create one for free here: `https://signup.sendgrid.com/`.

Open our Logic app designer and click New Step. Search for SendGrid, and you will see a list of all its actions (refer to Figure 3-25).

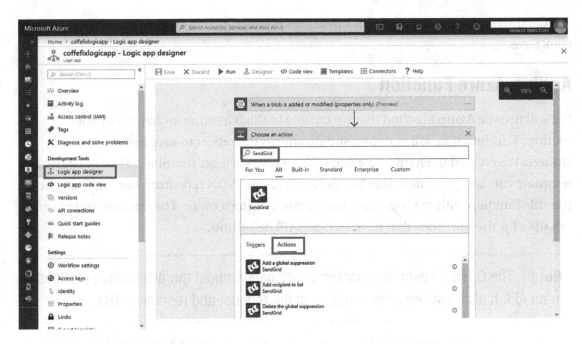

Figure 3-25. *SendGrid Actions*

By clicking Send email (v3), you can select any option, per your requirements. Give it a meaningful connection name. We used the name `coffeefixsendmail`, provided a valid SendGrid Api Key, and clicked Create (Figure 3-26). You can generate a new SendGrid Api Key from `https://app.sendgrid.com/settings/api_keys`.

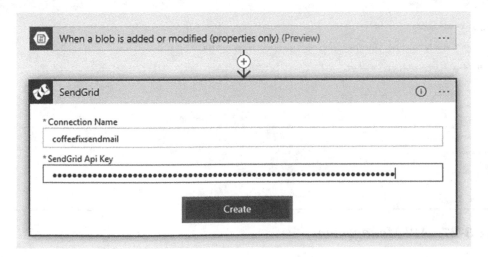

Figure 3-26. *SendGrid Connection Name and Api Key*

On the next screen, provide complete information and contents of the e-mail and click Save.

Adding Azure Function

We will use the Azure function that we created in the "Creating an Azure Function" section. This function will generate and download the report to save in on-premises storage. We created the Azure function with an HTTP trigger template. The HTTP trigger template can accept content that has the application/JSON type from our logic app. To use this function with our logic app, we require a custom route. The custom route is only possible for the functions that have an OpenAPI definition.

Note   The OpenAPI definition contains information about the available operations in an API. It also discloses the structure of the request and response data.

We will create an OpenAPI definition for our function using Azure API Management (we will discuss this in more detail later in this chapter). Select API Management from Platform features and create or select an existing definition. Complete the details and click Link API on the next screen (Figure 3-27).

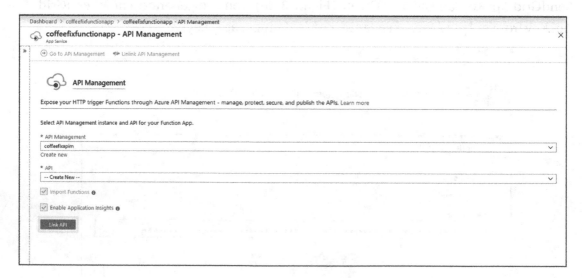

Figure 3-27. *API Management*

From the Import Azure Functions screen, select the Azure function. Note that you will see only functions that use the HTTP trigger. Leave the default values on Create from function app and click Create. Click Test, if you want to test the functionality. Click Download OpenAPI definition, and you will get a JSON file (Figure 3-28).

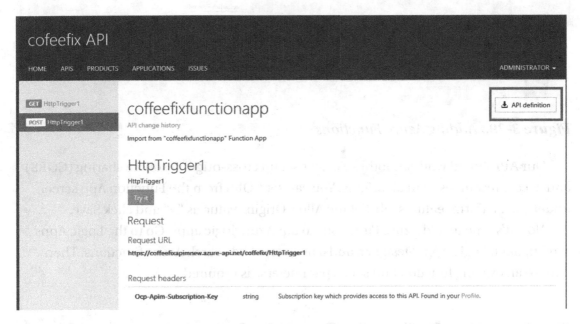

Figure 3-28. *Downloading OpenAPI definition*

Note   Cross-origin resource sharing (CORS) is a way to use restricted resources on a web page from outside the domain.

Only functions that have OpenAPI definition will be available (Figure 3-29).

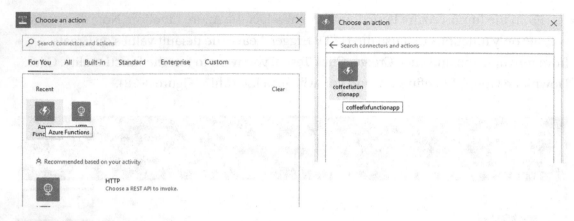

Figure 3-29. *Adding Azure Functions*

Our API should work smoothly. So, let's set up cross-origin resource sharing (CORS) and access resources from all origins. You can set CORS from the Function App screen, under the Platform features tab. Set the Allow Origins value as "∗" and click Save.

Now it's time to add Azure Functions to our Azure logic apps. Go to the Logic Apps screen, open Logic Apps Designer, add a new step, and search Azure functions. Then choose an existing function and set its parameters, as required.

Back to the CoffeeFix Console App

In previous sections, we have created our logic apps (to configure the workflow for sending e-mail on an updated blob and to call an Azure function to perform calculations) and Azure Functions. Now we will amend our CoffeeFix console app to work with Logic Apps.

We will continue with the CoffeeFix console app and make changes, per our new requirements. Let's add a new package, so that we can work and connect with Azure Blob Storage. We add the package from the Windows command prompt (Figure 3-30).

```
dotnet add package Microsoft.Azure.Storage.Blob
```

Figure 3-30. *Adding a package to Azure Storage Blob*

Note   You can also add the Microsoft.Azure.Storage.Blob package, by using the NuGet Package Manager console.

After this, we will add the following, using directives (see Listing 3-3).

Listing 3-3. Using directives

```
using Microsoft.Azure.Storage;
using Microsoft.Azure.Storage.Blob;
```

To connect with our Azure Blob Storage account, we need a connection string. The connection string can be found on the Azure portal. Open Storage Account and under Settings click Access key and copy Connection string (Figure 3-31).

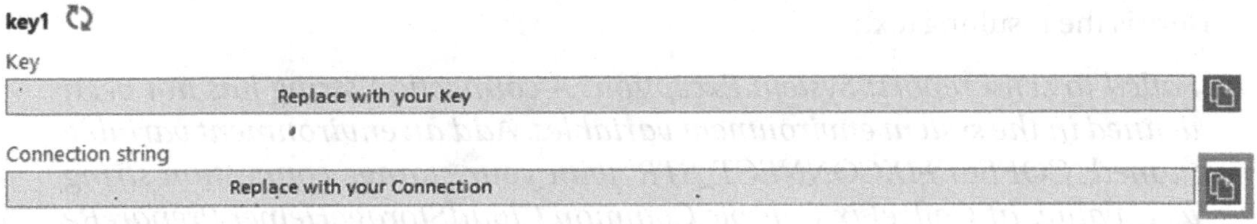

key1 ↻

Key

Replace with your Key

Connection string

Replace with your Connection

Figure 3-31. *Key and Connection string*

We added our connection string value to an environment variable of the local operating system (we are using Windows Operating System). Replace <addyourconnectionstringhere> from setx COFFEEFIXCONNECT_STR <addyourconnectionstringhere> with a valid storage connection string (Figure 3-32).

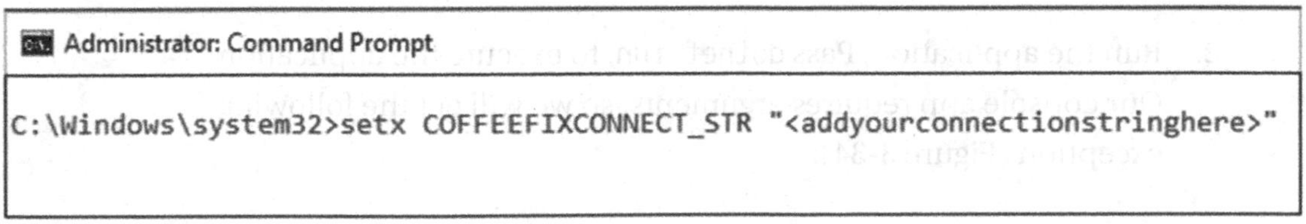

Administrator: Command Prompt

```
C:\Windows\system32>setx COFFEEFIXCONNECT_STR "<addyourconnectionstringhere>"
```

Figure 3-32. *Setting the environment variable*

The following statement helps us to retrieve the storage connection string from the environment variable:

```
string coffeeFixConnectionString = Environment.GetEnvironmentVariable
("COFFEEFIXCONNECT_STR");
```

The CoffeeFix console app will terminate if the system does not find the connection string (Figure 3-33).

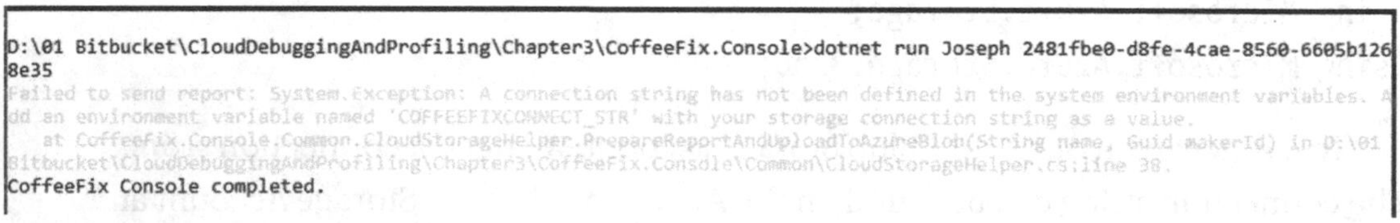

```
D:\01 Bitbucket\CloudDebuggingAndProfiling\Chapter3\CoffeeFix.Console>dotnet run Joseph 2481fbe0-d8fe-4cae-8560-6605b126
8e35
Failed to send report: System.Exception: A connection string has not been defined in the system environment variables. A
dd an environment variable named 'COFFEEFIXCONNECT_STR' with your storage connection string as a value.
   at CoffeeFix.Console.Common.CloudStorageHelper.PrepareReportAndUploadToAzureBlob(String name, Guid makerId) in D:\01
Bitbucket\CloudDebuggingAndProfiling\Chapter3\CoffeeFix.Console\Common\CloudStorageHelper.cs:line 38.
CoffeeFix Console completed.
```

Figure 3-33. *Exception due to unavailability of connection string*

Here is the resulting text:

Failed to send report: System.Exception: A connection string has not been defined in the system environment variables. Add an environment variable named 'COFFEEFIXCONNECT_STR' with your storage connection string as a value. at CoffeeFix.Console.Common.CloudStorageHelper.PrepareReportAndUploadToAzureBlob(String name, Guid makerId) in...line 38.

Test CoffeeFix Console App

Let's run our application, to see if it is working as expected. Open the command prompt and go to the folder in which the CoffeeFix console app is stored. Perform these steps:

1. Build the application. Enter dotnet build, to build our console application.

2. Run the application. Pass dotnet run, to execute the application. Our console app requires arguments, so we will get the following exception (Figure 3-34):

```
D:\01 Bitbucket\CloudDebuggingAndProfiling\Chapter3\CoffeeFix.Console>dotnet run
CoffeeFix Console requires two parameters: Store Supervisorname and the id of the coffee maker.
Example:
CoffeeFix.Console Kenneth Davis CB81F3C2-1182-4A5D-A941-52A80CEBE1D1
CoffeeFix Console completed.
```

Figure 3-34. *Parameters are required*

3. Provide the required argument. Pass command dotnet run
   Davis CB81F3C2-1182-4A5D-A941-52A80CEBE1D1 and note the
   result. This is the valid command for our console application.
   Figure 3-35 shows the results.

```
D:\01 Bitbucket\CloudDebuggingAndProfiling\Chapter3\CoffeeFix.Console>dotnet run Joseph 2481fbe0-d8fe-4cae-8560-6605b126
8e35
File is created C:\Users\aroraG\Documents\Report_2173450c-bdc6-49b5-a99a-99a568e62673.txt
Uploading to Blob storage as blob 'Report_2173450c-bdc6-49b5-a99a-99a568e62673.txt'
CoffeeFix Console completed.
```

Figure 3-35. *Successful run with valid input*

We added Listing 3-4 to upload the file to Azure Blob Storage. Method
PrepareReportAndUploadToAzureBlob is responsible to perform the Upload File
operation.

Listing 3-4. Upload a file to Blob Storage

```
public static async Task PrepareReportAndUploadToAzureBlob(string name,
Guid makerId)
{
    string coffeeFixConnectionString = Environment.GetEnvironmentVariable
    ("COFFEEFIXCONNECT_STR");
    CloudStorageAccount coffeeFixStorageAccount;
    if (CloudStorageAccount.TryParse(coffeeFixConnectionString, out
    coffeeFixStorageAccount))
    {
        CloudBlobClient cloudBlobClient = coffeeFixStorageAccount.
        CreateCloudBlobClient();
        CloudBlobContainer cloudBlobContainer = cloudBlobClient.
        GetContainerReference("container-reports");
        await cloudBlobContainer.CreateIfNotExistsAsync();

        //setting permissions are optional
        BlobContainerPermissions permissions = new BlobContainerPermissions
        {
            PublicAccess = BlobContainerPublicAccessType.Blob
        };
        await cloudBlobContainer.SetPermissionsAsync(permissions);
```

```
        Utility.name = name;
        Utility.makerId = makerId;
        Utility.PrepareReport();
        System.Console.WriteLine($"File is created {Utility.SourceFile}");
        System.Console.WriteLine("Uploading to Blob storage as blob '{0}'",
        Utility.localReportFileName);

        CloudBlockBlob cloudBlockBlob = cloudBlobContainer.
        GetBlockBlobReference(Utility.localReportFileName);
        await cloudBlockBlob.UploadFromFileAsync(Utility.SourceFile);
    }
    else
    {
        throw new Exception("A connection string has not been defined in
        the system environment variables. " +
"Add an environment variable named 'COFFEEFIXCONNECT_STR' with your
storage " +
"connection string as a value.");

    }
}
```

The preceding code (Listing 3-4) works like this:

- Gets the Connection string from the Environment variable.

- Connects the Azure Cloud Storage account and creates BlobClient.

- Adds Container.

- Sets permissions for the container.

- Generates Reportdata by using the GenerateRandomDataForReport method (Listing 3-5). This demonstrates that we have created random data.

Listing 3-5. Generate Reports Data

```
public static byte[] GenerateRandomDataForReport(string name, Guid makerId)
{
    var random = new Random();

    var report = new StoreReport
    {
        MakerId = makerId,
        Supervisor = name,
        UpTimeMeasure = random.Next(300, 22000),
        BeanCount = random.Next(100, 33000),
        WaterLevel = random.Next(0, 9),
        RandomMetricsA = Enumerable.Repeat(0, 500).Select(i => random.
        Next(0, 99)).ToArray(),
        RandomMetricsB = Enumerable.Repeat(0, 500).Select(i => random.
        Next(0, 99)).ToArray(),
        RandomMetricsC = Enumerable.Repeat(0, 500).Select(i => random.
        Next(0, 99)).ToArray(),
    };

    return Encoding.UTF8.GetBytes(JsonConvert.SerializeObject(report,
    Formatting.None));
}
```

- Saves to a local file.

- Uploads the local file to Azure Blob Storage.

- Causes Console app to execute and perform two tasks:

    - It creates a report and saves it to a local folder in the text file. This
      text file stores JSON data (Figure 3-36). You can view the JSON
      data with any JSON viewer, by opening the local file in any text
      editor from the local folder.

Figure 3-36. *JSON output*

- A report is uploaded to Azure Blob Storage. You can also check the file from the Azure portal. Go to your Azure Blob Storage and open the container, and you will find the same file (Figure 3-37).

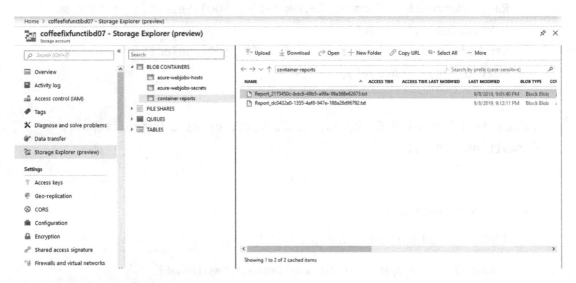

Figure 3-37. *Files stored*

- As soon as our Azure Blob updates, it triggers Logic Apps and initiates the e-mail (Figure 3-38).

Figure 3-38. *Sample mail*

- Finally, Logic App calls a function, and it sends a CoffeeFix store report to on-premises storage. Figure 3-39 shows the JSON output of the report.

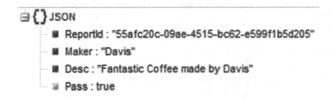

Figure 3-39. *JSON view of output*

We tested it and found that our CoffeeFix console application is working according to our requirements.

An Overview of API Management Services

With the help of the Azure API Management (APIM) service, we can publish, secure, transform, maintain, and monitor our APIs. Azure API Management provides an interface with which we can easily create an API dashboard for our customers. API Management manages the tasks related to API calls, such as authentication and authorization, rate limit, request and response transformation, logging, and tracing, and also other versions of APIs.

The complete system of API Management is built on the following three components:

- API gateway

- Admin portal

- Developer portal

Creating an API Management Service

From Azure portal, click Create a resource ➤ Integration ➤ API Management (Figure 3-40).

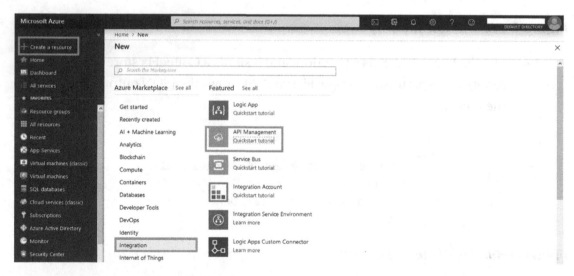

Figure 3-40. *Selecting API Management*

The next screen provides all the information required to create an API Management service. After inserting the relevant information, click Create (Figure 3-41).

Figure 3-41. *Creating API Management services*

API Management Products

Products in Azure API Management are similar to groups that contain one or more APIs. In other words, a product contains a usage quota and the terms of use for the APIs. Once a product is published, developers can subscribe to the product and begin to use its APIs. We've created a "Basic" product with which to group all free APIs with specific usage quotas. Click Create, then Publish, so that the product will be available on the Developer portal (Figure 3-42).

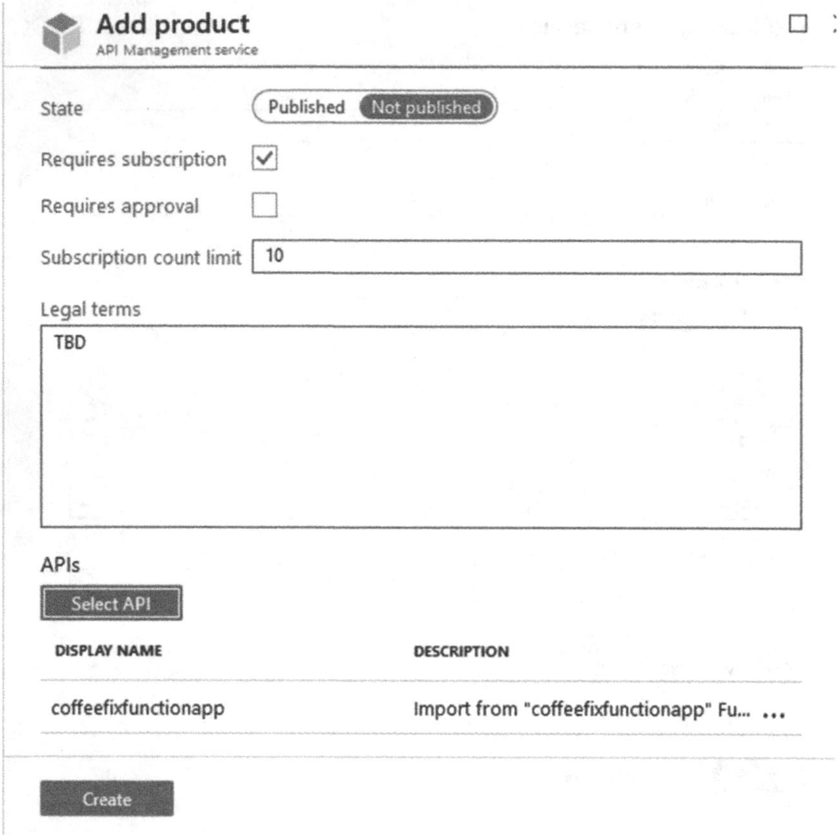

Figure 3-42. *Add product*

Once our product has been created, we can define policies for it, such as accepting only JSON requests or providing only XML responses, etc. To keep our example simple, we are not making any changes in product policy.

Adding a subscription for the Basic product allows developers to subscribe to the subscription package. To make our code simpler, we've added a Basic subscription, which is free for all subscribers (Figure 3-43).

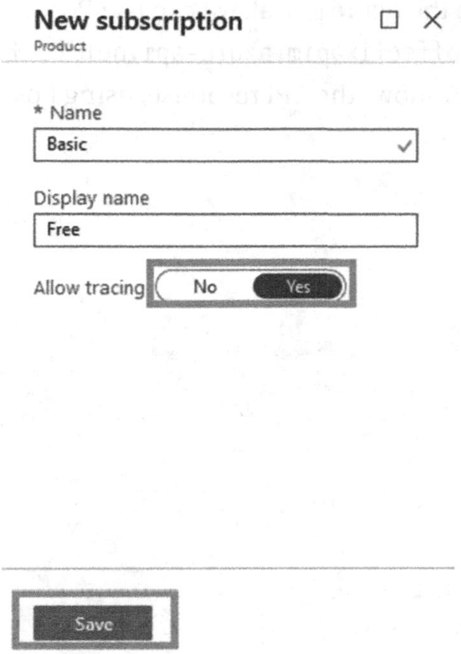

New subscription   □ ✕
Product

* Name

| Basic | ✓ |

Display name

| Free |

Allow tracing | No   **Yes** |

| Save |

Figure 3-43. *New subscription*

Subscriptions have subscription keys (Primary and Secondary). These keys are required in order to use APIs of products belonging to a subscription. Figure 3-44 shows the Subscription keys of Basic—Subscriptions.

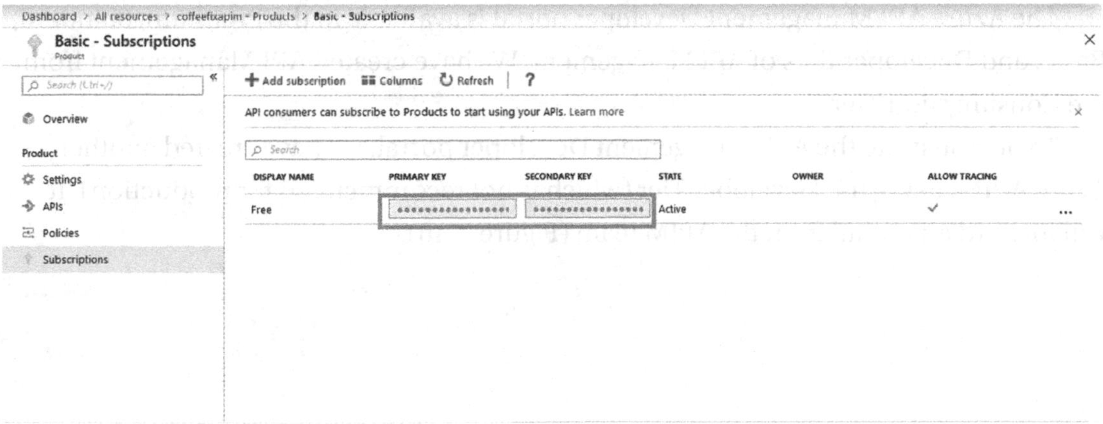

Figure 3-44. *Subscription keys*

To test our API outside the Azure portal, we can use Postman. Open Postman and test POST (`https://coffeefixapim.azure-api.net/coffeefixfunctionapp/HttpTrigger1`). Figure 3-45 shows the API response, using Postman.

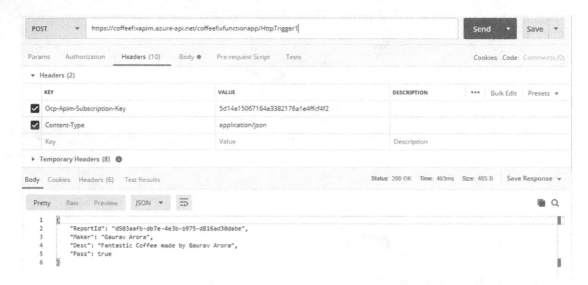

Figure 3-45. *Calling our API with Postman*

We have now reviewed API Management services and created APIs, products, and subscriptions from the Azure portal. Please note that most of the features discussed were being previewed at the time of writing this book.

The Azure API Management Developer portal is available in the Premium, Standard, Basic, and Developer tiers of API Management. We have created API Management from the Consumption Tier.

To demonstrate the API Management Developer portal, we have created another Azure APIM, using the Developer Tier (which is not recommended for production). It will forward an e-mail from the APIM team (Figure 3-46).

Azure API Management

Your Azure API Management instance **'coffeefixapimnew'** is ready to go! You can find it in the Azure portal.

To get started, follow this tutorial. It will show you how to create an API, define its operations and then test it in an interactive console. All in under 5 minutes.

These resources might be helpful too:
Documentation
Forum
Updates
Feature requests

Many thanks!
Azure API Management Team

Figure 3-46. *Sample e-mail from the Azure API Management team*

Our new Azure APIM service gives us built-in products and APIs. Do not change anything; keep the default values. Figure 3-47 shows the default products.

DISPLAY NAME	ACCESS CONTROL	STATE	
Starter	Administrators, Developers, Guests	Published	...
Unlimited	Administrators, Developers, Guests	Published	...

Figure 3-47. *APIM products*

We can go to the Developer portal and edit/update the components. The overview screen shows all the information related to the Azure APIM service (Figure 3-48).

[ ] Publisher portal   [ ] Developer portal   [ ] New developer portal (previ...   🗑 Delete

Resource group (change)
coffeefixfunctionapp

Status
Online

Location
Central India

Subscription (change)
Microsoft Azure Sponsorship

Subscription ID
580dbac4-cf41-460d-a17b-af7299f00c16

Tags (change)

apim : cost

Developer portal URL
https://coffeefixapimnew.portal.azure-api.net

Gateway URL
https://coffeefixapimnew.azure-api.net

Tier
Developer (No SLA)

Virtual IP (VIP) addresses
public: 104.211.77.42

Repository
◈ Disabled 🗋

Figure 3-48. *APIM overview*

We will open the Developer portal, to test our newly added APIs. The Developer portal provides samples and a way to test the API. You can modify the contents and layout of the Developer portal. In addition, the Publisher portal provides a way to add more content. Figure 3-49 shows the APIs (Developer portal) of our imaginary application, CoffeeFix.

Figure 3-49. *APIs (Developer portal)*

This section discussed Azure APIM services and provided an overview of its various components. Next, we will discuss how to use tags for billing.

Using Tags for Billing

Tags are used to organize resources logically, by using properties that we define. Tags can be associated to a resource or a group of resources directly. Tags can be very useful when we want to locate or select resources or groups of resources from within the following:

- The console
- Web portal
- PowerShell
- The API

Tags also help to organize resources for billing management. In this section, we will demonstrate this by setting up an Azure policy to `Append tag and its default value`. We will use Azure portal to set up the policy. Make sure you're logged in to your Azure account. In this example, we will use the Azure Sample policy available on GitHub (`https://github.com/Azure/azure-policy/tree/master/samples`).

You can initiate the new policy with a sample value from this link: `https://portal.azure.com/?#blade/Microsoft_Azure_Policy/CreatePolicyDefinitionBlade/uri/https%3A%2F%2Fraw.githubusercontent.com%2FAzure%2Fazure-policy%2Fmaster%2Fsamples%2Fbuilt-in-policy%2Fapply-default-tag-value%2Fazurepolicy.json`.

- Alternatively, you can click the following link for a blank policy: `https://portal.azure.com/?#blade/Microsoft_Azure_Policy/`.

From Azure portal, from the New Policy definition screen, make changes to suit your requirements. We are creating this policy for the category `compute` and the tag `costCenter`. In our sample JSON file, we amended these values, as shown in Listing 3-6.

Listing 3-6. Setting a policy

```
"parameters": {
    "tagName": {
        "type": "String",
        "metadata": {
```

```
      "description": "costCenter"
    }
  },
  "tagValue": {
    "type": "String",
    "metadata": {
      "description": "coffeefix"
    }
  }
}
```

In Listing 3-6, we have set a policy with `tagName` `CostCenter` and `tagValue` `coffeefix`. After all the necessary amendments, click Save, to create a policy definition. You should receive a notification of success, as shown in Figure 3-50.

Figure 3-50. *Notifications*

Summary

This chapter introduced serverless computing and Azure Functions and its implementations. We continued to evolve our imaginary application, CoffeeFix, and added various advantages and usages of serverless computing, by implementing Azure Functions. We also covered integration with respect to EIP, by using Azure Logic Apps. The sample application was extremely simple, but, we hope, provided some understanding as to how serverless computing can been used to ease the work experience. We also added the power of API Management to our sample application.

With the help of a bit of code, we discussed various advantages and important features of API Management. Finally, we discussed the magic of Azure Tags and how we can manage our costs by using these.

In the next chapter, we will monitor a solution, with the help of Application Insights. We will introduce the Application Insights blade and Log Analytics reporting. The Application Insights blade supports many types of applications and platforms, and its ability to simplify views is important for focusing on the specific concerns of a particular scenario. Log Analytics uses a query language built on the language supported by Azure Data Explorer, and Chapter 4 will offer some examples of generating reports.

CHAPTER 4

Application Insights

Using an Application Performance Management (APM) service effectively is essential to the health of modern solutions. An APM provides a means to gain a view of deployed applications that may span across data centers, as well as of cloud and on-premises applications. As modern solutions tend to be composed of more distributed systems, a sophisticated, flexible, and intuitive APM is necessary for maintaining the health of a solution and to gain a comprehensive view.

Application Insights is Microsoft's APM as a service offering. It includes powerful analytics, error detection, and visual tools to allow for a comprehensive view of running systems. Many of the Azure services provide support for sending telemetry to Application Insights, and a wide variety of platforms, including .NET, Node.js, and J2EE, are supported. Telemetry can be collected from both applications running in the cloud as well as on-premises.

This chapter introduces the basic mechanics of Application Insights, as well as how to use Log Analytics to report on the telemetry data collected. The CoffeeFix console application will be used to demonstrate features of Application Insights. There are many ways to send telemetry data, and using a console application is a good way to understand the building blocks of Application Insights in .Net Core applications. In subsequent chapters, other approaches will be shown.

This chapter introduces the Application Insights blade and Log Analytics reporting. The Application Insights blade supports many types of applications and platforms, and its ability to simplify the view is important for focusing on the specific concerns of a particular scenario. Log Analytics uses the Kusto query language, which is built on the language supported by Azure Data Explorer.

This chapter covers these topics in the following sections: "Creating Application Insights," "Adding a Telemetry Initializer," "Tracking Dependencies," "Tracking Exceptions," "Additional Telemetry Processing," "Viewing Application Insights Data in the Portal," and "View Analytics."

© Jeffrey Chilberto, Sjoukje Zaal, Gaurav Aroraa and Ed Price 2020
J. Chilberto et al., *Cloud Debugging and Profiling in Microsoft Azure*,
https://doi.org/10.1007/978-1-4842-5437-0_4

CoffeeFix

To illustrate using Application Insights, we will add the service to the CoffeeFix console application that sends information to the main office. Currently, the coffeemakers send back information periodically about how well they are performing, the conditions they are running under, and a status to indicate if they require maintenance. Different support operators monitor the status of the coffeemakers in their region and arrange for service technicians to service any coffeemakers that require maintenance. This system has worked reasonably well, but after several instances in which a coffeemaker fault was not detected promptly, the business is looking for a better way to monitor the coffeemakers.

In this scenario, we will add Application Insights to the CoffeeFix console application, to collect telemetry information.

Creating Application Insights

The first step is to provision an Application Insights service; we will use the Azure portal to achieve this. This service will capture telemetry data in a console application that we'll create later in the chapter.

In the portal, navigate to the Application Insights blade, either by using the search at the top of the screen or the Application Insights link on the left side menu (Figure 4-1).

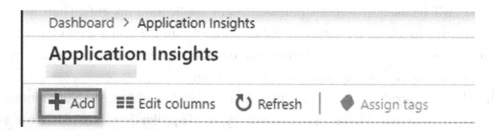

Figure 4-1. *Adding Application Insights*

Some basic information about the service is collected, and the following is an example for the CoffeeFix console application (Figure 4-2).

PROJECT DETAILS

Select a subscription to manage deployed resources and costs. Use resource groups like folders to organize and manage all your resources.

* Subscription ❶	Microsoft Partner Network ⌄
└── * Resource Group ❶	(New) ApplicationInsightsTestGroup ⌄
	Create new

INSTANCE DETAILS

* Name ❶	ApplicationInsightsTest ✓
* Region ❶	(Asia Pacific) Australia East ⌄

Figure 4-2. *Project details*

Once the service is created, the Instrumentation Key will be used later, when we create the .Net Console Application (Figure 4-3).

Resource group (change)	Status	Location
ApplicationInsightsTestGroup	---	West US 2
Subscription (change)	Subscription ID	Instrumentation Key
		b691cd6b-6157-4e4a-beea-033d0ac34d03
Tags (change)		
Click here to add tags		

Figure 4-3. *Copy the Instrumentation Key*

Later in this and subsequent chapters, we will explore different areas of the Application Insights blade. For now, we only need access to the Instrumentation Key on the Overview section.

Adding Insights to the CoffeeFix Console Application

Let's look at hooking up the CoffeeFix application to Application Insights. Working from the Chapter 2 solution, we will be using the Microsoft.ApplicationInsights NuGet package to send the telemetry to Application Insights.

The first step is to add the Microsoft.ApplicationInsights NuGet package. In the Package Manager Console, we will set the Default project to the CoffeeFix.Console application (Figure 4-4).

Figure 4-4. *The Package Manager Console*

The following command adds the NuGet package:

```
Install-Package Microsoft.ApplicationInsights
```

In our `Main` method, we set the Application Insights instrumentation key identified earlier:

```
TelemetryConfiguration configuration = TelemetryConfiguration.Active;
configuration.InstrumentationKey = "[replace with your key]";
```

The next step is to create an instance of `TelemetryClient` that will be used to send messages to Application Insights. In this example, we send a simple event message:

```
var telemetryClient = new TelemetryClient();
telemetryClient.TrackEvent("CoffeeFix.Console has started!");
```

As this is a simple example, we have to give Application Insights enough time to complete its activity, so we'll use a delay of five seconds to make sure the telemetry is pushed to our service, after performing a flush of the telemetry client:

```
telemetryClient.Flush();
Task.Delay(5000).Wait();
```

The following command shows the completed application with existing information elapsed:

```
using Microsoft.ApplicationInsights;
using Microsoft.ApplicationInsights.Extensibility;
using System;
using System.Threading.Tasks;

namespace CoffeeFix.Console
{
    class Program
    {
        static void Main(string[] args)
        {
```

```
// set the Application Insights key
TelemetryConfiguration configuration = TelemetryConfiguration.
Active;
configuration.InstrumentationKey = "[your key here]";

// this simulates a coffee make sending a message back to the
main website periodically
try
{
    var telemetryClient = new TelemetryClient();
    telemetryClient.TrackEvent("CoffeeFix.Console has started!");
    ...
    telemetryClient.Flush();
    Task.Delay(5000).Wait();
}
catch (Exception ex)
{
    ...
}
...
    }
  }
}
```

If all went well, then after running the application, a single trace message is sent to Application Insights. But how can you tell? The Application Insights menu bar should have been added automatically, and a message should be indicated, as shown in Figure 4-5.

Figure 4-5. *Application Insights control*

But if it was not added to the IDE automatically, then under the View menu, you can select the Application Insights Search menu in the Other Windows section. Using this option will load the Application Insights Search tab. At the top of the tab is a cog that allows you to select the Application Insights account (Figure 4-6).

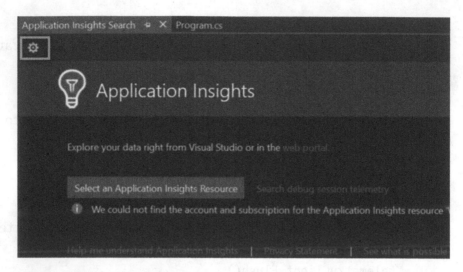

Figure 4-6. *Application Insights Search*

Once the account is selected, you can perform a search of the telemetry data that has been recorded. The following shows a search for all the telemetry recorded in the previous hour (Figure 4-7).

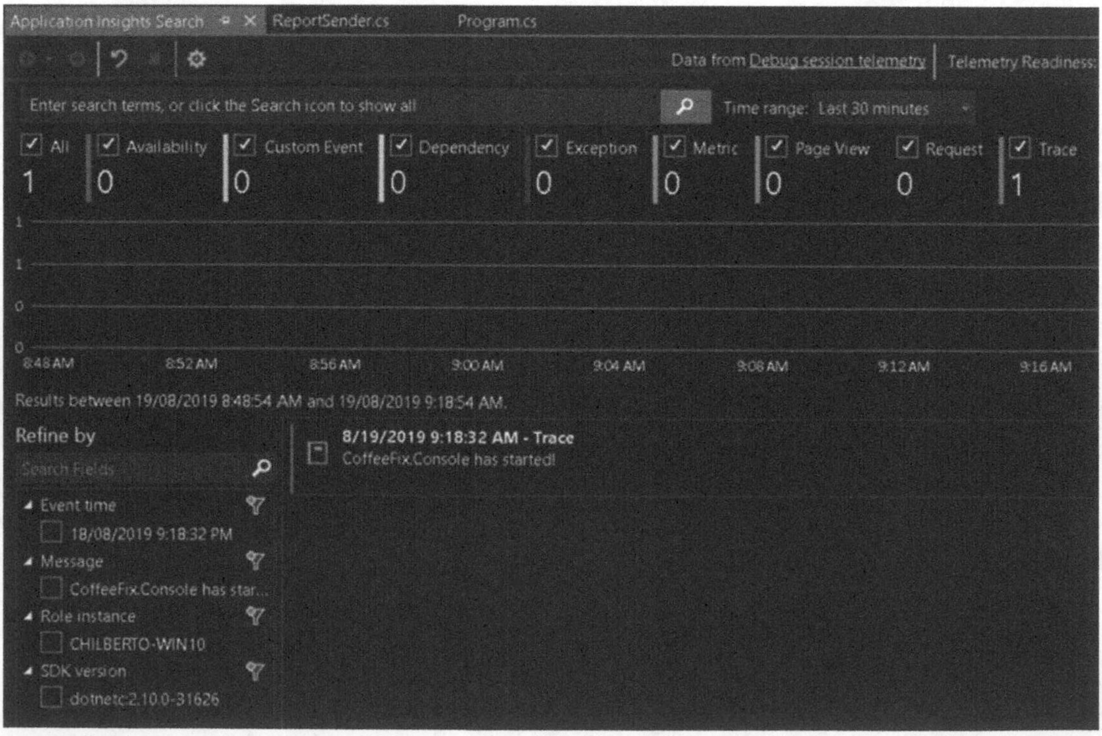

Figure 4-7. *The Application Insights Search results*

Expanding the event will display additional information about the event (Figure 4-8).

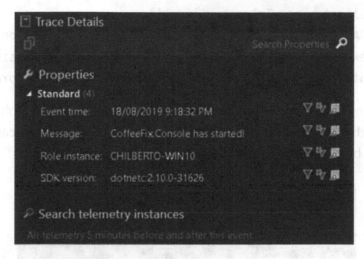

Figure 4-8. *The trace results*

Adding Custom Properties to Events

The next step we'll take is to add some information to our event. Fortunately, the TrackEvent method allows for additional information to be added in the form of two dictionaries (Figure 4-9).

```
//
// Summary:
//     Send an Microsoft.ApplicationInsights.DataContracts.EventTelemetry for display
//     in Diagnostic Search and in the Analytics Portal.
//
// Parameters:
//   eventName:
//     A name for the event.
//
//   properties:
//     Named string values you can use to search and classify events.
//
//   metrics:
//     Measurements associated with this event.
//
// Remarks:
//     Learn more
public void TrackEvent(string eventName, IDictionary<string, string> properties = null, IDictionary<string, double> metrics = null);
```

Figure 4-9. *The TrackEvent method*

For our example, let's add the assembly version to the starting event:

```
var telemetryClient = new TelemetryClient();
var version = Assembly.GetExecutingAssembly().GetName().Version.ToString();
var props = new Dictionary<string, string> { { "Version", version } };
telemetryClient.TrackEvent("CoffeeFix.Console has started!", props);
```

The preceding code determines the version from the running assembly, and it adds the version number as a property to the event. In the Visual Studio Application Insights Search, this can be viewed as follows (Figure 4-10).

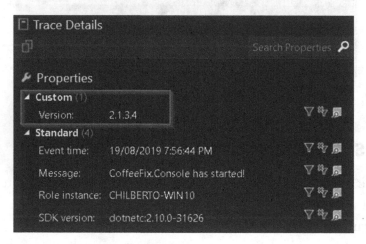

Figure 4-10. *Trace Details with Version*

Another important form of custom property is the metrics that allow for the data to be collected that are valuable to perform measurements across multiple events. As an example, we'll collect a new measurement of the amount of time that the console application took to run.

The first step is to create a StopWatch instance at the start of the application:

```
var watch = new Stopwatch();
watch.Start();
```

A new event is then added before the call to flush the telemetry, as shown in the following:

```
telemetryClient.TrackEvent("CoffeeFix.Console has ended!",
                    properties: props,
                    metrics: new Dictionary<string, double>
                    {
                        {
                            "ElapsedMilliseconds",
                            watch.ElapsedMilliseconds
                        }
                    });
```

In the Visual Studio Application Insights Search, this is also shown in the properties section of the event (Figure 4-11).

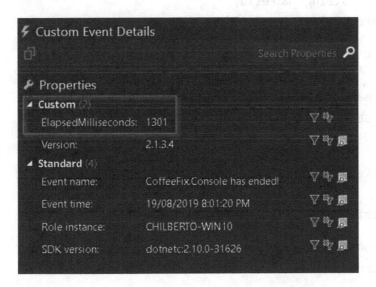

Figure 4-11. *Custom Event Details*

Being able to add custom properties to the telemetry will be used by the CoffeeFix team to identify important information about the coffeemakers deployed. We have added a version of the software running, as well as how long the application has taken to complete. The next section will explore using some of the context properties available in the reported telemetry.

Adding a Telemetry Initializer

Application Insights provides several convenient ways of extending the functionality. One of these is the ability to add initializers that are run each time the telemetry is tracked. The interface, ITelemetryInitializer, has a single method Initialize(). Take the following example:

```
using Microsoft.ApplicationInsights.Channel;
using Microsoft.ApplicationInsights.Extensibility;
using System;

namespace CoffeeFix.Console
{
    internal class TelemetryInitializer : ITelemetryInitializer
    {
        private string _makerId;
        private string _sessionId;

        public TelemetryInitializer(string userId)
        {
            _makerId = userId;
            _sessionId = Guid.NewGuid().ToString();
        }

        public void Initialize(ITelemetry telemetry)
        {
            var context = telemetry.Context;

            context.Session.Id = _sessionId;
            context.User.Id = _makerId;
        }
    }
}
```

This initializer sets the session ID and ID of the coffeemaker. One important thing to note is that the Initialize() method is run per event and not once. This is why the _sessionId is set in the constructor and not in the Initialize() method.

The initializer is added to the telemetry and will be applied to each new instance of TelemetryClient:

```
TelemetryConfiguration.Active.TelemetryInitializers
       .Add(new TelemetryInitializer(args.Length == 2 ?
                                 args[1] :
                                 "[unknown]"));
```

The CoffeeFix.Console application takes two parameters. The second is the ID of the coffeemaker. This is why if it is not supplied, then the value of "[unknown]" is used.

As expected, when the application is run, the account ID and session ID are now set (Figure 4-12).

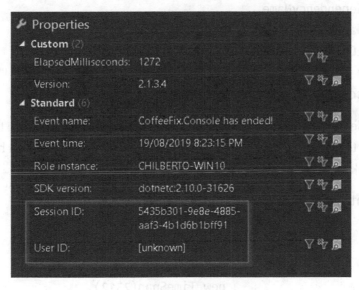

Figure 4-12. *The event with Session ID and User ID*

In the CoffeeFix.Console example, the TelemetryContext is empty, but when used in combination with other ApplicationInsights packages, the properties of the TelemetryContext will automatically be set. For example, when using the ASP.Net package, information about the web application will be set as part of each tracked web request.

Tracking Dependencies

Tracking dependencies of a running application is an important way of both measuring behavior and performance, as well as understanding a running application. This example manually adds a dependency, and like the preceding `TelemetryInitializer`, in subsequent chapters, these dependencies are tracked by the framework, without additional code having to be written.

A dependency can be tracked using the `TrackDependency` method, as shown in the following command:

```
public void TrackDependency(
     string dependencyTypeName,
     string dependencyName,
     string data,
     DateTimeOffset startTime,
     TimeSpan duration,
     bool success);
```

In the sample application, the following call will be made to illustrate the tracking of a successful call to a water sensor, including when the call was made and how long the dependency took to complete:

```
telemetryClient.TrackDependency("Application",
                                "WaterSensor",
                                "IsSystemOnline?",
                                DateTime.UtcNow,
                                new TimeSpan(2312),
                                true);
```

This is tracked, as indicated in the following image, in Application Insights Search (Figure 4-13).

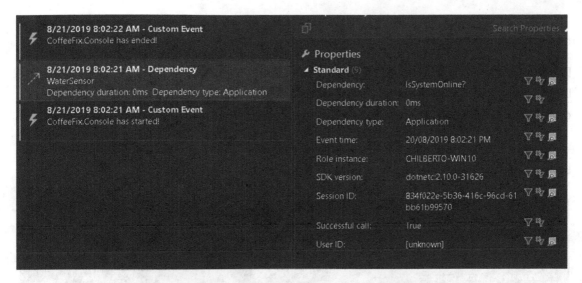

Figure 4-13. *The Dependency trace*

Note that the account ID and session ID are set for both the events and the dependencies by the initializer that we defined earlier.

Manually adding dependencies is good for some unusual dependencies, but let's take tracking dependencies one step further and add an additional NuGet package:

```
Install-Package Microsoft.ApplicationInsights.DependencyCollector -Version
2.10.0
```

This package automatically tracks the following dependencies:

Dependencies	Details
HTTP	Both HTTP and HTPPS calls
WCF	HTTP bindings
SQL	SqlClient calls
Azure Storage	Calls made with the Azure Storage Client to Blob, Table, and Queue
EventHub Client	Versions 1.1 and above supported
ServiceBus Client	Versions 3.0 and above supported
Azure Cosmos DB	HTTP/HTTPS supported

The dependency is added by constructing an instance and initializing with the current configuration. For example:

```
DependencyTrackingTelemetryModule dependencyTracking = new
DependencyTrackingTelemetryModule();
dependencyTracking.Initialize(TelemetryConfiguration.Active);
```

When the CoffeeFix.Console application is now run, we can see both the water sensor and the call to the API are tracked (Figure 4-14).

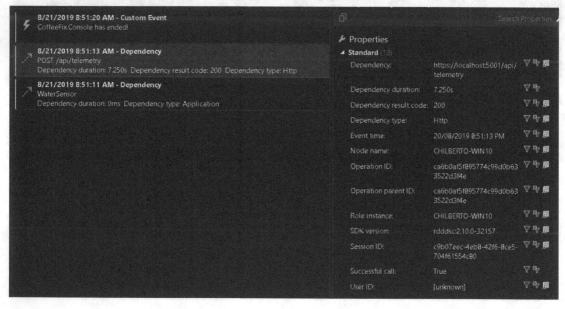

Figure 4-14. *The trace details*

Tracking Exceptions

Tracking failures in deployed applications is a common requirement for monitoring solutions. Application Insights supports this with the TrackException method:

```
public void TrackException(Exception exception,
                           IDictionary<string, string> properties = null,
                           IDictionary<string, double> metrics = null);
```

In the CoffeeFix.Console application, we add a catch to `ReportSender` when the report is sent back to the main web site:

```
}
catch (Exception ex)
{
    var telemetryClient = new TelemetryClient();
    telemetryClient.TrackException(ex);
}
```

This results in the exception being sent to Application Insights, as shown in Figure 4-15.

Figure 4-15. *The Exception trace*

Let's highlight some things in the exception details recorded. The first is that the stack trace is recorded, including the file and line number in which the error occurred. As expected, the exception type and message are recorded in the properties, as well as the account ID and session ID from our initializer.

Another useful feature are the shortcuts at the bottom, allowing for a view of the other telemetry recorded in the session, or viewing all the telemetry recorded around this event. This feature is very valuable when trying to identify a possible cause or situation that leads up to the exception being thrown (Figure 4-16).

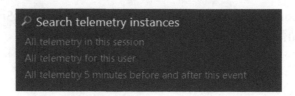

Figure 4-16.   *Search telemetry instances*

Clicking All telemetry in this session will filter the result by session ID, as illustrated in Figure 4-17.

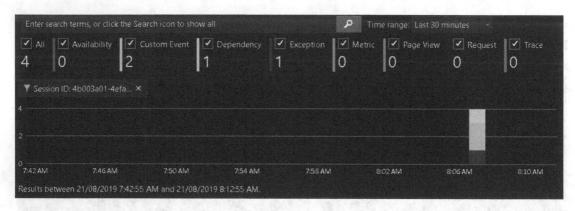

Figure 4-17.   *Filtering telemetry*

Though this is a simple example, the value of being able to filter to the session can be shown by the resulting four messages (Figure 4-18).

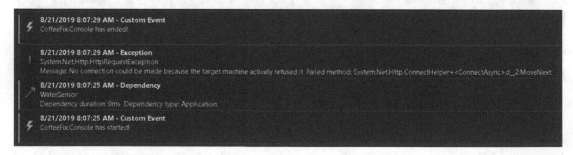

Figure 4-18.   *The filtered telemetry result*

Additional Telemetry Processing

As we have seen, Application Insights has several means of being extended. We have seen the ability to add custom properties to all messages, using an initializer, as well as adding custom properties and metrics to a specific message in the `TrackException` and `TrackEvent` methods. Another common way of extending the telemetry is by using `ITelemetryProcessor` instances. These are primarily used for filtering messages before they are sent to Application Insights, but they could also be used to alter the telemetry, by adding, removing, or altering properties, if required. Generally, they are used to either reduce cost by sending less messages or to reduce the number of messages within Application Insights.

In our example, we remove the `"CoffeeFix.MyConsoleApp has started!"` event from being sent. The first step is to create an instance of `ITelemetryProcessor`:

```
internal class MyTelemetryProcessor : ITelemetryProcessor
{
    private ITelemetryProcessor Next { get; set; }

    public MyTelemetryProcessor(ITelemetryProcessor next)
    {
        this.Next = next;
    }

    public void Process(ITelemetry item)
    {
        var eventTelemetry = item as EventTelemetry;

        if (eventTelemetry != null &&
            eventTelemetry.Name == " CoffeeFix.MyConsoleApp has started!")
        {
            // skip this item
            return;
        }

        this.Next.Process(item);
    }
}
```

In the preceding example, we are simply matching on the name of the telemetry event, and if it matches our starting message, we do not continue handling the event.

The next step is to add to the active configuration's telemetry processor the active configuration:

```
var builder = TelemetryConfiguration.Active.TelemetryProcessorChainBuilder;
builder.Use((next) => new MyTelemetryProcessor(next));
builder.Build();
```

Note in the example that we are adding to a chain of telemetry processors, meaning we can have a collection of post processing that runs sequentially for every event.

Sampling

The example of the telemetry processor targeted a single event to be removed and differs from the feature Sampling. Sampling is the recommended way to reduce the amount of telemetry traffic, as it keeps the gathered metrics more statistically accurate. Our example removed specific events from being sent, while Sampling will only send a certain percentage of the telemetry, or a sampling. For high-scale applications, this provides a view of the performance and behavior of the application, while reducing both the cost of telemetry traffic, as well as storage. Chapter 6 will provide an example of Sampling while covering Web Applications.

Disabling Tracing When Developing

There are several ways to disable tracing when developing an application and/or in situations in which you want to stop sending telemetry. A common approach is to not set the instrumentation key. Also, there is a DisableTelemetry property on the active configuration, as shown in the following:

```
TelemetryConfiguration.Active.DisableTelemetry = true;
```

It's pretty simple but worth mentioning, as in larger teams, this could cause unwanted cost and tracking.

Example Test Suite

This section takes the CoffeeFix.Console application and simulates a scenario, by using PowerShell to run the console application, as if it was being executed by multiple coffeemaker instances.

The final version of the CoffeeFix.Console application has been updated to support the test scenario, in order to generate more interesting telemetry in Application Insights. Let's revisit some key components of the solution.

First, the initialization of the telemetry has been added to a method and is run when the application first starts:

```
private static TelemetryClient ConfigureTelemetry(string coffeeMakerId)
{
    // set the Application Insights key
    TelemetryConfiguration configuration = TelemetryConfiguration.Active;
    configuration.InstrumentationKey = "[kcy]";
    TelemetryConfiguration.Active.TelemetryInitializers
                        .Add(new TelemetryInitializer(coffeeMakerId));

    var builder = TelemetryConfiguration.Active.TelemetryProcessorChainBuilder;
    builder.Use((next) => new MyTelemetryProcessor(next));
    builder.Build();

    DependencyTrackingTelemetryModule dependencyTracking =
                        new DependencyTrackingTelemetryModule();
    dependencyTracking.Initialize(TelemetryConfiguration.Active);

    return new TelemetryClient();
}
```

The ConfigureTelemetry() method first sets the instrumentation key. The custom TelemetryInitializer is then added to provide context to the coffeemaker that is sending the report. The next step adds the MyTelemetryProcessor to the telemetry processor chain, in order to remove our superfluous starting event. Then the dependency tracking module is added to track the generic web service calls. And, finally, an instance of the TelemetryClient is returned.

The following PowerShell script was created to generate some activity:

```
$sw = [system.diagnostics.stopwatch]::StartNew()

$coffeemakers = @()
1..20 | ForEach-Object { $coffeemakers += [guid]::newguid() }

for($i=1; $i -le 100; $i++)
{
    if((Get-Random -Maximum 20) -eq 1)
    {
        $address = "https://localhost:5004"
    }
    else
    {
        $address = "https://localhost:5001"
    }

    $id = $coffeemakers[(Get-Random -Maximum 19)]

    write-host "loop number $i" $sw.Elapsed
    cmd.exe /C "dotnet run --no-build $address $id"
    sleep (Get-Random -Maximum 15)
}
```

The script runs the scenario 100 times and is set to fail 5% (1 in 20) of the time, by sending to the incorrect endpoint. The ID of the coffeemaker will be taken from a collection of 20 randomly created values. A small delay was also introduced, using the sleep command.

The next section will view these events in the portal.

Viewing Application Insights Data in the Portal

Now that we have generated some activity, let's look at how this is visualized in the portal. After logging into the portal, navigate to the Application Insights blade. Our application is very simple, so some of the Application Insights will be either missing information or appear incomplete. As we explore other applications in later chapters, we will revisit sections of the portal, to complete the picture of how to visualize applications in the Azure portal.

Application Map

The default overview doesn't have any useful information with our current setup, so first navigate to Application map in the Investigate section (Figure 4-19).

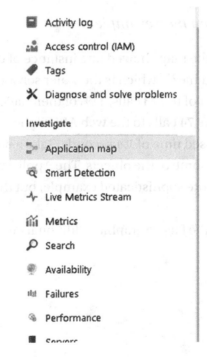

Figure 4-19. Application map

This provides an interactive map of our application (Figure 4-20).

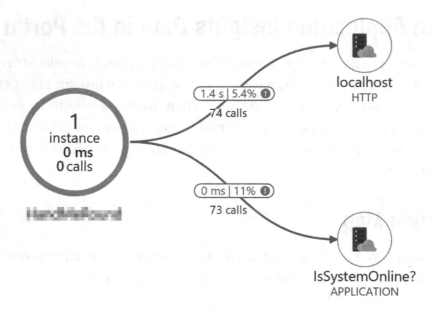

Figure 4-20. *An application map example*

When viewing the data, the map showed one instance of the application running with 73 calls to `"IsSystemOnline?"`, which is the water sensor. This is shown as an Application dependency. Out of the 73 calls, 11% of them failed. Also, at the time of running the query, there were 74 calls to the web API, with 5.4% of them resulting in a failure and an average elapsed time of 1.4 seconds. Take a moment to explore the Application map by clicking some of the objects. The Application map will provide a richer experience with a more sophisticated example, but this should illustrate the potential.

For example, by clicking the failure graphic, additional detail is provided (Figure 4-21).

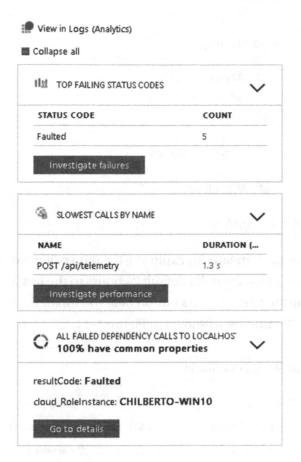

Figure 4-21. *The telemetry options*

The detail provides several ways of investigating the telemetry further. We will look at these later, but note the View in Logs (Analytics) link (at the top of the list), as well as the options to view the Top Failing Status Codes, Slowest Calls by Name, and the All Failed Dependency Calls.

Metrics

The second feature we will explore with this example is the Metrics section, from which we can get a view of the information that has been recorded (Figure 4-22).

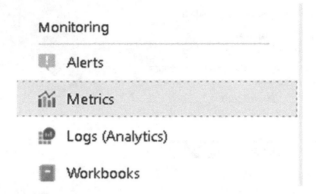

Figure 4-22. *The Metrics option*

Metrics provides a quick means for exploring the data collected visually. The first step to take is to set our range from the default 24 hours to the last 30 minutes of activity. You do this by clicking the Last 24 hours button near the top of the section and then switching to the Last 30 minutes, as shown in Figure 4-23.

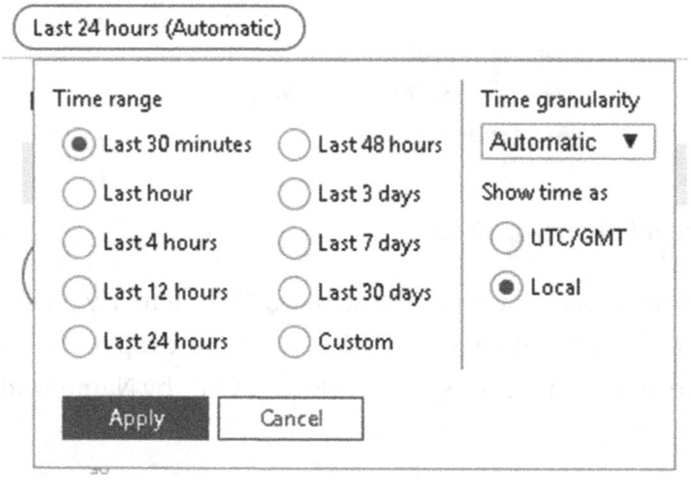

Figure 4-23. *Setting the time range*

Example 1: Line Chart on Custom Metric

Next, let's add a metric to our chart. Adding a metric is done using multiple comboboxes. These comboboxes support searching, so to create a shortcut to adding a metric, type in the start of the metric name, as shown for ElapsedMilliseconds (Figure 4-24). (Do you remember the custom metric we sent in at the end of a session?)

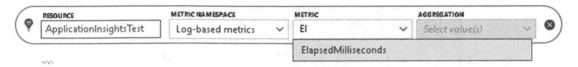

Figure 4-24. *Selecting the elapsed milliseconds metric*

Go ahead and add the metric for the average elapsed milliseconds (Figure 4-25).

Figure 4-25. *Adding the elapsed millisecond metric*

The result is illustrated in Figure 4-26.

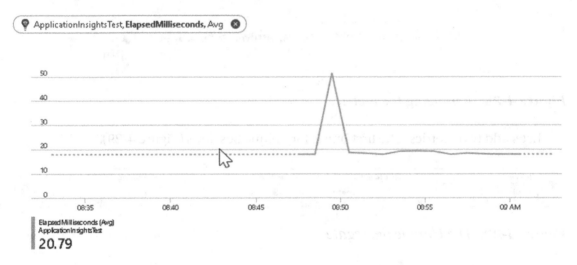

Figure 4-26. *The elapsed millisecond metric view*

Have a quick look at the graph, and you will notice a couple of nice features. The first is that the graph is responsive, so when you hover over points, the value is reflected in the bottom legend. Also, the graph periodically refreshes, making this a useful chart for pinning to a dashboard, and conveniently, there is a button at the top of the graph to pin it (Figure 4-27).

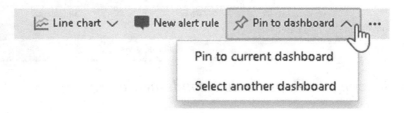

Figure 4-27. *Pin to dashboard*

Example 2: Measuring Failures

The next example will compare the number of failures to the number of sessions. In our context, a session represents a single run of the application. Note: You can remove the previous metric by clicking the remove button on the metric, as shown in Figure 4-28.

Figure 4-28. *Removing the metric*

Let's add two metrics. The first one is for unique Sessions (Figure 4-29).

Figure 4-29. *The Unique aggregate*

The second metric is for the sum of Exceptions (Figure 4-30).

Figure 4-30. *The Sum aggregate*

First, we change the chart type from Line chart to Bar chart. The supported chart types—Line, Area, Bar, and Scatter—visually depict the data differently, and we feel the Bar chart depicts this information more clearly. This is done using the drop-down menu at the top right of the chart (Figure 4-31).

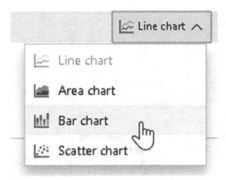

Figure 4-31. *Selecting the chart type*

The following is an illustration of what this looks like (Figure 4-32).

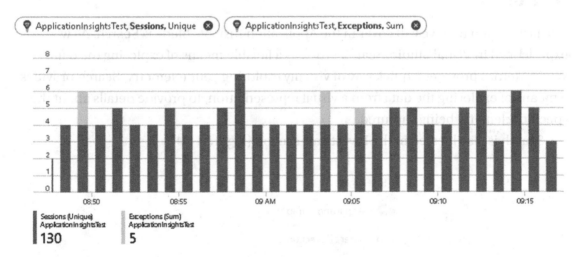

Figure 4-32. *The stacked bar example*

And like the Line chart, the Bar chart supports an interactive experience, as shown when one of the bars is hovered over (Figure 4-33).

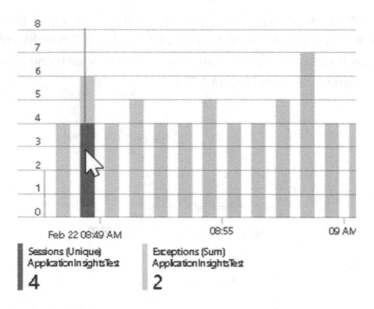

Figure 4-33. *A dynamic graph example*

Search

The last section that we will cover in the Application Insights blade is Search. As we experienced in Visual Studio, Search provides a flexible means of exploring the data. While Metrics provides a quick way of visually exploring your telemetry, Search provides a means of exploring the data from a visual representation, to provide details about the specific telemetry being captured.

Search is also located in the Investigate section (Figure 4-34).

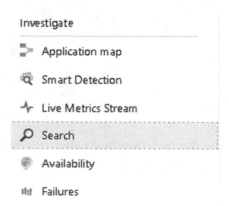

Figure 4-34. *The Search option*

The following screenshot illustrates the value of Search (Figure 4-35).

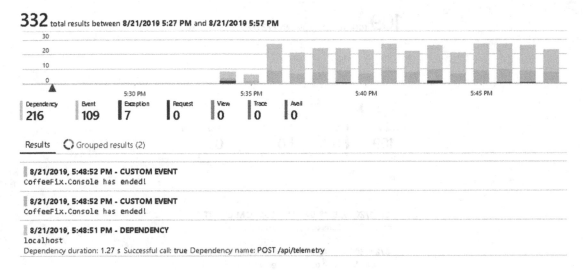

Figure 4-35. *The Search results example*

A graphical stacked bar chart provides a quick view of the type and quantity of the telemetry that has been collected. The chart differs from Metrics on a couple of points. First, it does not auto-refresh, and it only supports the single type of chart. But it does support the ability to interact with the chart, by hovering over the bars to get a quick, filtered result on only the relevant data. Another great feature is the ability to search over the range of results for telemetry, containing terms in the property values. For example, the following screenshot shows the chart after the results have been filtered for all telemetry with the term *ended* (Figure 4-36).

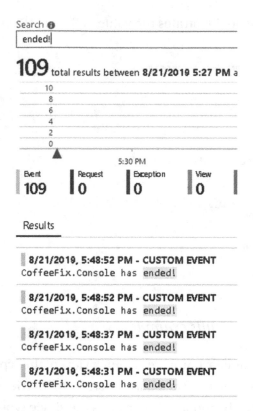

Figure 4-36. *A filtering search example*

The other significant distinction between Metrics and Search is that Search also provides a way of exploring the results in more detail. For example, by clicking a row in the Results section, additional details are displayed, including a means of looking at the properties associated with the telemetry. Note the user and session ID associated with the event (Figure 4-37).

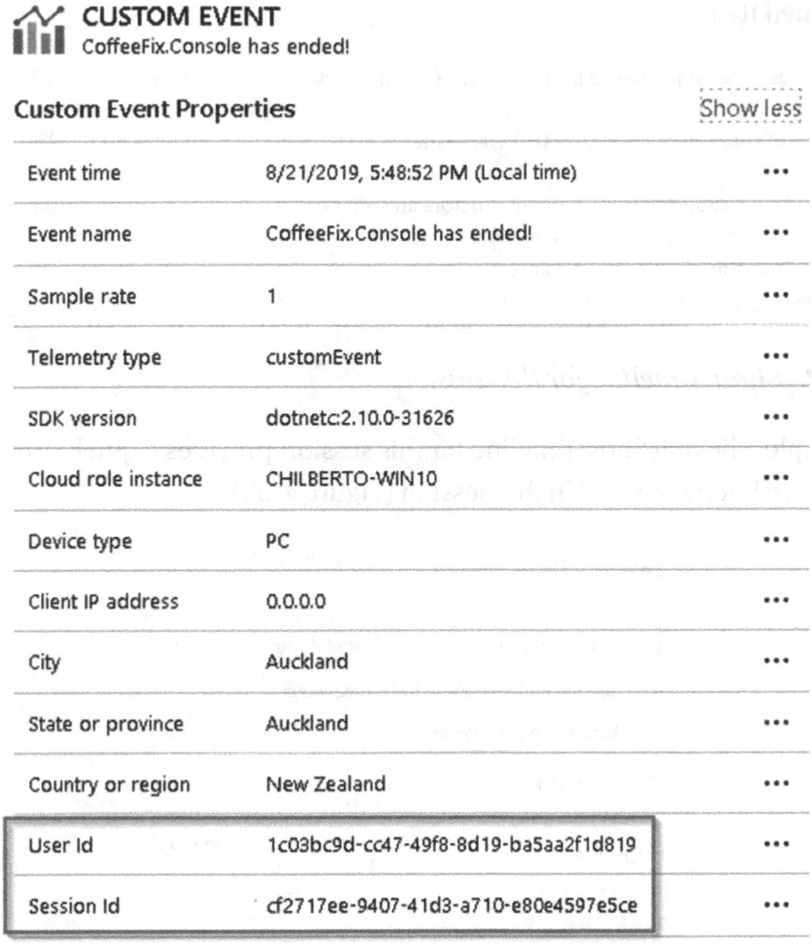

CUSTOM EVENT
CoffeeFix.Console has ended!

Custom Event Properties   Show less

Event time	8/21/2019, 5:48:52 PM (Local time)	•••
Event name	CoffeeFix.Console has ended!	•••
Sample rate	1	•••
Telemetry type	customEvent	•••
SDK version	dotnetc:2.10.0-31626	•••
Cloud role instance	CHILBERTO-WIN10	•••
Device type	PC	•••
Client IP address	0.0.0.0	•••
City	Auckland	•••
State or province	Auckland	•••
Country or region	New Zealand	•••
User Id	1c03bc9d-cc47-49f8-8d19-ba5aa2f1d819	•••
Session Id	cf2717ee-9407-41d3-a710-e80e4597e5ce	•••

Figure 4-37. *The Custom Event details*

There are several ways of exploring the data and events in Search. For example, there are convenient links to explore the related items (Figure 4-38).

Related Items

☰	Show what happened before and after this dependency in User Flows	ⓘ
↗	All available telemetry for this user session	ⓘ
↗	All available telemetry 5 minutes before and after this event	ⓘ
◱	Show timeline for this session	ⓘ

Figure 4-38. *Show timeline for this session*

For example, clicking Show timeline for this session provides a quick summary of the events that have been recorded in this session (Figure 4-39).

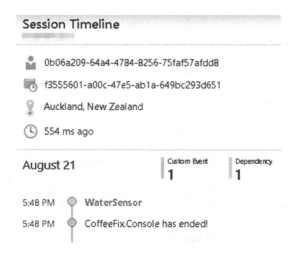

Figure 4-39. *The Session Timeline example*

Application Insights Blade

In this section, we looked at the Application Map, Metrics, and Search features in the Application Insights blade. All three features offer a different way to view the metrics data that has been collected for an application. Application Map is a great way of visually getting a topography of the application and its dependencies, as well as a means of exploring the telemetry, by drilling into the graph for more detail. Metrics allows for interactive graphs to be quickly developed, while Search provides a means of exploring the telemetry more thoroughly.

In subsequent chapters, additional features of the Application Insights blade will be explored, and additional examples will be provided to cover the Application Map, Metrics, and Search in different levels of detail.

View Analytics

View Analytics is a rich environment for querying and visualizing the data in Application Insights. It uses the Kusto Query Language (KQL), which has an SQL feel and only supports read-only queries. The syntax is designed to be easy to read and lends itself well to handling queries against large data sets.

The View Analytics environment provides a rich design environment for building queries supporting both visual representation of entities as well as syntax highlighting. The environment also provides features for visualizing the data with tables and charts. So, let's start exploring.

Table View

To start using View Analytics, select the Analytics option on the Overview section (Figure 4-40).

Figure 4-40. *The Analytics option*

To become more familiar with Analytics, let's start exploring by simply viewing some of the data that has been collected. In the Schema section, hover over the customEvents table and click the eye link that appears (Figure 4-41).

Figure 4-41. *Generating a base query*

This provides a query to select the top 50 entries in the customEvents table, as shown by the query in the editor:

```
customEvents
| limit 50
```

This should provide a result containing the first 50 entries that match the criteria of the time range. See Figure 4-42.

▷ Run   (Time range: **Last 30 minutes**)

```
customEvents
| limit 50
```

Completed. Showing results from the last 30 minutes.

☰ TABLE   ‖ CHART │ Columns ⌄

Drag a column header and drop it here to group by that column

	timestamp [UTC]	name	itemType	customDimensions	customMeasurements
>	2019-08-21T05:34:36.899	CoffeeFix.Console has ended!	customEvent	{"Version":"2.1.3.4"}	{"ElapsedMilliseconds":5361}
>	2019-08-21T05:34:54.182	CoffeeFix.Console has ended!	customEvent	{"Version":"2.1.3.4"}	{"ElapsedMilliseconds":5342}
>	2019-08-21T05:35:52.682	CoffeeFix.Console has ended!	customEvent	{"Version":"2.1.3.4"}	{"ElapsedMilliseconds":10051}
>	2019-08-21T05:35:54.875	CoffeeFix.Console has ended!	customEvent	{"Version":"2.1.3.4"}	{"ElapsedMilliseconds":3383}
>	2019-08-21T05:36:04.652	CoffeeFix.Console has ended!	customEvent	{"Version":"2.1.3.4"}	{"ElapsedMilliseconds":4043}
>	2019-08-21T05:36:10.457	CoffeeFix.Console has ended!	customEvent	{"Version":"2.1.3.4"}	{"ElapsedMilliseconds":3564}
>	2019-08-21T05:36:11.463	CoffeeFix.Console has ended!	customEvent	{"Version":"2.1.3.4"}	{"ElapsedMilliseconds":3529}
>	2019-08-21T05:36:20.202	CoffeeFix.Console has ended!	customEvent	{"Version":"2.1.3.4"}	{"ElapsedMilliseconds":3309}

Figure 4-42. *A Custom Events analytics example*

The result is displayed in a table, with default columns selected. Let's de-select some of the columns that are always blank, by using the Columns drop-down, as shown in Figure 4-43.

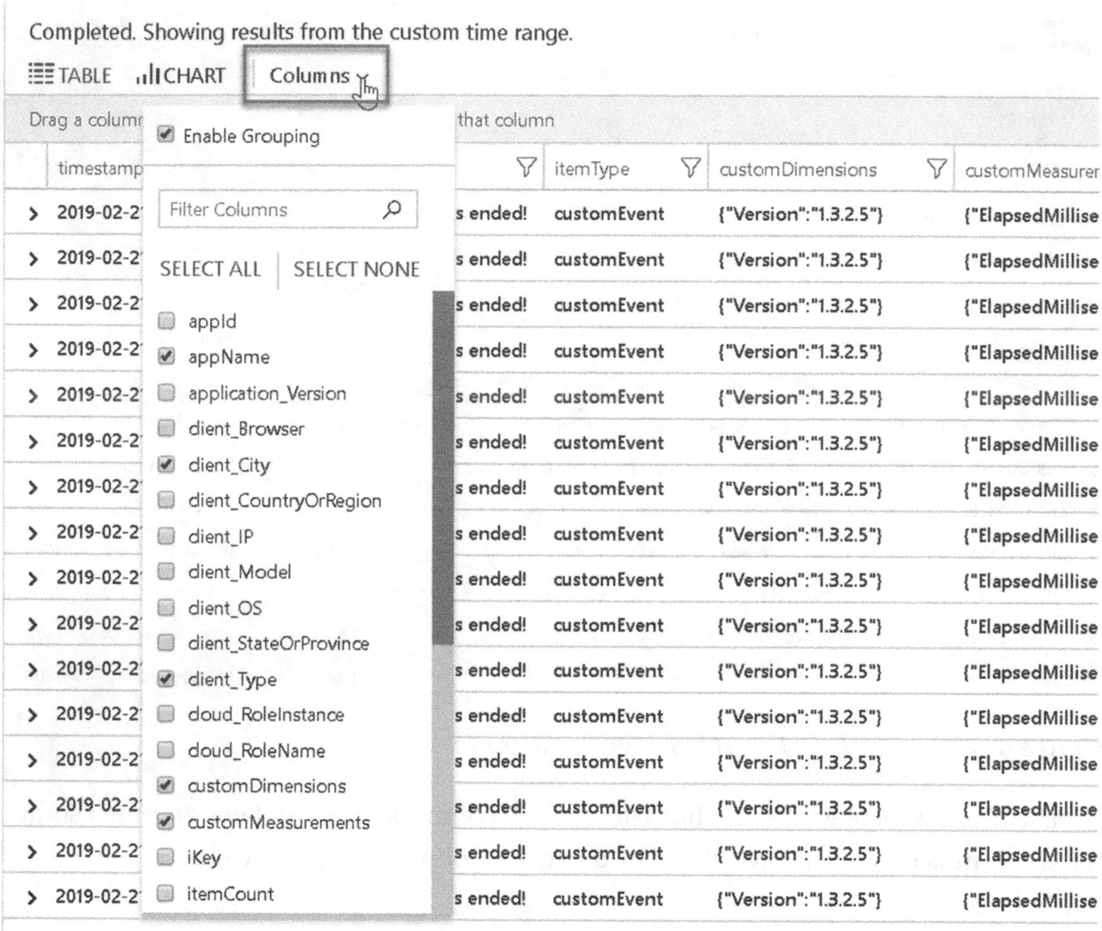

Completed. Showing results from the custom time range.

Figure 4-43. *Column selection*

Common KQL Expressions

This section will run through some common KQL expressions to get us used to writing these queries.

limit

As illustrated in the preceding example, limit is used to return up to a specific number of rows.

order by

We have seen the `limit` operator already. Now let's change this query from the first 50 entries to the last 50 entries, by adding an `order  by` clause on the timestamp column, as follows:

```
customEvents
| limit 50
| order by timestamp desc
```

where

Another common operator is the `where` clause, and the following example filters the data to where the user ID is set to a particular coffeemaker:

```
customEvents
| where user_Id   == "a246a369-9f50-4b8a-bb20-da0d69d2ee12"
| limit 50
| order by timestamp desc
```

The order of operators is very important. For example, when we run this query against our result, we can see four rows returned (Figure 4-44).

timestamp [UTC]	name	itemType	customDimensions	customMeasurements
> 2019-08-21T05:48:28.127	CoffeeFix.Console has ended!	customEvent	{"Version":"2.1.3.4"}	{"ElapsedMilliseconds":3746}
> 2019-08-21T05:47:07.767	CoffeeFix.Console has ended!	customEvent	{"Version":"2.1.3.4"}	{"ElapsedMilliseconds":3589}
> 2019-08-21T05:41:46.255	CoffeeFix.Console has ended!	customEvent	{"Version":"2.1.3.4"}	{"ElapsedMilliseconds":3984}
> 2019-08-21T05:37:24.756	CoffeeFix.Console has ended!	customEvent	{"Version":"2.1.3.4"}	{"ElapsedMilliseconds":4055}

Figure 4-44. *A Custom Events query example*

If we switch the `limit` and `where` operators, we see a different result (Figure 4-45).

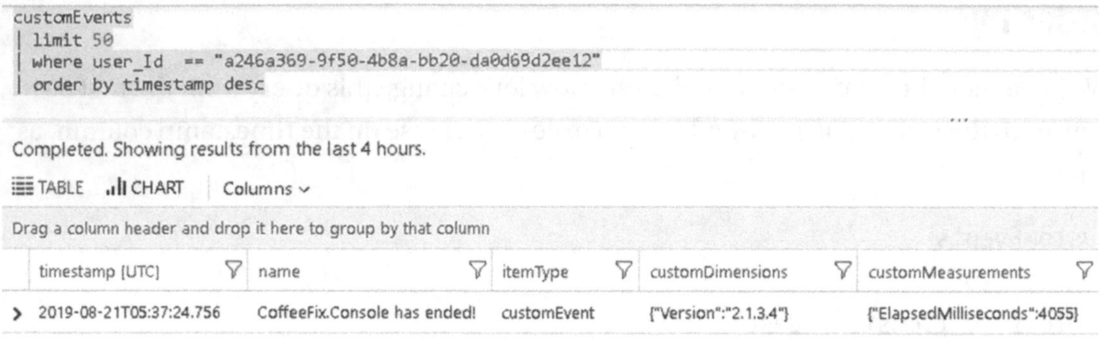

```
customEvents
| limit 50
| where user_Id == "a246a369-9f50-4b8a-bb20-da0d69d2ee12"
| order by timestamp desc
```

Completed. Showing results from the last 4 hours.

⊞ TABLE ⬛ CHART   Columns ⌄

Drag a column header and drop it here to group by that column

timestamp [UTC]	name	itemType	customDimensions	customMeasurements
> 2019-08-21T05:37:24.756	CoffeeFix.Console has ended!	customEvent	{"Version":"2.1.3.4"}	{"ElapsedMilliseconds":4055}

Figure 4-45. *A where clause example*

This is because the where clause was changed to being applied to the first 50 results instead of to the entire set of data.

summarize

Another common operator is the summarize operation, which is used to aggregate the results. For example, if we want to determine who has been using our application the most, we could perform a summarize on the user account ID, as follows:

```
customEvents
| summarize count(user_Id) by user_Id
| order by count_user_Id desc
| limit 10
```

Note that the limit has been set to 10, and we are ordering by the count descending, to give us the following result (Figure 4-46).

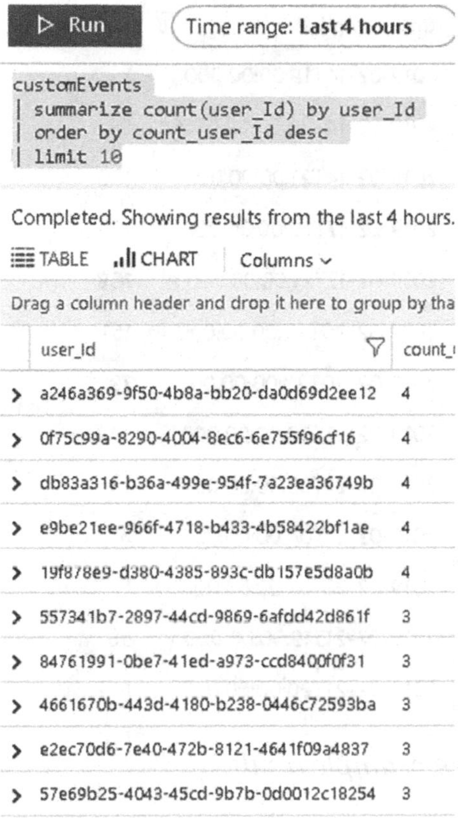

Figure 4-46. *A summarize example*

We are just scratching the surface of summarize. There are many aggregate functions, such as average (avg), maximum value (max), minimum value (min), summation (sum), standard deviation (stdev), and others.

Here is a great feature of summarize: bin. Using bin, we can determine the busiest periods of our application, by creating a summary per hour of the activity. Think of bin as a box, collection, or group. Here is the code:

```
customEvents
| summarize count() by bin(timestamp, 1h)
| order by timestamp asc
```

And here's a sample result of the query run across our data (Figure 4-47).

timestamp [UTC]	count_
> 2019-02-14T19:00:00.000	1
> 2019-02-14T20:00:00.000	93
> 2019-02-14T21:00:00.000	100
> 2019-02-17T20:00:00.000	100
> 2019-02-17T21:00:00.000	108
> 2019-02-20T22:00:00.000	151
> 2019-02-20T23:00:00.000	73
> 2019-02-21T00:00:00.000	198
> 2019-02-21T02:00:00.000	1
> 2019-02-21T04:00:00.000	61
> 2019-02-21T05:00:00.000	1
> 2019-02-21T19:00:00.000	56
> 2019-02-21T20:00:00.000	144

Figure 4-47. *A summarize example result*

union

Linking tables together is also a common task, and KQL makes this easy. The following example shows a search across the custom events, exceptions, and dependencies for all the records relating to a coffeemaker:

```
union customEvents, exceptions, dependencies
| where user_Id == "a246a369-9f50-4b8a-bb20-da0d69d2ee12"
| order by timestamp
```

Here is a sample of the results (Figure 4-48).

timestamp [UTC]	name	itemType	customDimensions	customMeasurements	operation_Id	operation_ParentId
> 2019-08-21T05:48:28.127	CoffeeFix.Console has ended!	customEvent	["Version":"2.1.3.4"]	["ElapsedMilliseconds":3746]		
> 2019-08-21T05:48:26.732	POST /api/telemetry	dependency			547925887b695b48b79ee2366312e10c	547925887b695b48b79ee2366312e10c
> 2019-08-21T05:48:25.412	WaterSensor	dependency				
> 2019-08-21T05:47:07.767	CoffeeFix.Console has ended!	customEvent	["Version":"2.1.3.4"]	["ElapsedMilliseconds":3589]		
> 2019-08-21T05:47:06.570	POST /api/telemetry	dependency			068ac6eff7b29d47ae89153ef804db83	068ac6eff7b29d47ae89153ef804db83
> 2019-08-21T05:47:05.283	WaterSensor	dependency				
> 2019-08-21T05:41:46.255	CoffeeFix.Console has ended!	customEvent	["Version":"2.1.3.4"]	["ElapsedMilliseconds":3984]		
> 2019-08-21T05:41:44.830	POST /api/telemetry	dependency			a761d717f0a706428d4278d65cdbb5e6	a761d717f0a706428d4278d65cdbb5e6
> 2019-08-21T05:41:43.273	WaterSensor	dependency				
> 2019-08-21T05:37:24.756	CoffeeFix.Console has ended!	customEvent	["Version":"2.1.3.4"]	["ElapsedMilliseconds":4055]		
> 2019-08-21T05:37:23.458	POST /api/telemetry	dependency			2c8f7e3b2a82e54690102a0b59de8f97	2c8f7e3b2a82e54690102a0b59de8f97
> 2019-08-21T05:37:21.801	WaterSensor	dependency				

Figure 4-48. *A union example*

Features

There are some features of Analytics that should be highlighted.

Time Zone

The time zone will default to UTC, and to switch to a local time zone, we use the settings option at the top right of the page (Figure 4-49).

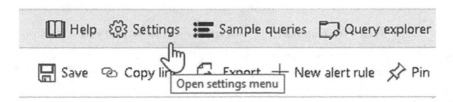

Figure 4-49. *Opening the Settings menu*

The display time zone can be set on this dialog box, as well as the default paging of the table view and whether the results should default to being sorted by the timestamp (Figure 4-50).

Settings

Date & Time

Display time zone

(UTC +13:00) Auckland, Wellington

Sort results

Sort results by TimeGenerated (Log Analytics) / timestamp (App Insights)

| On | Off |

Table view

Set # of rows per page

50

Figure 4-50. *Settings Date & Time*

Export

The ability to export a result to CSV and to Power BI is supported under the option at the top right of the page (Figure 4-51).

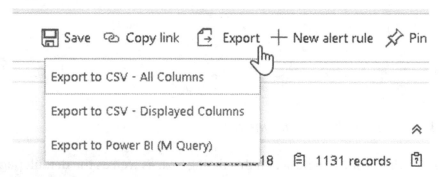

Figure 4-51. *The Export to options*

Saved Queries

The ability to save queries and maintain a collection of queries is built into the Analytics page. To save a query, use the Save option, which is at the top right of the page (Figure 4-52).

Save
Copy link
Export

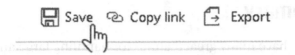

Figure 4-52. *The Save query button*

This allows for a query to be saved and retrieved later. A query requires a name and can be saved to a private collection or to a shared collection of queries (Figure 4-53).

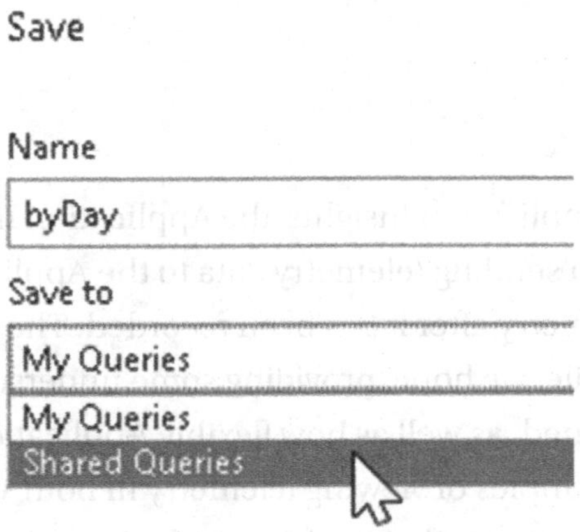
Save
Name
byDay
Save to
My Queries
My Queries
Shared Queries

Figure 4-53. *Shared queries*

To retrieve a saved query, use the Query explorer located at the top right of the page (Figure 4-54)

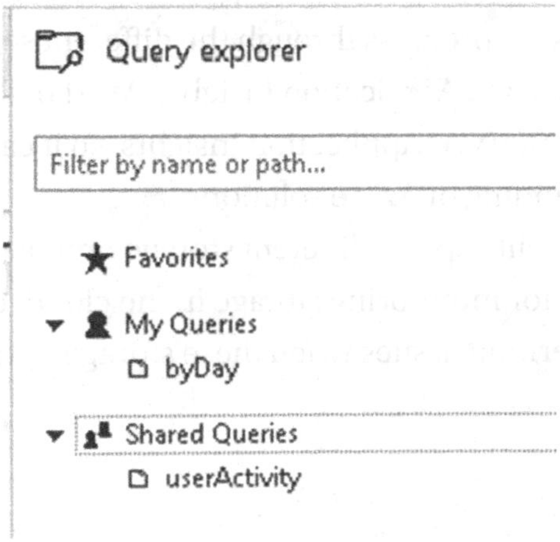
Query explorer
Filter by name or path...
Favorites
My Queries
byDay
Shared Queries
userActivity

Figure 4-54. *Query explorer*

Analytics Summary

Analytics and the KQL have many great features for handling large amounts of telemetry data. In this section, we have covered some of the features of running KQL queries against the gathered data. The table view is a flexible grid for viewing the results, and we covered some of the more common KQL operators. As we progress through the different Azure services, Analytics and KQL will play an important role in understanding the telemetry collected by Application Insights.

Summary

This chapter introduced Application Insights, the Application Insights blade, and View Analytics. We covered both sending telemetry data to the Application Insights service, as well as viewing the telemetry after it has been recorded. The sample application was kept extremely simple, while, we hope, providing some understanding as to how the framework has been designed, as well as how flexible Application Insights is at being extended. We provided examples of viewing telemetry in both Visual Studio and the Azure portal. We highlighted several of the features for investigating telemetry data. We covered View Analytics and the Kusto Query Language (KQL), including some examples that provide additional ways of exploring the telemetry data.

The value of Application Insights really becomes apparent with distributed systems at scale. Without using an APM, such as Application Insights, building a bespoke logging and monitoring system, with a rich feature set, quickly becomes impractical, due to the required cost and effort. As we progress through the different services offered in Azure, we will continually come back to Application Insights. Most of the services in Azure have native support to send telemetry to Application Insights, so it can be viewed as a central way of gaining an understanding of Azure solutions.

In the next chapter, we will explore different storage options available in Azure and different features available for monitoring storage in the cloud, detecting issues, and understanding how to determine issues when these storage options are being used.

CHAPTER 5

Azure Web Apps

Azure offers numerous possibilities for hosting applications. In this chapter, we are going to look at Azure Web Apps. We will cover the different App Service plans that are available and what the characteristics are for the different App Service plans. We will then dive into the different debugging and profiling options that there are for Web Apps, such as Log Analytics, Profiling from Visual Studio, and more.

Azure Web Apps

Azure Web Apps is part of Azure App Service, and it allows you to host your web sites and applications in Azure. Besides web sites and applications, you can also host your Web APIs and your mobile back ends inside Azure Web Apps. You can use a programming language of your choice for developing applications. At the time of writing, Azure Web Apps supports .NET, .NET Core, Java, Ruby, Node.js, PHP, and Python. Those applications are hosted on Windows or Linux virtual machines (VMs) that are fully managed by Microsoft and can easily be scaled using out-of-the-box features.

Besides scaling, you can leverage other Azure features, such as security, load balancing, and insights and analytics. You can also use the DevOps capabilities, such as continuous integration and deployment from Azure DevOps, GitHub, Docker Hub, and other resources, SSL certificates, package management, staging environments, and custom domains.

App Service Plans

Azure Web Apps are hosted in App Service plans. You can configure all the required settings, such as the compute resources, which region you want to deploy your apps in, and the costs, inside an App Service plan. You can choose between free plans, which are most suitable for development applications and where you share all the resources with

147

© Jeffrey Chilberto, Sjoukje Zaal, Gaurav Aroraa and Ed Price 2020
J. Chilberto et al., *Cloud Debugging and Profiling in Microsoft Azure*,
https://doi.org/10.1007/978-1-4842-5437-0_5

other customers, to paid plans, where you can set the available CPU, choose whether to host your apps on Linux or Windows VMs, and more.

Azure offers the following service plan options:

- *Dev/Test*: Free and Shared are both part of this service plan option. Your app runs in a shared environment, on the same VM as other apps. This environment can also include apps from other Azure customers and users. Each app has a CPU quota, and there is no ability to scale up or out. The Free App Service plan can host up to 10 apps, and the shared plan can host up to 100 apps. These App Service plans are most suited for development and test environments or apps with less traffic. There is no SLA support for these two plans. The Shared service plan offers the ability to add custom domains. The service plan is shown in Figure 5-1.

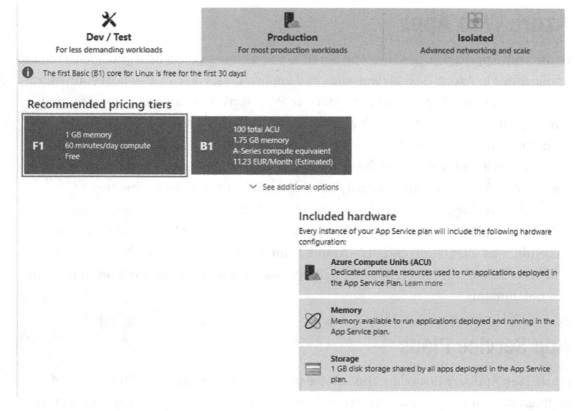

Figure 5-1. *Free and Shared App Service plans*

- *Production*: There are three options:

    - *Basic*: The Basic tier is the first tier, from which you can choose between different pricing ranges. It offers three tiers, and the available cores and RAM double for each tier. Apps run on dedicated Linux or Windows VMs, and the compute resources are only shared between apps that are deployed inside the same App Service plan. This App Service plan supports SSL and custom domains. The Basic tier can host an unlimited number of apps, with a maximum of three instances. It offers scaling to three instances, but you must do this manually. This tier is most suitable for development and test environments, as well as applications with less traffic.

    - *Standard*: The Standard tier also has three tiers to choose from. It offers custom domains and SSL support, can also host an unlimited number of apps, offers autoscaling for up to ten instances, and offers five deployment slots, which can be used for testing, staging, and production apps. It also provides daily backups and support for Azure Traffic Manager.

    - *Premium*: Premium offers two types of tiers, Premium and Premium V2. They both offer all the features of the Standard tier, but the Premium tier offers extra scaling instances and deployment slots. The Premium V2 tier runs on Dv2-series VMs, which have faster processors and SSD drives. This drastically increases the performance of your application. This tier can host an unlimited number of apps and offers autoscaling for up to 20 instances. The dedicated compute plans in the Azure portal are shown in Figure 5-2.

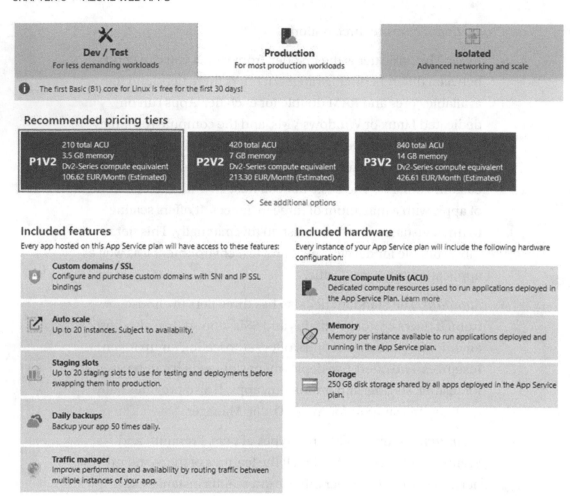

Figure 5-2.   Production App Service plans

- *Isolated*: The isolated tier offers full isolation for mission-critical workloads that must run in a virtual network. Your applications run in a private environment with dedicated VMs. This tier can host an unlimited number of apps, and you can scale up to 100 instances. This can be 100 instances in one App Service plan or 100 different App Service plans. To create a private environment, App Service uses App Service Environment (ASE), which will be covered in the next chapter. All apps run on Dv2-series VMs, so this tier offers high-performance capabilities. The isolated App Service plan is most suitable for apps that require complete isolation because of high-security demands, but also need to use all the capabilities that Azure Web Apps offers, such as autoscale and deployment slots. The isolated service plan is shown in Figure 5-3.

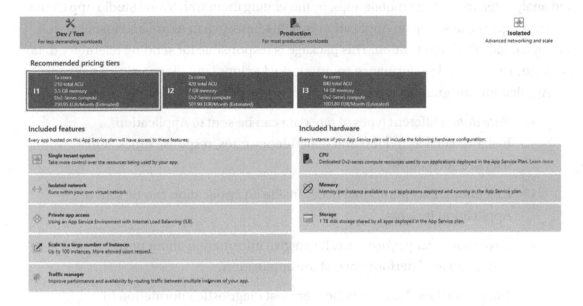

Figure 5-3. *Isolated App Service plans*

Note   You should be aware that App Service Environments are expensive. If you create one for testing purposes, then delete it as soon as possible.

Having introduced the different App Service plans that you can use for hosting your applications, we will now look into the different debugging and profiling capabilities. We will start with Application Insights.

Application Insights

Application Insights is an extensible Application Performance Management (APM) service for web developers on multiple platforms. You can use it to monitor your live web application. Application Insights automatically detects performance anomalies, and it includes powerful analytics tools to help you diagnose issues and understand how people are using your app.

It works for apps that are built on a variety of platforms, including .NET, Node.js, and Java EE, hosted on-premises, hybrid, or any public cloud. It integrates with your DevOps process and has connection points to a variety of development tools. It can even monitor and analyze telemetry from mobile apps, by integrating them with Visual Studio App Center.

Developers can set up an Application Insights Resource in Azure and install a package inside their application. This package is responsible for sending telemetry data to Azure. You can add performance counters, docker logs, and diagnostic logs as well.

Application Insights can monitor the following:

- *Rate data*: Different types of rate data can be sent to Application Insights, such as request and dependency rates, response times, and user session counts.

- *Exceptions*: Exceptions that occur inside an application can be sent to Application Insights.

- *Page views and performance*: It can give information about page views and load performance of the application.

- *Diagnostic logs*: This sends Docker Host diagnostic information to Application Insights and traces logging from applications.

- *AJAX calls*: This is the performance of AJAX calls and failed requests and response time.

- *Custom events*: You can create custom events in your applications as well.

Adding Logging to the CoffeeFix Web App

We are going to use the CoffeeFix application for this, which has a Web App that we are going to deploy to Azure. However, the first step is adding Log Analytics to the Web App. We are going to do this from Visual Studio.

Adding Application Insights to the Web App

To get started with this demonstration, in Visual Studio open the CoffeeFix solution from the Chapter 5 folder. You will see that this application consists of a console app and a web app. In this demo, we are going to focus on the web app.

1. In the Solution Explorer, right-click the CoffeeFix.Web application.
    Then select Add ➤ Application Insights Telemetry (Figure 5-4).

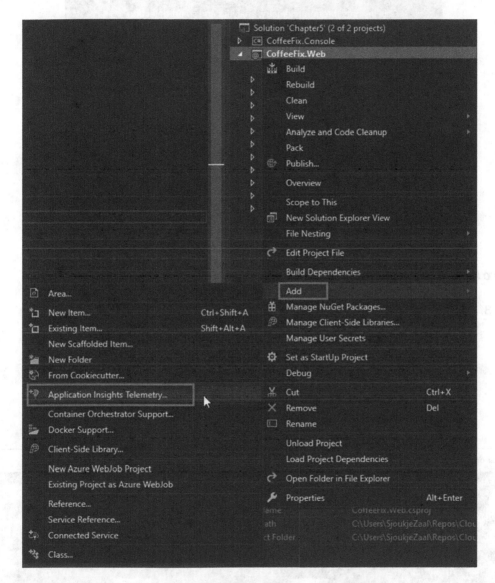

Figure 5-4. *Adding Application Insights to your application*

2. In the next screen, click the Get Started button (Figure 5-5).

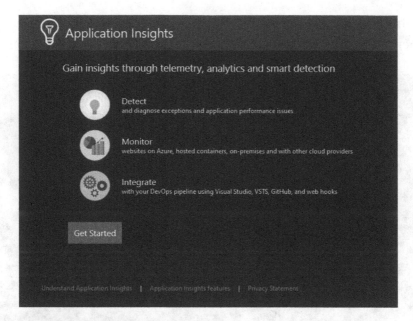

Figure 5-5. *The Application Insights wizard*

3. In the next screen, you must register your application in Azure and create an Applications Insights workspace. This will all be handled for you by Visual Studio. The Application Insight SDK will be added to the Visual Studio solution as well. If you are not signed in to Azure yet, first add your credentials and select the right subscription (Figure 5-6).

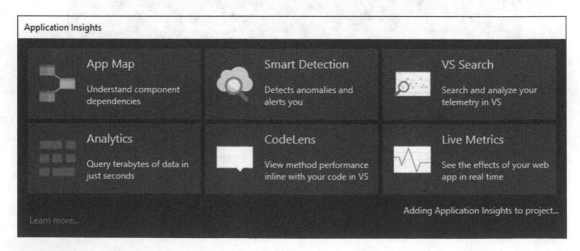

Figure 5-6. *Application Insights capabilities*

4.   After registration (Figure 5-7), build the project. We can now deploy our web app to Azure.

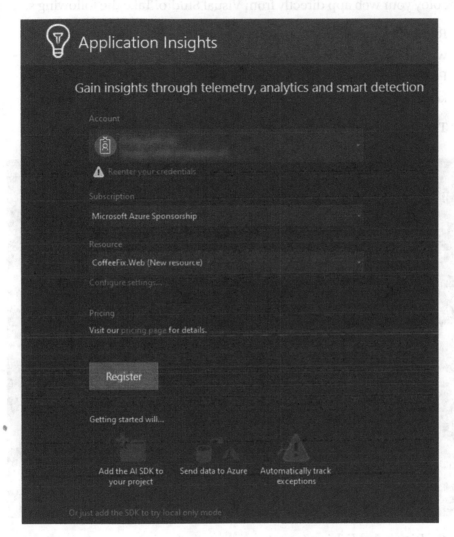

Figure 5-7. *Registering Application Insights*

5.   Click Register.

Deploy the Web App

You can deploy your web app directly from Visual Studio. Take the following steps:

1. Right-click the project name and click Publish. The publishing wizard opens, and you can select how you want to deploy your app. For this demo, select App Service in the left menu (Figure 5-8), and keep the default selection, Create New, selected.

2. Then click Publish immediately.

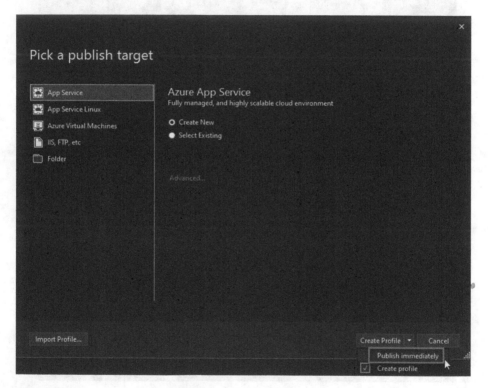

Figure 5-8. *Pick a publishing target*

3. In the next screen, keep the default name, select a subscription, create a new resource group, and call it ProductWebAppGroup. Under Hosting Plan, click New. In the next screen, you can provide a name for the hosting plan and select the subscription. Create a new resource group and call it CoffeeFixWeb. Then create a new hosting plan and select the East US region. Select the S1 size (Figure 5-9).

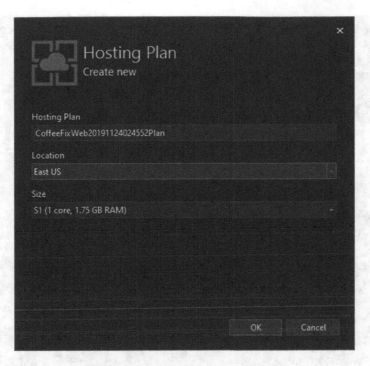

Figure 5-9. *Creating a new App Service plan*

Note For an overview of all the different plans, sizes, and prices, you can refer to the following web site: `https://azure.microsoft.com/en-us/pricing/details/app-service/windows/`.

---

4. Click OK, as shown in Figure 5-9.

5. The hosting plan screen closes. In the previous screen, we don't have to set Application Insights, because we already did this manually. Click Create, to let Visual Studio create the publishing profile and to publish the app to Azure (Figure 5-10).

Figure 5-10. *Creating a new App Service*

After publishing, your browser automatically loads the published site (Figure 5-11).

Figure 5-11. *A deployed application*

Now that our app is published to Azure, we can monitor it from the Azure portal.

Monitoring Your App Using Application Insights and Azure Monitor

Application Insights is part of Azure Monitor. Azure Monitor delivers a solution for collecting, analyzing, and acting on telemetry from your cloud and on-premises environments. It helps you understand how your applications are performing and proactively identifies issues affecting them and the resources they depend on.

To view the telemetry that is collected for our application, we must take the following steps:

1. Open the Azure portal, by navigating to `https://portal.azure.com/`.

2. In the left menu, click Monitor, then under Insights, select Applications. You will now see our app in the overview (Figure 5-12).

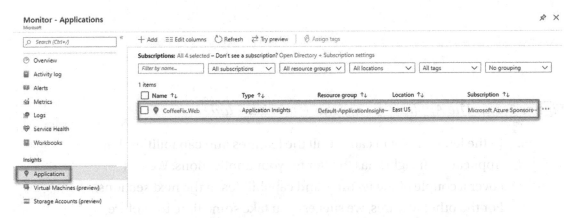

Figure 5-12. *Application Insights in Azure Monitor*

3. Select the application, and you will be redirected to the Application Insights workspace that we created in Visual Studio in the previous section.

4. In the Overview blade, you can see the failed requests, Server response time, Server requests, and the Availability of the web app (Figure 5-13).

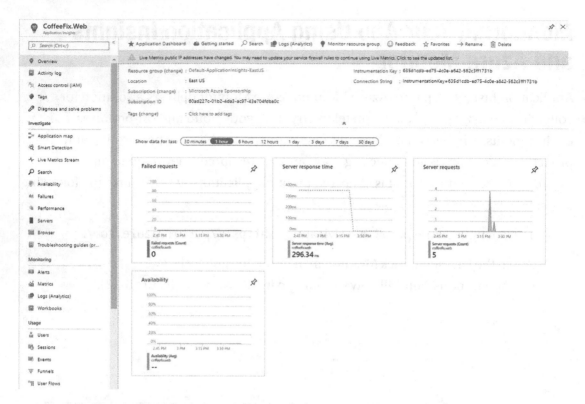

Figure 5-13. *The Application Insights Overview blade*

5. In the left menu, you can see all the features and capabilities that Application Insights has to offer for your applications. We will cover a couple of the features and capabilities in the next sections. For the other features, we suggest you take some time to explore them and get familiar with them.

Live Metrics

The Live Metrics stream from Application Insights gives you the ability to monitor and diagnose your in-production web application. You can select and filter multiple metrics and performance counters, which you can watch in real time for your application. Exceptions and failed requests can be inspected using stack traces.

Live Metrics offers the following features:

•   When releasing a new version of your application or fixing a bug, you can watch the performance and failure counts of the app.

•   You can monitor the effect of load tests and diagnose the issues live.

- You can get exception traces immediately, as they happen.

- Filters can be created to easily identify a server that is having issues focus on particular test sessions, or filter out known issues.

- You can experiment with filters to find the most relevant KPIs.

- The Windows performance counter can be monitored live (Figure 5-14).

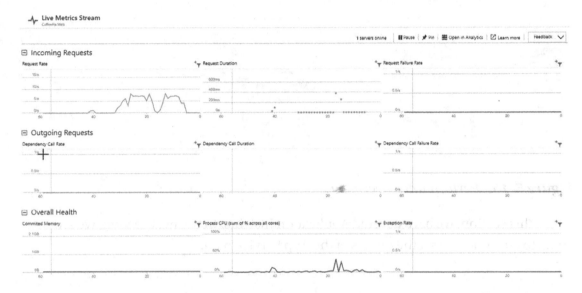

Figure 5-14. *The Live Metrics overview*

Performance

The Performance blade of Application Insights gives an overview of all the performance details for the different operations in your application. By identifying those operations with the longest duration, you can diagnose potential problems or best target your ongoing development, to improve the overall performance of the application.

It shows the count and average duration of each operation for the application. You can use this information to identify those operations that most impact users. In the following example (Figure 5-15), based on the CoffeeFix application, the GET /css/ site.css and GET /index require some further investigation because of their relatively high duration and number of calls. Other operations may have a higher duration but were rarely called, so the effect of their improvement would be minimal.

Figure 5-15.   *Performance overview*

In this section, we have covered Application Insights. In the next section, we are going to cover how to set the quotas of the App Service plan.

Monitoring Apps in App Service Plans

In addition to the information that you can get with Application Insights and Azure Monitor, you can also monitor apps on the App Service plan level. For instance, you can view the limits of the App Service plan, the CPU performance of the app, or the amount of memory that it is using. The App Service plan offers Quotas, Alerts, and Metrics for this.

In the next sections, we are going to cover these three aspects.

Quotas

Apps that are hosted in App Service plans have certain limits on the resources they can use. The limits are defined by the App Service plan that's associated with the app. These limits are called quotas.

If the app is hosted in a *Free* or *Shared* plan, the limits on the resources that the app can use are defined by quotas. Quotas for Free or Shared apps are CPU, the total amount of CPU allowed for an app per day (CPU Day) or per five-minute interval (CPU Short). Other quotas are Memory, Bandwidth, and Filesystem. Apps that are hosted in *Basic*, *Standard*, and *Premium* plans only have the Filesystem quota.

If an app exceeds the *CPU (Short)*, *CPU (Day)*, or *Bandwidth* quota, the app is stopped until the quota resets. During this time, all incoming requests will result in an HTTP 403 error.

Metrics

Metrics provide information about the behavior of the app or the App Service plan. In the Metrics blade in the Azure portal, you can filter on different metrics (Figure 5-16). Some of these metrics are as follows:

- *Average Response Time*: The average time it takes for the app to serve a request (in seconds)

- *CPU Time*: The amount of CPU consumed by the app (in seconds)

- *HTTP*: The count of requests resulting in different HTTP status codes

- *Average memory working*: The average amount of memory used by the app

- *Connections*: The number of bound sockets existing in the sandbox (w3wp.exe and its child processes)

- *Data in/out*: The amount of incoming and outgoing bandwidth consumed by the app

- *Current Assemblies*: The current number of Assemblies loaded across all AppDomains in this application

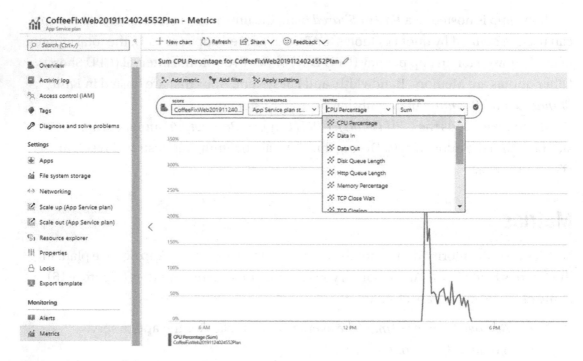

Figure 5-16. *Filtering on CPU Percentage*

Alerts

Metrics for an app or an App Service plan can be used to set up alerts. Alerts are typically created when you want to receive notifications when specific changes occur to the app or App Service plan, such as when the App Service plan reaches a certain limit. You can then receive a notification via an SMS or e-mail. You can also create alert rules that automatically take certain action, such as autoscaling based on the CPU of the app.

In the next demonstration, we are going to set up an alert when the application reaches the maximum CPU. We will then receive a notification e-mail. Follow these steps:

1. Open the App Service plan of the CoffeeFix application in the Azure portal.

2. In the left menu, select Alerts.

3. In the top menu, click + New alert rule.

4. The resource is automatically selected, which is the App Service plan. We first must add a Condition. Click the Add button under Condition. Then select the Signal type, CPU Percentage (Figure 5-17).

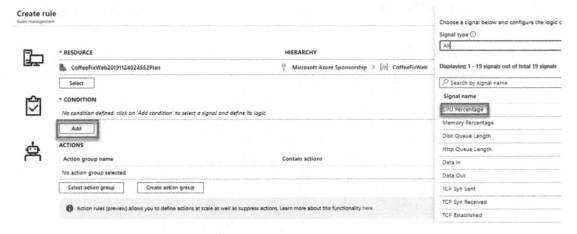

Figure 5-17. *Creating an alert condition*

5. For the Operator, select Greater than; for the Aggregation type, select Average; and set the Threshold value to 80%. This means that the alert rule will fire when more than 80% of the CPU power is used (Figure 5-18).

Figure 5-18. *Configuring the condition*

6. Click Done.

7. Then create a new action group. An action group is a collection of notification preferences. Call the Action group: CoffeeFixActionGroup; assign the short name: CoffeeFix. Next, select the right Subscription and Resource group. Create an action, such as in the following image (Figure 5-19).

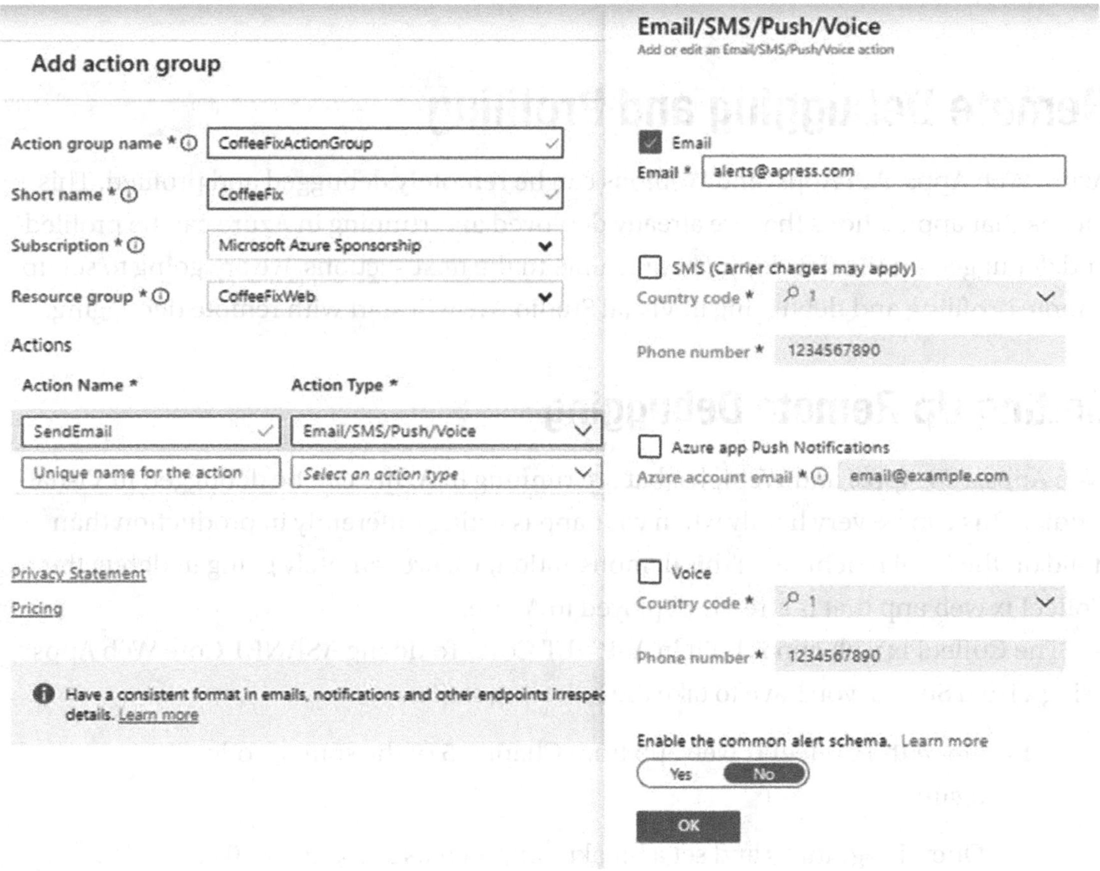

Figure 5-19. *Configuring the Action group*

8. Click OK and again, to create the action group.

9. At last, we must give the alert a name. Call it CoffeeFixAlert and set the required severity level. Click Create alert rule.

We have now configured an alert rule that will fire when the CPU reaches a limit of 80%. An e-mail will then be sent to the configured e-mail address.

In the next section, we are going to look at how we can debug applications that are already deployed and running in Azure.

Remote Debugging and Profiling

Azure Web Apps, API Apps, and WebJobs can be remotely debugged and profiled. This means that applications that are already deployed and running in Azure can be profiled and debugged on the development machine. In the next sections, we are going to set up remote profiling and debugging in Visual Studio. We will start with remote debugging.

Setting Up Remote Debugging

Web Apps, API Apps, and WebJobs that are running in Azure can be debugged in Visual Studio. This can be very handy when your app is acting differently in production than it did on the local machine. In this demonstration, we are remotely going to debug the CoffeeFix web app that is already deployed to Azure.

The CoffeeFix web app is built in ASP.NET Core. To debug ASP.NET Core Web Apps using Visual Studio, you have to take the following steps:

1. Open the CoffeeFix web app from Chapter 5 of the source code again.

2. Open Program.cs and set a breakpoint, such as in Figure 5-20.

```
 1💡  ⊟using System;
 2      using System.Collections.Generic;
 3      using System.IO;
 4      using System.Linq;
 5      using System.Threading.Tasks;
 6      using Microsoft.AspNetCore;
 7      using Microsoft.AspNetCore.Hosting;
 8      using Microsoft.Extensions.Configuration;
 9     ⌊using Microsoft.Extensions.Logging;
10
11     ⊟namespace CoffeeFix.Web
12      {
              0 references
13     ⊟      public class Program
14             {
                  0 references | 0 exceptions
15     ⊟          public static void Main(string[] args)
16                 {
17                     CreateWebHostBuilder(args).Build().Run();
18                 }
19
                   1 reference | 0 exceptions
20     ⊟          public static IWebHostBuilder CreateWebHostBuilder(string[] args) =>
21                     WebHost.CreateDefaultBuilder(args)
22                         .UseStartup<Startup>();
23             }
24      }
25
```

Figure 5-20. Setting a breakpoint

3. We deployed a release build when we deployed the app to Azure.
    Right-click the CoffeeFix.Web application and click Publish. Then
    click the Edit button, as shown in Figure 5-21.

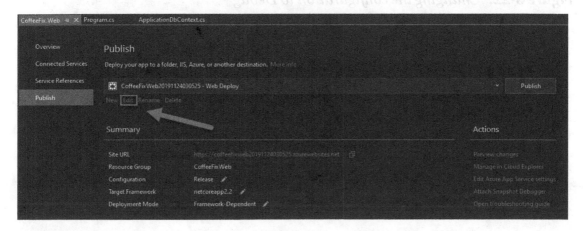

Figure 5-21. Editing the deployment profile

4.   Go to Settings, change the configuration to Debug, and click Save
     (Figure 5-22).

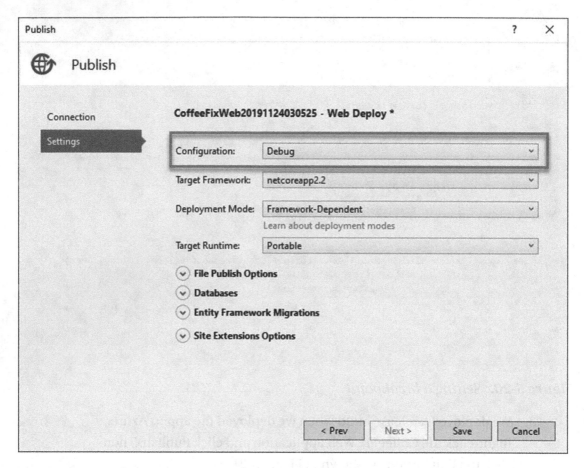

Figure 5-22. *Changing the configuration to Debug*

5.   Publish the application again.

6.   Open Cloud Explorer in Visual Studio (View ➤ Cloud Explorer).

7.   Select the subscription, expand App Services, then your Resource
     group, and then right-click the app's node and click Attach
     Debugger (Figure 5-23).

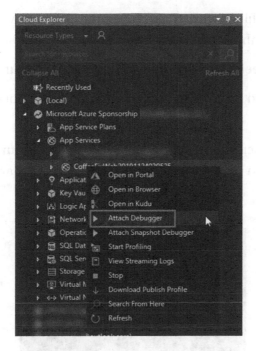

Figure 5-23. *Attaching the debugger*

8. The browser automatically opens to your home page running in Azure. You might have to wait 20 seconds or so while Azure sets up the server for debugging. This delay only occurs the first time you run in debug mode on an app in a 48-hour period. When you start debugging again in the same period, there isn't a delay.

9. Visual Studio stops on the breakpoint, and the code is running in Azure, not on your local computer. Press F5 to continue running.

Setting Up Remote Profiling

Azure Web, API Apps, and WebJobs can also be remotely profiled. The latency of HTTP requests might be higher than normal, your process might be running slower, or the CPU usage might be higher than expected. Then you can remotely profile your process and get the CPU sampling call stacks to analyze the process activity and code hot paths directly from Visual Studio.

To set up remote profiling, we first must open the CoffeeFix web application again in Visual Studio. Then take the following steps:

1. Open the CoffeeFix web app from Chapter 5 of the source code.

2. Open the Cloud Explorer in Visual Studio (View ➤ Cloud Explorer).

3. Select the subscription, expand App Services, then your Resource group, and then right-click the app's node and click Start Profiling (Figure 5-24).

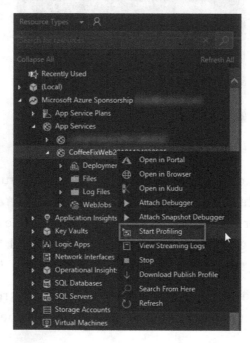

Figure 5-24. *Start Profiling*

4. The remote profiling session starts, and you can run your scenario. The CPU samples are collected in Azure for your process.

5. Make sure that there is some load on your app running in Azure. After a couple of minutes, click the Stop Profiling button, to stop the remote profiling session (Figure 5-25).

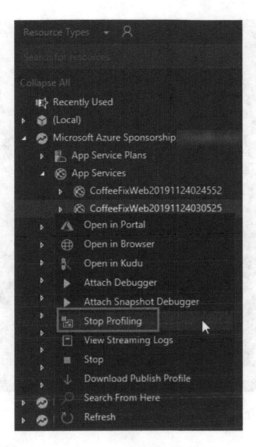

Figure 5-25. *Stop Profiling*

6. The profiling data collected in your Azure Web App is downloaded and opened in Visual Studio 2019 (Figure 5-26). You can drill down to get more information.

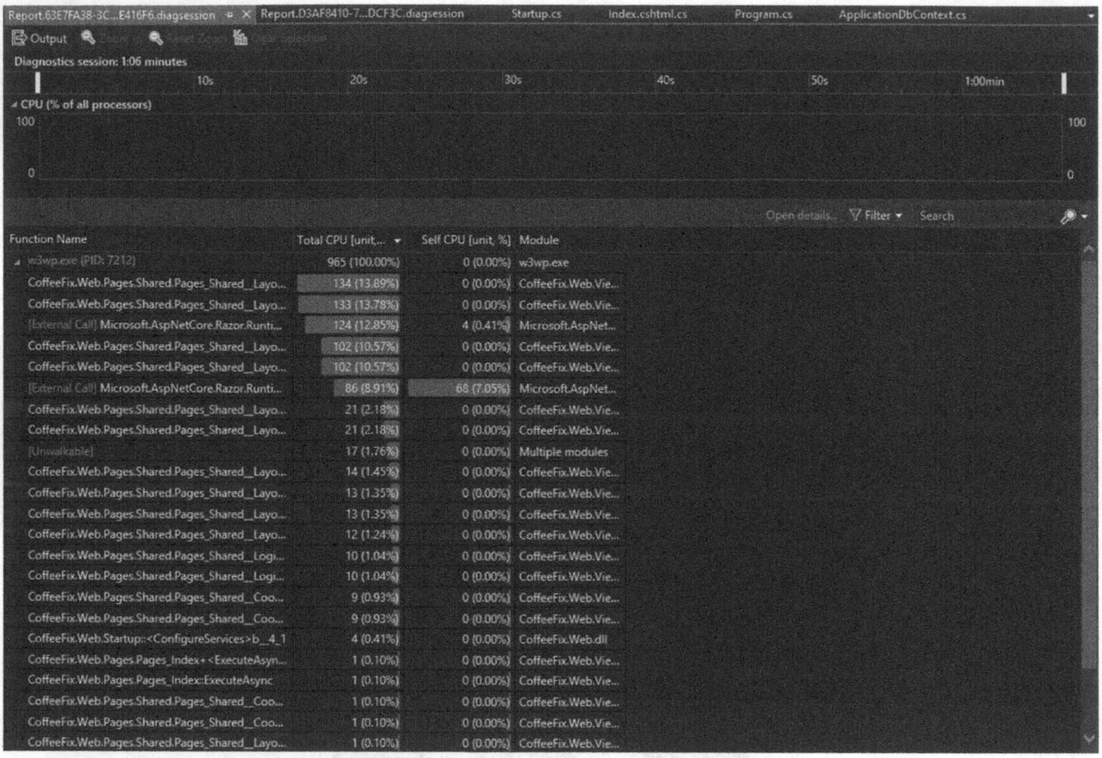

Figure 5-26. *Diagnostics profiling report in Visual Studio*

Summary

In this chapter, we have covered profiling and debugging in Azure Web Apps. We started this chapter by describing the different App Service plans. We then enabled Application Insights for the CoffeeFix web app and deployed to Azure. Finally, we looked at the different debugging and monitoring capabilities that are offered for Web Apps.

In the next chapter, we are going to cover databases and storage.

Useful Links

The following articles are all available from Microsoft. They will give you more relevant information on all the topics covered in this chapter:

- "Azure App Service plan overview," https://docs.microsoft.com/
  en-us/azure/app-service/overview-hosting-plans, November 8,
  2017.

- "Monitor apps in Azure App Service," `https://docs.microsoft.com/`
  `en-us/azure/app-service/web-sites-monitor`, January 10, 2019.

- "Troubleshoot an app in Azure App Service using Visual Studio,"
  `https://docs.microsoft.com/en-us/azure/app-service/`
  `troubleshoot-dotnet-visual-studio`, August 28, 2016.

- "Remote Debug ASP.NET Core on IIS in Azure in Visual Studio,"
  `https://docs.microsoft.com/en-us/visualstudio/debugger/`
  `remote-debugging-azure?view=vs-2019`, May 20, 2018.

CHAPTER 6

Databases and Storage

Azure offers many different useful storage solutions. It offers Microsoft databases, as well as different open source ones. In addition to databases, Azure offers other storage solutions, such as NoSQL storage, table storage, file storage, queues, and blob storage. In this chapter, we are going to look into the different databases and storage solutions that Azure has to offer.

Databases

Azure offers different types of databases that you can use for your data and applications. In addition, Azure offers various data stores for data analytics and big data. In the following sections, we are going to describe the different types of databases that Azure offers and the different characteristics of each database and data store.

Azure SQL Database

Azure SQL Database offers a relational database in the cloud. It offers the code base as an SQL server on-premises, However, by using the SaaS solution, you don't have to manage the underlying platform, operating system, or buy any licenses.

Azure SQL Database offers scalability without causing any downtime for your databases. It offers column-based indexes, which make queries perform much faster. Built-in monitoring and built-in intelligence increase the performance of your database automatically, and disaster recovery is provided by automatic backups and point-in-time restores. You can also use active geo-replication, for global applications.

© Jeffrey Chilberto, Sjoukje Zaal, Gaurav Aroraa and Ed Price 2020
J. Chilberto et al., *Cloud Debugging and Profiling in Microsoft Azure*,
https://doi.org/10.1007/978-1-4842-5437-0_6

Azure SQL Database offers the following features:

- *Elastic database pools*: Elastic pools are a feature that helps in managing and scaling databases that have unpredictable usage demands. All databases in an elastic pool are deployed on the same database server and share the same resources. By managing a pool of databases and not an individual database, they can share performance and scaling. The performance of this tier is expressed in elastic Database Transaction Units (eDTUs).

- *Individual databases*: These are a good fit if you have a database with predictable performance. Scaling is done for each database separately. The performance of this tier is expressed in Database Transaction Units (DTUs).

Azure Database for MySQL

Azure Database for MySQL is an implementation of the MySQL open source relational database in the cloud. The Azure offering provides the same functionality and capabilities as MySQL Community Edition.

The MySQL database is widely used by PHP developers and for a lot of PHP applications, such as the open source CMS WordPress. MySQL offers the following features and capabilities:

- *ACID compliancy*: It offers atomicity, consistency, isolation, durability (ACID) transactions. This ensures that there is no data loss in the case of failure. MySQL offers ACID compliancy when using InnoDB and NDB Cluster Storage engines. InnoDB has been the default MySQL storage engine since version 5.6.

- *Performance*: MySQL can underperform for heavy loads and when it must execute complex queries. It is most suitable for web-based projects that require simple, straightforward data transactions.

- *Security*: MySQL offers security based on access-Control lists (ACLs) for all connections, queries, and other operations. It offers some support for SSL-encrypted connections between MySQL clients and servers.

- *NoSQL features*: MySQL only offers JSON data-type support and no support for indexing JSON.

- *Programming languages*: MySQL drivers support most programming languages.

By running your MySQL databases on Azure, in addition to all the features and capabilities that MySQL offers, Microsoft offers automatic scaling, high availability, encryption for data at rest, automatic backup, point-in-time restoration for up to 35 days, enterprise security and compliance, and more.

Azure Database for PostgreSQL

Azure Database for PostgreSQL is an implementation of the open-source relational database, PostgreSQL, in the cloud. It is also based on the community version of the open-source PostgreSQL database engine. PostgreSQL offers capabilities similar to MySQL, but there are differences.

It offers the following features and capabilities:

- *ACID compliancy*: It offers ACID transactions.

- *Performance*: It supports a variety of performance optimizations and is most suitable for systems that require the execution of complex queries and where read and write speeds are crucial. PostgreSQL performs well in OLTP/OLAP systems and with business intelligence applications.

- *Security*: PostgreSQL offers role-based and inherited role-based security. It offers native SSL support for client/server communications, and it offers row-level security.

- *Concurrency*: PostgreSQL has full multiversion concurrency control (MVCC) support and is extremely responsive in high-volume environments.

- *NoSQL features*: PostgreSQL supports JSON and other NoSQL features, such as native XML support, JSON indexing, and key-value pairs with HSTORE.

- *Extensibility*: PostgreSQL offers support for extensibility, such as adding new functions, types, new index types, and more.

- *Programming languages*: PostgreSQL offers programming language extensions in the form of connectors, for most programming languages.

Cosmos DB

Azure Cosmos DB is Microsoft's globally distributed, multi-model database service. Cosmos DB enables users to independently and elastically scale throughput and storage across any number of Azure regions worldwide. This makes Cosmos DB most suitable for applications and resources that must scale globally. Cosmos DB supports the following APIs:

- *Programming languages*: Cosmos DB offers programming language extensions for JavaScript, .NET, R, C/C++, Java, Perl, Python, Ruby, Tcl, and more.

- *SQL API*: With the SQL API, you can use SQL queries as a JSON query language against the data set inside Cosmos DB. Because Cosmos DB is schemaless, it provides autoindexing of the JSON documents. Data is stored on SSD drives for low latency, and it is lock-free, so you can create real-time queries for your data. Cosmos DB also supports writing stored procedures, triggers, and user-defined functions (UDFs) in JavaScript, and it supports ACID transactions inside a collection.

- *MongoDB API*: MongoDB is an open source document database that provides high performance, high availability, and automatic scaling by default. Using it inside Cosmos DB provides automatic sharding, indexing, replication, and encryption of your data on top of this. MongoDB also provides an aggregation pipeline, which can be used to filter and transform the data in multiple stages. It also supports creating a full-text index, and you can integrate it easily with Azure search and other Azure services as well.

- *Gremlin (Graph) API*: The Gremlin API is part of the Apache TinkerPop project, which is an open source Graph computing framework. A Graph is a way of storing objects (nodes), based on relationships. Each object can have multiple relations with other objects. You can interact with the data using JavaScript.

- *Table API*: The Azure Table API can be used for applications that are written for using Azure table storage but require premium features, such as global distribution, automatic indexing, low latency, and high throughput.

- *Cassandra API*: The Cassandra API can be used for applications that are written for Apache Cassandra. Apache Cassandra is an open source distributed NoSQL database that offers scalability and high availability. Cosmos DB offers no additional operations management, SLA, or automatic indexing.

In the future, new APIs will be added to Cosmos DB.

In the next section, we are going to create an Azure SQL Database from the Azure portal.

Creating an Azure SQL Database from the Azure Portal

To create an Azure SQL Database from the Azure portal, take the following steps:

1. Open the Azure portal, by navigating to `https://portal.azure.com/`.

2. Select Create a resource, then select SQL Database from the menu (Figure 6-1).

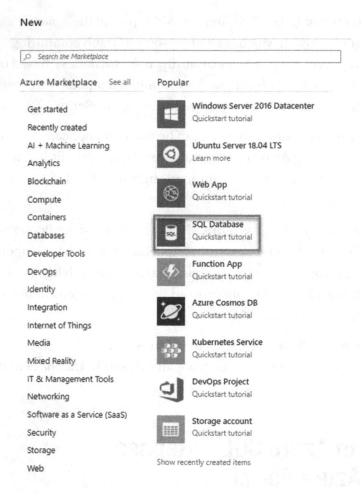

Figure 6-1. *Creating a new Azure SQL Database server*

3. In the Create SQL Database blade, add the following values:

a. *Subscription.* Select a subscription.

b. *Resource group.* Create a new one and call it AzureSQLResourceGroup.

c. *Database name.* AzureSQL

d. *Server.* Create a new one with the following properties (Figure 6-2):

Server name: apresssql1

Server admin login: apressadmin

Password: P@ssWord

Location: East US

Click Select.

Figure 6-2. *Specifying Azure SQL Database server configuration values*

    e. Want to use SQL elastic pool?: No.

    f. Compute + Storage: Select Basic (Figure 6-3).

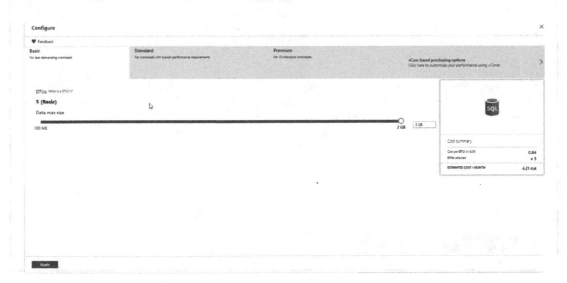

Figure 6-3. *Select Basic Storage*

    g. Then select Apply.

The configurations will now look like the following image (Figure 6-4).

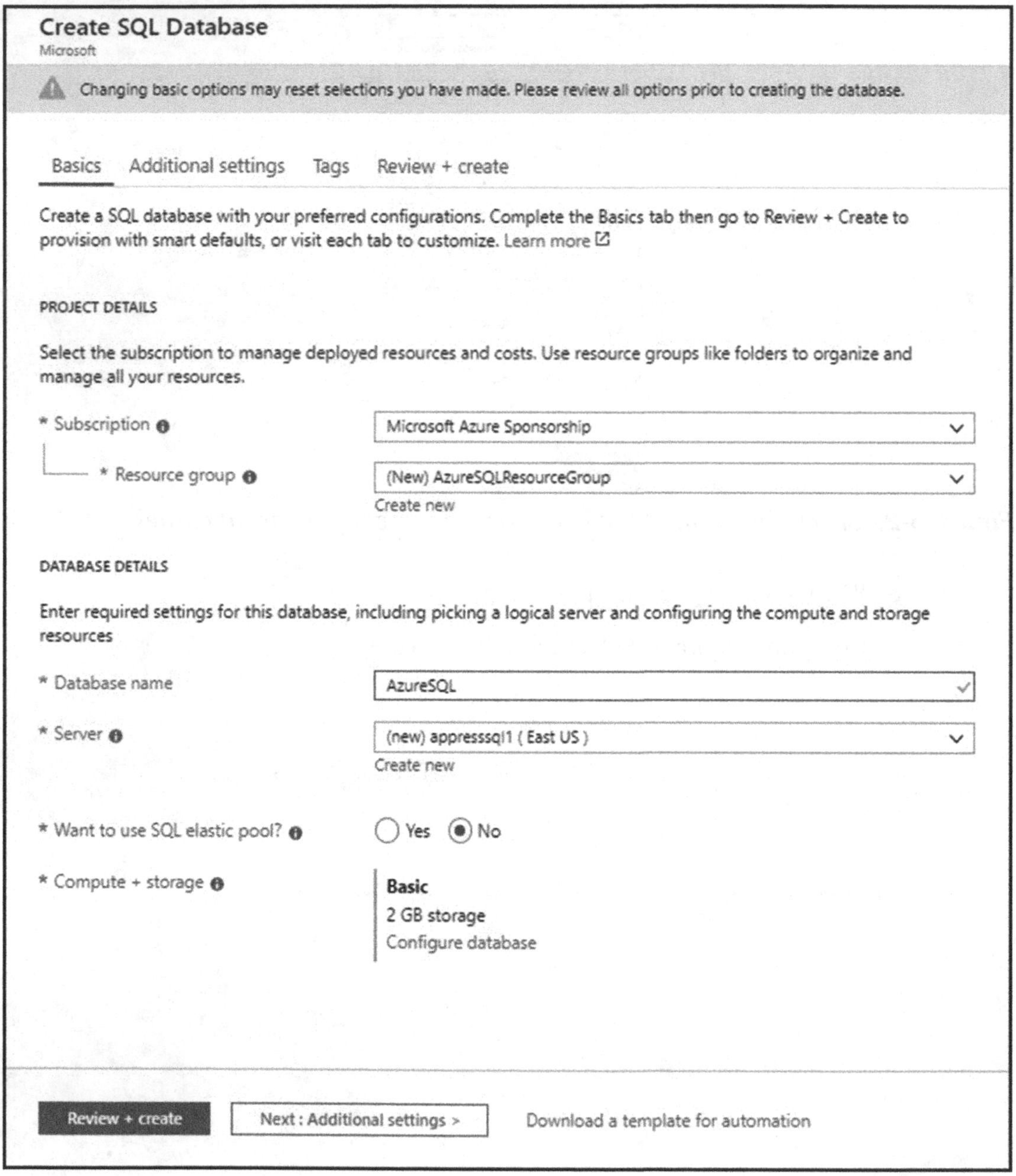

Create SQL Database
Microsoft

⚠ Changing basic options may reset selections you have made. Please review all options prior to creating the database.

Basics   Additional settings   Tags   Review + create

Create a SQL database with your preferred configurations. Complete the Basics tab then go to Review + Create to provision with smart defaults, or visit each tab to customize. Learn more ☑

PROJECT DETAILS

Select the subscription to manage deployed resources and costs. Use resource groups like folders to organize and manage all your resources.

* Subscription ❶	Microsoft Azure Sponsorship ⌄
└── * Resource group ❶	(New) AzureSQLResourceGroup ⌄
	Create new

DATABASE DETAILS

Enter required settings for this database, including picking a logical server and configuring the compute and storage resources

* Database name	AzureSQL ✓
* Server ❶	(new) appresssql1 (East US) ⌄
	Create new
* Want to use SQL elastic pool? ❶	◯ Yes ⦿ No
* Compute + storage ❶	**Basic**
	2 GB storage
	Configure database

Review + create   Next : Additional settings >   Download a template for automation

Figure 6-4. *Creating a new Azure SQL database*

4.   Click Review + create and then Create, to create the new database.

Now that we have a database in place, we can look at how to manage it from the Azure portal.

Managing Your Azure SQL Database from the Azure Portal

After your database is created, you can open the overview blade of that database as a starting point for managing your database. To go to the overview blade, select Go to resource (Figure 6-5).

Figure 6-5. *Navigating to the newly created resources*

In the overview blade, in the left menu, there are several configurations that can be set for this database. We are going to cover scaling and the query editor in the next sections.

Specifying a Server-Level IP Firewall Rule

Initially, all access to your Azure SQL server is blocked by the SQL Database firewall. To access a database server, you must specify one or more server-level IP firewall rules that enable access to your Azure SQL server. We are going to use this database in Chapter 7 as well, where we are going to create an Azure MVC Web App that connects to the database.

Therefore, we must add a firewall rule, to allow our public IP address to access the Azure Database server.

To set the firewall rule from the Azure portal, take the following steps:

1. From the database overview page, click Set server firewall from the top menu (Figure 6-6).

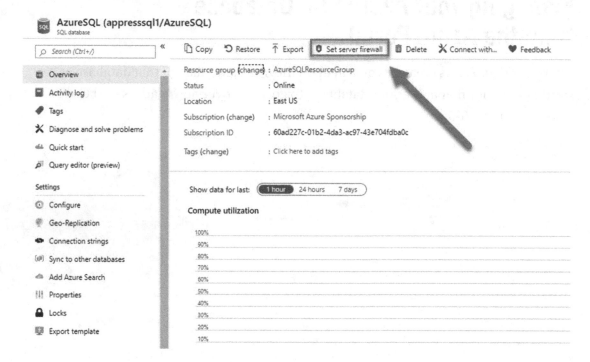

Figure 6-6. *Setting the server firewall*

2. Then click + Add client IP. A new rule is created, and your public on-premises IP address is automatically added to the Start IP and End IP fields (Figure 6-7).

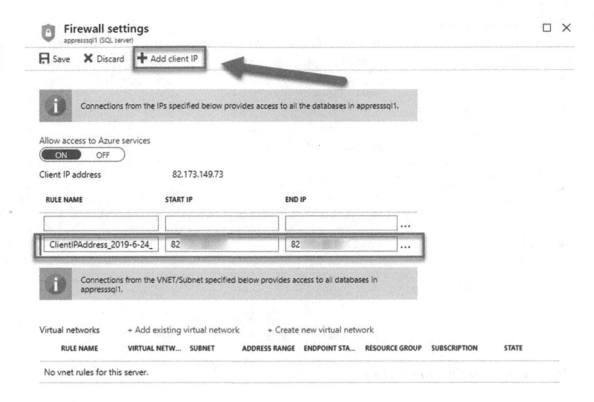

Figure 6-7. *Adding the client IP address*

3. Click Save.

Scaling Your Database

Azure SQL Database supports two types of scaling: vertical scaling (with which you can scale up or down the database by adding more compute power) and horizontal scaling (with which you can add more databases and divide the database over multiple database nodes). You can scale your databases to do the following:

1. Configure the scaling of your database. In the left menu, select Configure (Figure 6-8).

Figure 6-8. *Configuring scaling*

2. In the next screen, you can choose different tiers for your
    database. When we created the database, we chose the Basic
    tier. For this demonstration, pick the Standard tier and increase
    the Data max size to 500 MB, as shown in the following image
    (Figure 6-9).

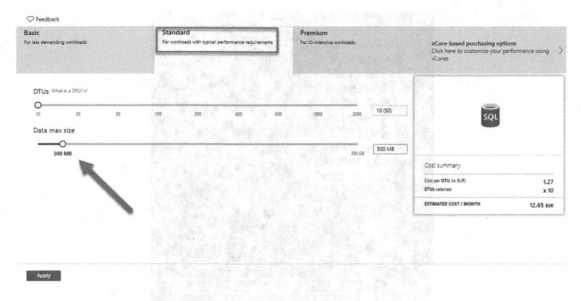

Figure 6-9. *Scaling down the database*

Note   You can also scale the amount of DTUs. For more information about DTUs, refer to the "Useful Links" section at the end of this chapter.

---

3.   Click Apply to save this setting.

We have now covered how to scale your database. In the next section, we will look at the CoffeeFix sample application.

Updating the CoffeeFix Application

In this demonstration, we are going to move the on-premises SQL database to our Azure SQL database that we created in the previous section. Therefore, we must update the following pieces of code:

1.   Open the CoffeeFix application from the Chapter 6 source code folder.

2.   Then open the CoffeeFix.Web application and select Data ➤ Migrations. Open the 00000000000000_CreateIdentitySchema.cs file (Figure 6-10).

189

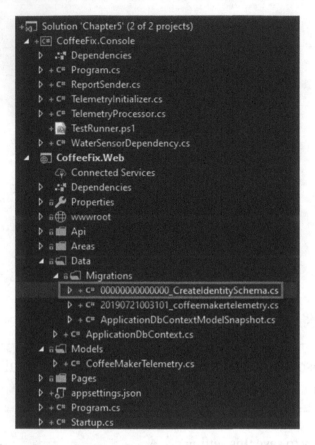

Figure 6-10. *Scaling down the database*

3. This class contains the code that creates the table in the database, using the Migration namespace from Entity Framework (EF). This way, EF creates a new table that matches the model inside the application. However, you should be aware that it will result in the loss of data.

4. We must change the database connection string in the appsettings.json file, to let EF create this database in our Azure SQL database. Therefore, switch back to the overview page of the database in the Azure portal and, in the left menu, under Settings, select Connection strings (Figure 6-11).

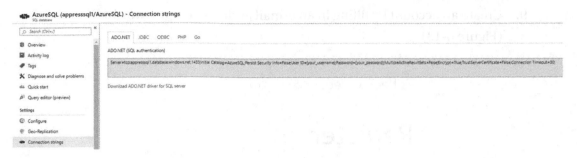

Figure 6-11. *Retrieving the connection string*

5.   Copy the connection string, open the `appsettings.json` file in Visual Studio, and replace the connection string in the file. This will look like the following:

```
{
  "ConnectionStrings": {
    "DefaultConnection": "Server=tcp:apresssql1.database.
    windows.net,1433;Initial Catalog=AzureSQL;Persist Security
    Info=False;User ID={your_username};Password={your_password};
    MultipleActiveResultSets=False;Encrypt=True;TrustServer
    Certificate=False;Connection Timeout=30;"
  },
```

6.   Then replace the user ID and password with the values that we used to create the database: apressadmin and P@ssWord.

7.   Now build and run your application.

8.   When the application is opened in the browser, click the Register button at the top right menu (Figure 6-12).

Figure 6-12. *Running the application*

9. Create an account by filling in an e-mail address and password (Figure 6-13).

Figure 6-13. *Registering for a new account*

10. Click Register.

11. Next, an error page is displayed, stating that there is something wrong with the database (Figure 6-14).

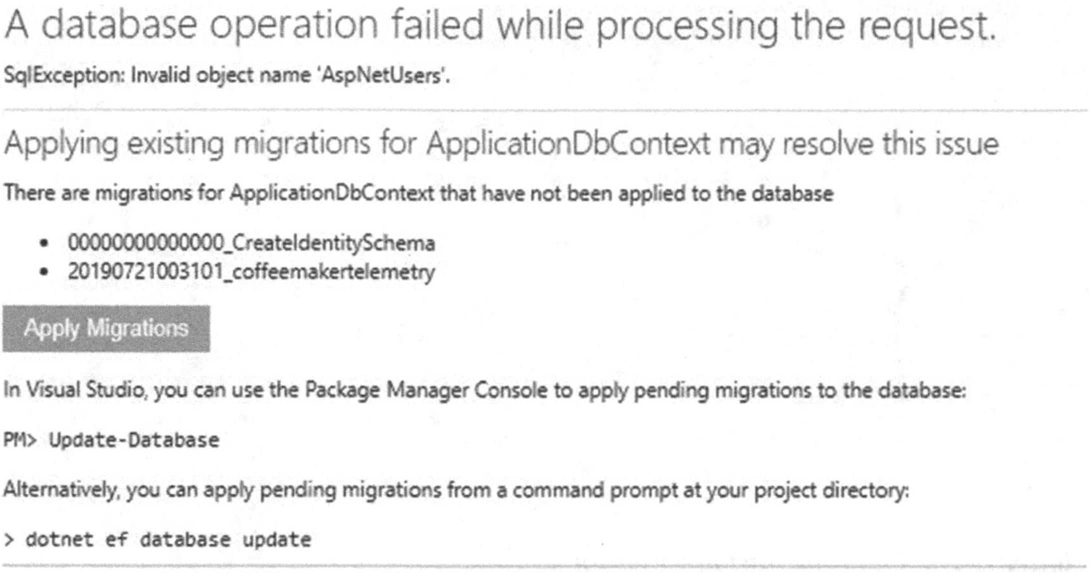

A database operation failed while processing the request.

SqlException: Invalid object name 'AspNetUsers'.

Applying existing migrations for ApplicationDbContext may resolve this issue

There are migrations for ApplicationDbContext that have not been applied to the database

- 00000000000000_CreateIdentitySchema
- 20190721003101_coffeemakertelemetry

`Apply Migrations`

In Visual Studio, you can use the Package Manager Console to apply pending migrations to the database:

`PM> Update-Database`

Alternatively, you can apply pending migrations from a command prompt at your project directory:

`> dotnet ef database update`

Figure 6-14. *Creating a new database*

12. There are two ways to solve this. You can click the Apply Migrations button, or you can open the Visual Studio command prompt and update the database from there. For this demo, we are going to create the tables by clicking the Apply Migrations button. Click the button.

13. The database and tables will now be created in the Azure SQL database.

14. We can check the database and tables in the Query editor in the Azure portal. To open this, select Query editor (Preview) from the SQL database overview page in the Azure portal (Figure 6-15).

Figure 6-15. *Opening the Query editor*

15. Next, we must authenticate to the server. Log in with the admin credentials that we provided when we first created the database (Figure 6-16).

Welcome to SQL Database Query Editor

SQL server authentication

Login *

apressadmin

Password *

••••••••

OK

OR

Active Directory authentication

Continue as SZaal@outlook.com

Figure 6-16. *Signing in to the database*

16. Open the tables section, and you will see the tables that are created (Figure 6-17).

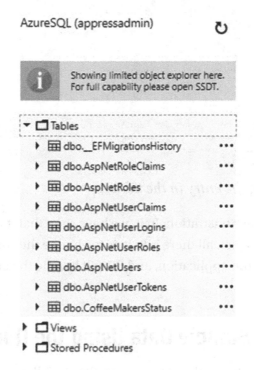

Figure 6-17. *Created database tables*

17. Switch back to the application and refresh the browser. Log in with your credentials and register again. You will see that the application now works as expected (Figure 6-18).

Figure 6-18. *Running the application*

18. When you switch back to the Azure portal again, right-click the AspNetUsers table, and then click Select Top 1000 Rows, you will see that the user has been added to the table (Figure 6-19).

Figure 6-19. *Checking the entry in the table*

This concludes the demonstration. In it, we have seen that it is very simple to move this database to Azure. In fact, all there is to it, is to change the connection string to the Azure database and run the application, and EF will handle the creation of the tables f or you.

Ingesting Some Sample Data Using the Query Editor

By the time of writing this book, the SQL Query editor is still in preview. It offers an easy way to execute SQL queries on your Azure SQL database or Azure SQL Data Warehouse directly from the Azure portal.

In the next demonstration, we are going to use the Query editor to ingest some data in the database. We can then monitor the database later.

1. With the Query editor still open, add the following script to add rows to the CoffeeMakerStatus table in the database. (This SQL query is also added to the source code for Chapter 6.) You can adjust the amount of rows, if needed.

```
declare @id int
select @id = 1
while @id >= 1 and @id <= 10000
```

```
begin
    insert INTO dbo.CoffeeMakersStatus(CoffeeMakerId, Date,
    Status, DataFileName)
    values(NEWID(), GETDATE(), 1, 'SampleData')
    select @id = @id + 1
end
```

We have now created in the database some rows in the CoffeeMakerStatus table. In the next section, we are going to monitor the database.

Monitoring and Performance Tuning for the Azure SQL Database

Azure SQL Database provides tools and methods to monitor usage, add or remove resources (such as CPU, memory, and I/O), troubleshoot potential problems, and make recommendations to improve the performance of the database. Azure also provides features that can automatically fix problems in the databases.

The database can adapt to the workload automatically, using Automatic. But there may still be some custom issues that require troubleshooting. For this, Azure SQL Database provides tools to monitor the database performance and to troubleshoot performance problems. These are covered in the upcoming sections.

Azure SQL Database offers the following tools and options to monitor and troubleshoot database performance:

- *Azure portal*: Select the Azure SQL database from the Azure portal. On the overview page, you will see the Monitoring chart, on which DTU consumption is shown by default. Select Edit to change the time range and the values that are shown. For single databases and elastic pools only, use Query Performance Insight to identify the queries that use the most resources.

- *SQL Server Management Studio*: SQL Server Management Studio can also provide a lot of useful reports, such as the performance dashboard. These reports can be used to monitor the resource usage and identify top resource-consuming queries. You can use Query Store to identify queries whose performance has regressed.

- *SQL Database Advisor*: You can use this tool to view recommendations to help you create and drop indexes, parameterize queries, and fix schema problems. This feature is available in single database and elastic pools only.

- *Azure SQL Intelligent Insights*: This tool can be used to automatically monitor database performance. When a performance problem is detected, a diagnostic log is generated. The log provides details and a root cause analysis (RCA) of the problem. A performance-improvement recommendation is provided, when possible.

- *Automatic tuning*: Azure SQL Database can automatically fix problems, using autotuning. Use dynamic management views (DMVs), extended events, and Query Store for help with more detailed troubleshooting of performance problems.

Note   More information about the tools that are covered here can be found in the "Useful Links" section at the end of this chapter.

Monitoring Database Performance

Azure SQL Database provides tools to monitor the performance of the database. It can monitor the following resources:

- *CPU usage*: Here, you can monitor whether the database is reaching 100% of the CPU usage. High CPU usage might indicate that the database or instance should be upgraded to a higher service tier.

- *Wait Statistics*: Use sys.dm_os_wait_stats (Transact-SQL) on the database, to determine how long queries are waiting. Queries can be waiting on resources, queue waits, or external waits.

- *IO usage*: Check to see if the database is reaching the IO limits of the underlying storage.

- *Memory usage*: The amount of memory available for the database or instance is proportional to the number of vCores. Make sure the memory is sufficient for the workload.

Monitoring the Performance of the Database from the Azure Portal

One option for monitoring the database performance in the Azure portal is to use Metrics. To access Metrics, take the following steps:

1. Go to the overview page of the Azure SQL Database that we have used for the CoffeeFix application.

2. Click Metrics in the left-hand menu. Based on the sample data that we have ingested in the database, you can filter on certain metrics here.

3. You can filter on CPU usage by selecting the CPU percentage in the Metric drop-down (Figure 6-20).

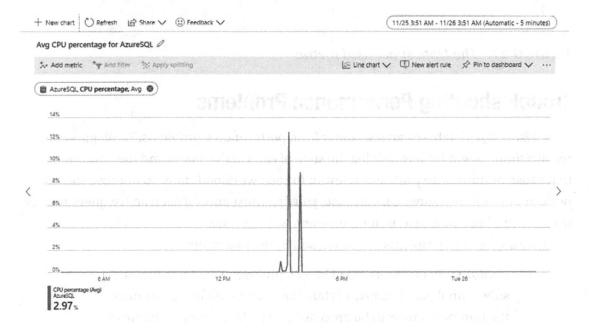

Figure 6-20. *CPU metric*

4. Another example is the Data space used metric (Figure 6-21).

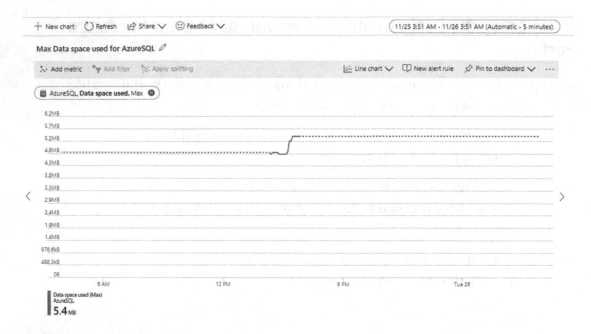

Figure 6-21. *The Data space used metric*

Troubleshooting Performance Problems

Your Azure SQL database can also suffer from performance problems. To diagnose and resolve these, begin by determining the state of each active query and the conditions that cause performance problems relevant to each workload state. To improve the performance of the Azure SQL database, you first must know if each active query request from the application is in a running state or a waiting state.

Running related problems can be caused by the following:

- *Compilation problems*: SQL Query Optimizer might produce a suboptimal plan because of stale statistics, an incorrect estimate of the number of rows to be processed, or an inaccurate estimate of the required memory. If you know the query was executed faster in the past or on another instance (either a managed instance or a SQL Server instance), compare the actual execution plans, to see if they're different. Try to apply query hints or rebuild statistics or indexes to get the better plan. Enable automatic plan correction in Azure SQL Database, to automatically mitigate these problems.

- *Execution problems*: If the query plan is already optimal, there is a good chance that it is already hitting the database's resource limits, such as log write throughput. It can also be using fragmented indexes that should be rebuilt. Execution problems can also occur when a large number of concurrent queries require the same resources.

Waiting related problems can be caused by the following:

- *Blocking*: One query might hold the lock on objects in the database, while others try to access the same objects. You can identify blocking queries by using dynamic management views (DMVs) or monitoring tools.

- *IO problems*: It can also be the case that queries are waiting for the pages to be written to the data or log files. For this, you can check the following wait statistics in the DMV: `INSTANCE_LOG_RATE_GOVERNOR, WRITE_LOG, or PAGEIOLATCH_*`

- *Temp DB problems*: When there are temporary tables used in queries, or there are TempDB spills in the plans, the queries can have a problem with the TempDB throughput.

- *Memory-related problems*: When there is not enough memory for the workload, the queries can receive less memory then required. In some cases, built-in intelligence in Query Optimizer will fix memory-related problems.

In the next section, we are going to monitor the Azure SQL Database performance, using DMVs.

Monitoring Performance of the Azure SQL Database Using Dynamic Management Views (DMVs)

To monitor the performance using DMVs, we must go back to our Azure database in the Azure portal. Follow these steps:

1. Open the Query editor again. We are going to run several queries to monitor the performance.

2. This first query retrieves the top-10 active CPU-consuming queries on our database:

```
SELECT TOP 10 GETDATE() runtime, *
FROM(SELECT query_stats.query_hash, SUM(query_stats.cpu_time)
'Total_Request_Cpu_Time_Ms', SUM(logical_reads) 'Total_Request_
Logical_Reads', MIN(start_time) 'Earliest_Request_start_Time',
COUNT(*) 'Number_Of_Requests', SUBSTRING(REPLACE(REPLACE(MIN(que
ry_stats.statement_text), CHAR(10), ' '), CHAR(13), ' '), 1, 256)
AS "Statement_Text"
    FROM(SELECT req.*, SUBSTRING(ST.text, (req.statement_start_
    offset / 2)+1, ((CASE statement_end_offset WHEN -1 THEN
    DATALENGTH(ST.text)ELSE req.statement_end_offset END-req.
    statement_start_offset)/ 2)+1) AS statement_text
        FROM sys.dm_exec_requests AS req
            CROSS APPLY sys.dm_exec_sql_text(req.sql_handle) AS
            ST ) AS query_stats
    GROUP BY query_hash) AS t
ORDER BY Total_Request_Cpu_Time_Ms DESC;
```

3. The next query identifies the data and log IO usage:

```
SELECT end_time, avg_data_io_percent, avg_log_write_percent
```
```
FROM sys.dm_db_resource_stats
ORDER BY end_time DESC;
```

4. The last query is going to identify memory grant wait performance issues:

```
SELECT wait_type,
        SUM(wait_time) AS total_wait_time_ms
FROM sys.dm_exec_requests AS req
    JOIN sys.dm_exec_sessions AS sess
        ON req.session_id = sess.session_id
WHERE is_user_process = 1
GROUP BY wait_type
ORDER BY SUM(wait_time) DESC;
```

5. The output of the last query can look like the following image (Figure 6-22).

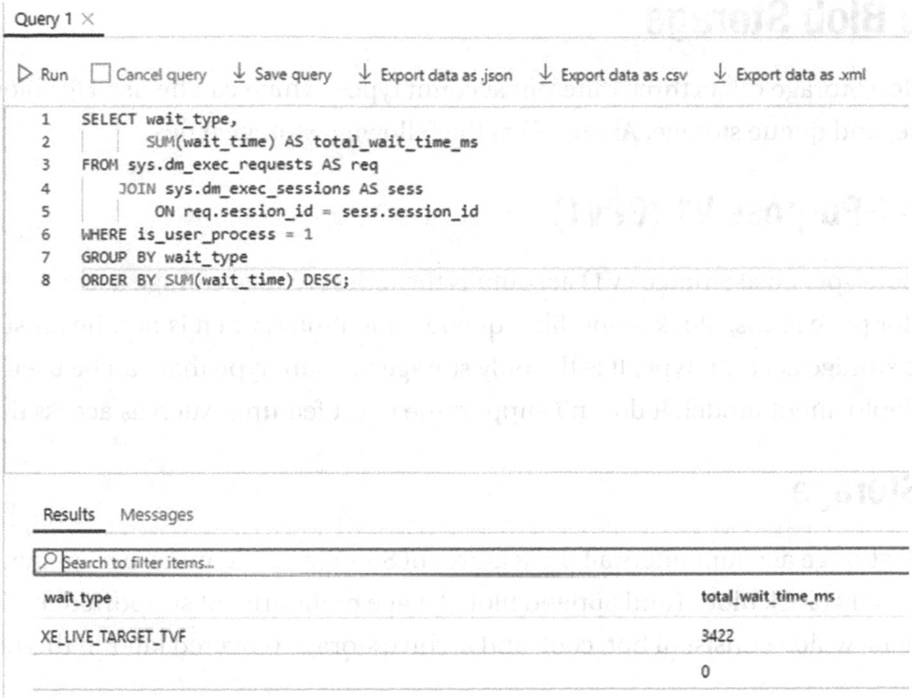

Query 1 ×

▷ Run   ☐ Cancel query   ↓ Save query   ↓ Export data as .json   ↓ Export data as .csv   ↓ Export data as .xml

```
1    SELECT wait_type,
2          SUM(wait_time) AS total_wait_time_ms
3    FROM sys.dm_exec_requests AS req
4        JOIN sys.dm_exec_sessions AS sess
5          ON req.session_id = sess.session_id
6    WHERE is_user_process = 1
7    GROUP BY wait_type
8    ORDER BY SUM(wait_time) DESC;
```

Results   Messages

🔍 Search to filter items...

wait_type	total_wait_time_ms
XE_LIVE_TARGET_TVF	3422
	0

Figure 6-22. *Total wait time in seconds*

Note   These are some examples of the different queries that you can run on the database, to monitor performance. In the "Useful Links" section, you can find the URL to the web site on which you can find more queries to use for monitoring your databases.

This concludes the database part of this chapter. In the next part, we are going to cover Azure Storage and what capabilities it has to offer.

Azure Storage

Every application requires some sort of storage solution. Azure offers several different types of storage, from storing files and documents to storing data sets. The first step is to create a Storage Account. When you create a storage account, you have to determine whether you want your data to be accessible locally or globally. Another consideration is which account type to choose.

Azure Blob Storage

Azure Blob Storage offers three different account types, which can be used for blob, table, file, and queue storage. Azure offers the following storage types.

General-Purpose V1 (GPv1)

The General-purpose Storage (V1) account is the oldest type of storage account. It offers storage for page blobs, block blobs, files, queues, and tables, but it is not the most cost-effective storage account type. It is the only storage account type that can be used for the classic deployment model. It doesn't support the latest features, such as access tiers.

Blob Storage

The blob storage account offers all the features of StorageV2 accounts, except that it supports only block blobs (and append blobs). Page blobs are not supported. It offers access tiers, which consist of hot, cool, and archive storage (covered later in this chapter).

General-Purpose V2 (GPv2)

StorageV2 is the newest type of storage account, and it combines V1 storage with Blob Storage. It offers all the latest features, such as access tiers for blob storage, with a reduction in costs. Microsoft recommends using this account type over the V1 and blob storage account types.

V1 storage accounts can be upgraded to V2.

Note   For more information on pricing and billing for these different account types, you can refer to the following pricing page: `https://azure.microsoft.com/en-us/pricing/details/storage/`.

Storage Replication Types

Azure uses Storage Replication types to ensure durability and high availability. This protects your storage accounts from unplanned and planned events, such as network or power outages, natural disasters, and terrorism. It also ensures that during these types of events, your storage account still meets the SLA.

The data from a storage account can be replicated within the same data center, the same region, across zonal data centers, and across different regions. These replication types are named Locally Redundant Storage (LRS), Zone Redundant Storage (ZRS), Geo-Redundant Storage (GRS), Geo-Zone-Redundant Storage (GZRS), and Read-Access Geo-Redundant Storage (RA-GRS). They are covered in more detail in the following sections.

Locally Redundant Storage

LRS is the cheapest option, which replicates the data three times within the same data center. When you make a write request to your storage account, it is synchronously written during this request to all three replicas. The request is committed when the data is completely replicated. With LRS, the data is replicated across multiple update domains and fault domains, within one storage scale unit.

Zone Redundant Storage

ZRS replicates three copies, across two or three data centers. The data is written synchronously to all three replicas in one or two regions. It also replicates the data three times inside the same data center in which the data resided, just as with LRS. It's only available in regions that have availability zones.

Geo-Redundant Storage

GRS replicates the data three times within the same region, as with ZRS, as well as three copies to other regions, asynchronously.

Geo-Zone-Redundant Storage

Geo-zone-redundant storage (GZRS) uses the high availability of ZRS with protection from regional outages, as provided by GRS. (At the time of writing this book, GZRS is still in preview.) The data is replicated across three Azure availability zones in the primary region and also replicated to a secondary geographic region, for protection from regional disasters. To make a regional pair, each Azure region is paired with another region within the same geographic area.

Read-Access Geo-Redundant Storage

RA-GRS maximizes availability for your storage account. It provides read-only access to the data in the secondary location, in addition to geo-replication across two regions.

Access Tiers

Blob storage accounts use access tiers to determine how frequently data is being accessed. You are billed based on the access tier that you select for your blob storage account. Azure offers three storage access tiers: hot, cool, and archive.

Hot

The hot access tier is most suitable for storing data that is accessed frequently in active use. For example, you could store images and style sheets for a web site inside the hot access tier. The storage costs for this tier are higher than those of the other access tiers, but you pay less for accessing the files.

Cool

The cool access tier is most suitable for storing data that is not accessed frequently (less than once in 30 days). Compared to the hot access tier, the cool tier has lower storage costs, but you pay more for accessing the files. This tier is most suitable for storing backups and older content that is not viewed often.

Archive

The archive storage tier is set on the blob level and not the storage level. It has the lowest costs for storing data and the highest cost for accessing data, compared to the hot and cool access tiers. This tier is for data that will remain in the archive for at least 180 days, and it will take a couple of hours of latency before it can be accessed. This tier is most suitable for long-term backups or compliance and archive data.

A blob in the archive tier is offline and cannot be read (except for the metadata), copied, overwritten, or modified.

Azure Table Storage

Azure table storage is based on a NoSQL data store, and it can be used for a large amount of semistructured, non-relational data. It is more cost-effective than relational databases, because it stores the data on cheaper servers that provide horizontal scale and high performance.

NoSQL uses a schemaless design, and data is stored, based on key/attribute values. You can store flexible data sets in it, and it can store any number of entities in a table, up to the maximum capacity of the storage account (which is 500TB).

Azure table storage is most suitable for data sets that don't require complex joins, stored procedures, and foreign keys. You can access the data using the OData protocol and LINQ Queries.

Azure Queue Storage

With Azure queue storage, you can create a message queue, which can be used for applications and other Azure resources. Message queues offer an asynchronous communication mechanism, whereby a sender adds a message to the queue, which can be received by the receiver when requested. Applications and other Azure resources can benefit from this, because they can decouple components, which can scale independently from one another.

Azure File Storage

With Azure files, you can create file shares in the cloud. You can access your files using the Server Message Block (SMB) protocol, which is an industry standard that can be used on Linux, Windows, and macOS devices. Azure files can also be mounted, as if on a local drive on these same devices. They can be cached for fast access on Windows Server, using Azure File Sync (preview).

File shares can be used across multiple machines, which makes them suitable for storing files or data that are accessed from multiple machines, such as tools for development machines, configuration files, or log data. Azure File share is part of the Azure Storage Client Libraries and offers an Azure Storage REST API, which can be leveraged by developers in their solutions.

Azure Disk Storage

The disks that are used for VMs are stored in Azure blob storage as page blobs. Azure stores two disks for each VM: the actual operating system (VHD) of the VM and a temporary disk that is used for short-term storage. This data is erased when the VM is turned off or rebooted.

There are two different performance tiers that Azure offers: standard disk storage and premium disk storage. Standard disk storage offers HDD drives to store the data on and is the most cost-effective storage tier from among those you can choose. With premium disk storage, your data is stored on SSDs.

Creating an Azure Storage Account with a Blob Container Using CLI

In this demonstration, we are going to create a storage account using CLI. For this, we are going to use Azure Cloud Shell. Therefore, take the following steps:

1. Open the Azure portal, by navigating to `https://portal.azure.com/`.

2. In the top-right menu, select Azure Cloud Shell. Switch to Bash.

3. Add the following line of code to create a new resource group in Azure:

```
az group create \
    --name ApressStorageRG \
    --location 'East US'
```

4. Add the following line of code to create the storage account:

```
az storage account create \
    --name apressblobstorage \
    --resource-group ApressStorageRG \
    --location 'East US' \
    --sku Standard_ZRS \
    --encryption blob
```

5. Then display your storage account keys:

```
az storage account keys list \
    --account-name ApressBlobStorage \
    --resource-group ApressStorageRG \
    --output table
```

6. The output looks like the following image (Figure 6-23).

```
sjoukje@Azure:~$ az storage account keys list \
>     --account-name ApressBlobStorage \
>     --resource-group ApressStorageRG \
>     --output table
KeyName    Permissions    Value
---------  -------------  --------------------------------------------------------------------------------------
key1       Full           ZMHTSGSgOvswVQCwtDyKO1dbyY3Zmgr/T4h2iGZ2flt8rwDuV4pzpcktSsXXDRtbvVl+w1GCJUnI2ZjHlZvdVA==
key2       Full           /N6TQtzXy51y3QQR8c7ZdKz05vChzbu0V/zZtnL/GHGa4sDrTvWtFJCO5kZdZiexC30Qwqwt+ltGjLl9/DcVKQ==
sjoukje@Azure:~$ ▌
```

Figure 6-23. *Storage account keys*

7. Set the AZURE_STORAGE_ACCOUNT and AZURE_STORAGE_KEY
    environment variables. Copy the first key from the preceding
    output:

```
export AZURE_STORAGE_ACCOUNT=apressblobstorage
export AZURE_STORAGE_KEY="<account-key>"
```

8. Then you have to create the blob container:

```
az storage container create --name apress-container
```

9. Create a blob:

```
vi helloworld
```

10. When the file opens, press Insert. Type "Hello world," then press
    Esc. Next, type ":x," then press Enter.

11. Upload the blob 500 times to the blob container, using the following code:

```
for i in `seq 1 500`;
do
        az storage blob upload \\
                --container-name apress-container \\
                --name helloworld$i \\
                --file helloworld
done
```

It can take some time before all the files are uploaded. To check the files in the blob storage container, you can navigate to the blob container in the Azure portal and check the Storage Explorer (Figure 6-24).

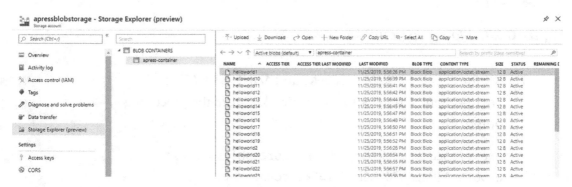

Figure 6-24. *The u ploaded blobs*

Monitoring Your Storage Services

All your storage accounts can easily be monitored from Azure. Azure delivers a unified view of your Azure Storage services' performance, capacity, and availability.

Storage capacity and performance can be observed in two different ways: viewed directly from a storage account or viewed from Azure Monitor.

Both ways offer a consistent experience. Only Azure Monitor is capable of monitoring different storage accounts at once. They both offer the following capabilities:

- *Drill down analysis:* You can drill down into a specific storage account, to help diagnose issues or perform detailed analysis by category—availability, performance, failures, and capacity.

- *At scale perspective*: This shows a snapshot view of the availability, based on the health of the storage service or the API operation. It shows both the total number of requests that the storage service receives and latency showing the average time the storage service or API operation type is taking to process requests.

- *Customizable*: You can customize the metrics you want to see, modify or set thresholds that align with your limits, and save as your own workbook. Charts in the workbook can be pinned to the Azure dashboard.

Monitoring Your Storage Account with Azure Monitor for Storage

Azure Monitor for Storage allows comprehensive monitoring of all your Azure Storage accounts in one solution. (At the time of writing this book, this feature is still in preview.) It can give you actionable knowledge on the health and performance of Storage accounts at scale, with the capability to focus on hotspots and diagnose latency, throttling, and availability issues.

In the next demonstration, we are going to look at some of the features and capabilities that Azure Monitor has to offer for your storage accounts:

1. Open the Azure portal, by navigating to `https://portal.azure.com/`.

2. In the left-hand menu, select Monitor. Under the Insights section, select Storage Accounts.

3. You will see an overview Workbook of the different storage accounts in the selected subscription. The table displays interactive storage metrics and service availability states for up to ten storage accounts, grouped within the subscription (Figure 6-25).

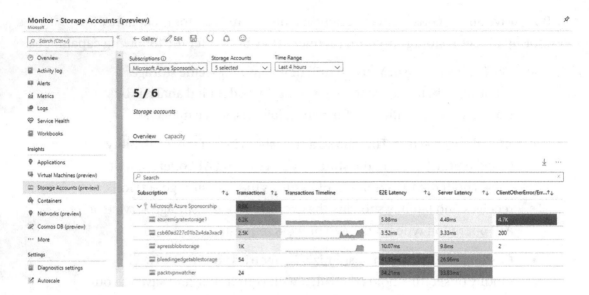

Figure 6-25. *An overview workbook of Storage Accounts*

4. You can filter the results, based on the options you select from the following drop-down lists:

- *Subscriptions*: Only the subscriptions that have storage accounts will be listed in this overview.

- *Storage accounts*: Ten storage accounts are preselected here, by default. A maximum of 200 of storage accounts can be returned, if you select multiple storage accounts.

- *Time range*: This displays the last four hours by default.

5. By selecting a value in the columns Availability, E2E Latency, Server Latency, and transaction error type/Errors, you will be redirected to a report that is tailored to specific types of storage metrics that match the column selected for that storage account (Figure 6-26).

Figure 6-26. *Part of the tailored report for the apressblobstorage account*

Note For more information about the workbooks for each category, refer to the URL in the "Useful Links" section.

Summary

In this chapter, we have covered the different types of databases and storage accounts. We have added a database to our application and then used the Query Editor to generate some load on the database. We then looked at the different monitoring and troubleshooting options that are available for Azure SQL databases. In the storage account section, we created a blob storage account and uploaded blobs using a CLI script. We then looked at the monitoring capabilities that Azure Monitor for Storage has to offer.

In the next chapter, we are going to cover Azure Active Directory.

Useful Links

The following articles, all available from Microsoft, will give you more relevant information on all the topics covered in this chapter. Some links provide more advanced information, such as, for example, on setting up a data architecture and more.

- "Service tiers in the DTU-based purchase model," `https://docs.microsoft.com/en-us/azure/sql-database/sql-database-service-tiers-dtu`, November 25, 2019.

- "Scale single database resources in Azure SQL Database," `https://docs.microsoft.com/en-us/azure/sql-database/sql-database-single-database-scale`, April 25, 2019.

- "Monitor database performance," `https://docs.microsoft.com/en-us/azure/sql-database/sql-database-monitor-tune-overview#monitor-database-performance`, January 24, 2019.

- "Monitoring performance Azure SQL Database using dynamic management views," `https://docs.microsoft.com/en-us/azure/sql-database/sql-database-monitoring-with-dmvs`, December 18, 2018.

- "Find and apply performance recommendations," `https://docs.microsoft.com/en-us/azure/sql-database/sql-database-advisor-portal`, December 18, 2018.

- "Monitoring your storage service with Azure Monitor for Storage," `https://docs.microsoft.com/en-us/azure/azure-monitor/insights/storage-insights-overview`, August 14, 2019.

- "Monitor a storage account in the Azure portal," `https://docs.microsoft.com/en-us/azure/storage/common/storage-monitor-storage-account`, July 30, 2018.

- "Detailed storage workbooks," `https://docs.microsoft.com/en-us/azure/azure-monitor/insights/storage-insights-overview#detailed-storage-workbooks`, August 18, 2019.

CHAPTER 7

Identity Security with Azure Active Directory

In this chapter, we are going to cover identity security with Azure Active Directory (Azure AD). We will cover what Azure AD has to offer for securing your identities and applications, such as Microsoft Graph, Azure AD Business-to-Business (B2B), and Azure AD Business-to-Consumer (B2C). We are also going to secure our application that we created in the previous chapter, using Azure Active Directory. We are going to secure the CoffeeFix web application using Azure AD, and then we are going to look at the different monitoring and troubleshooting capabilities.

Azure Active Directory

Azure Active Directory (AD) offers directory and identity management from the Microsoft Cloud. It offers traditional username and password identity management and roles and permissions management. In addition, it offers more enterprise-grade security features, such as multifactor authentication (MFA) and basic application monitoring, solution monitoring, and alerting capabilities. Azure AD can easily be integrated with your on-premises Active Directory to create a hybrid infrastructure.

Azure AD offers the following pricing plans:

- *Free*: This offers the most basic features, such as support for up to 500,000 objects, SSO, support for Azure AD Connect synchronization, and standard security reports.

- *Basic*: This offers no object limit, SLA of 99.9%, groups, self-service password reset, and support for the Application Proxy.

© Jeffrey Chilberto, Sjoukje Zaal, Gaurav Aroraa and Ed Price 2020
J. Chilberto et al., *Cloud Debugging and Profiling in Microsoft Azure*,
https://doi.org/10.1007/978-1-4842-5437-0_7

- *Premium P1*: This offers Advanced Reporting, MFA, MDM auto-enrollment, Cloud app discovery, and Azure AD Connect Health.

- *Premium P2*: Identity protection and Privileged Identity Management are offered.

Note   For a detailed overview of the different pricing plans and all the features that are offered for each plan, refer to the following pricing page: `https://azure.microsoft.com/en-us/pricing/details/active-directory/`. Note that Azure AD Premium is part of the Enterprise Mobility + Security Suite.

Azure AD can also be used in your custom apps and APIs and for authorizing your users and securing your resources. It offers support for industry standard protocols, such as OAuth2.0 and OpenID Connect, and it supports authentication for single- and multi-tenant applications.

Azure AD offers two different endpoints that can be leveraged in your custom applications:

- *V1 endpoint*: This endpoint offers support for Microsoft work or school accounts only, and it uses the Azure portal to register the apps in Azure AD. It uses the Azure Active Directory Library (ADAL) SDK to authenticate users within the application.

- *V2 endpoint*: This offers support for both Microsoft work or school accounts and personal accounts, such as Outlook.com. It also offers a new registration portal, located at `apps.dev.microsoft.com`, and that makes it much easier to register your application in Azure AD. It uses the Microsoft Authentication Library (MSAL) to authenticate your users within the application. Using this endpoint, you can create one single App ID for multiplatform apps. If your applications consist of a separate web, Android, or iOS app, they can all use the same App ID. You can use dynamic consent, whereby you grant permissions only at the time you need them in the application itself and not up front when registering the app in Azure AD.

Microsoft Graph

Microsoft Graph is a set of APIs that connects multiple Azure services and provides a single endpoint for developers to use in their custom applications.

Microsoft Graph is made up of relationships between the various Azure services. By calling the endpoint for a user that is added to Azure AD, you can retrieve the documents the user is working on, find his/her manager, retrieve the user's meetings, get a list of devices that the user has, and much more.

Azure AD is integrated in Microsoft Graph as well, but it can be used for more than Azure AD features. In fact, nearly all SaaS products of Azure use Azure AD, such as Office 365, Intune, Dynamic 365, and Azure SQL. All these Azure services are integrated in Microsoft Graph and can be used inside your apps and APIs.

Microsoft Graph offers two different endpoints: the v1.0 endpoint, which consists of all the APIs that are generally available, and the beta endpoint. The beta endpoint offers APIs that can still change over time.

Note   To get started with the Graph API and register your app in Azure AD, refer to: `https://developer.microsoft.com/en-us/graph`. This is a great starting point, from which you can also download secure sample applications for multiple programming languages. For an overview of all the Azure services that are integrated in Microsoft Graph, you can refer to the preceding web site as well.

Azure Active Directory Business-to-Business

Azure AD B2B is a feature on top of Azure Active Directory that enables organizations to work safely with external users. To be added to Azure B2B, external users don't have to add a Microsoft work or personal account to an existing Azure AD tenant. All sorts of accounts can be added to Azure B2B. You also don't have to configure anything in the Azure portal to use B2B. This feature is enabled by default for all Azure AD tenants.

Azure B2B is integrated with Office 365 for external sharing. It also provides APIs that can be leveraged inside custom applications, to let both internal and external users authenticate.

Azure AD Free features are available for external users at no cost. However, if you want external users to use Azure AD Premium features, such as MFA and conditional access, you must have enough Azure AD Premium licenses, with a ratio of 5:1. This means that for every Azure AD Premium license, you can add five external users. For example, if your organization wants to add 50 external users to Azure B2B, you should purchase 10 Azure AD Premium licenses.

Azure AD B2B offers the following features:

- *Groups*: You can create groups for external users. You can use dynamic groups as well. Administrators can set up rules to populate groups, based on user attributes.

- *Conditional access*: With conditional access, you can set certain conditions for your users. You can require external users to use multifactor authentication, allow them access only to certain applications, or permit access only from certain locations.

- *Sharing policies*: The ability to invite external users is not limited to administrators. You can use policies to delegate permissions to other external users. You can grant the Guest Inviter role to a user, who is then allowed to send invites.

- *Auditing and reporting*: Just as with normal users, there are also auditing and reporting capabilities. You can look into the invitation history and acceptance details.

Azure Active Directory Business-to-Consumer

Azure AD B2C is a cloud identity-management solution for mobile and web applications. It offers out-of-the-box authentication providers that can be leveraged from within your apps and custom APIs, using only the MSAL, which is used in other Azure AD applications as well (via the V2 endpoint).

This means that developers don't have to add additional SDKs manually. That is all handled by Microsoft. Next, to the authentication providers that are offered by Microsoft, it also allows the ability to add your own authentication providers.

Azure AD B2C offers the following authentication providers:

- *Social accounts*: These include Facebook, Google, LinkedIn, and others.

- *Enterprise accounts*: These use open standards protocols, such as OpenID or SAML.

- *Local accounts*: These are accounts that use an e-mail address/username and password.

Your application must be registered inside the Azure B2C tenant. After registration, built-in policies can be configured for the app, with which you can enable different authentication methods, set claims, enable MFA, or create a password reset policy that the app can use.

You then add the required configuration settings for the application that is registered in the Azure B2C tenant to your code. All the previously mentioned settings can then be used without any further configuration.

In the next section, we will demonstrate how to add users and groups to Azure AD.

Adding Users and Groups to Azure AD

In this demonstration, we are going to add some users to Azure AD, create a security group, and add a user to the group. Take the following steps:

1. Open the Azure portal, by navigating to `https://portal.azure.com/`.

2. In the left-hand menu, click Azure Active Directory, then, under Manage, select Users.

3. In the top menu, click + New user (Figure 7-1).

Figure 7-1. *Adding a new user*

4. Fill in the name of the user and the display name. Then select
    Profile and fill in the first name, last name, job title, and
    department (Figure 7-2).

Figure 7-2. *Specifying user values*

5. Now, when you click the Create button, the user is going to be created as a normal user, without any permissions in Azure. If you want to give the user certain permissions during creation, you can click the User link under Groups and roles (Figure 7-2). There, you can assign the required permissions to the user directly (Figure 7-3).

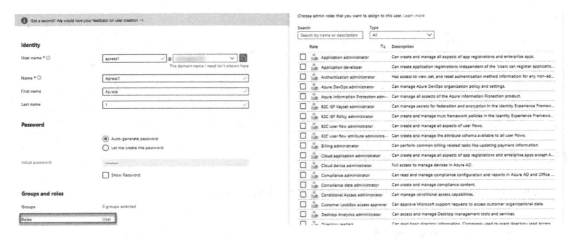

Figure 7-3. *Adding user permissions*

6. We are not going to assign the permissions directly to the user, because we are going to create a group. This group will be created for all the users of the CoffeeFix application, who we are going to secure later in this chapter. Click Create to add the user to Azure AD.

7. Go back to the overview blade of Azure AD. Under Manage, select Groups (Figure 7-4).

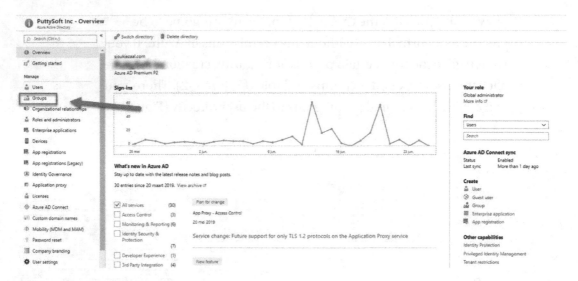

Figure 7-4. *The Groups overview page*

8. In the top menu, click + New group (Figure 7-5).

Figure 7-5. *Adding a new group*

9. Specify the following values:

    - *Group type*: Security

    - *Group Name*: CoffeeFix

    - *Group description*: Users of the CoffeeFix application

    - *Membership type*: Assigned

10. Then click Members. Search for the user that you created in the previous step and select it (Figure 7-6).

Figure 7-6. *Creating the group and adding a member*

11. Click Select, and then Create.

We have now created a new user, created a group, and added the user to the group. These are basic operations through which you can gain additional understanding of how to add users and groups in Azure AD. In the next section, we are going to undertake some more advanced actions. We are going to enable Azure AD authentication for our CoffeeFix web app.

Securing the CoffeeFix Web App Using Azure Active Directory

This demonstration is divided into three parts. First, we are going to make the code changes to the application, and then we are going to register the application. Finally, we are going to make some minor changes to the application, to update it with the registered values and to deploy it to Azure.

Adding Azure AD Authentication to the CoffeeFix Web App

We are going to use the OpenIDConnect and MSAL libraries to secure the application and to prepare it. To update the CoffeeFix web app so that it can authenticate to Azure AD, you must take the following steps:

1. In Visual Studio, open the CoffeeFix application from the Chapter 7 source code folder.

2. Open the NuGet package Manager console and add the following:

   ```
   Install-Package Microsoft.AspNetCore.Authentication.
   AzureAD.UI -Version 2.0.0
   ```

3. Microsoft.AspNetCore.Authentication middleware uses the Startup class that is executed when the hosting process initializes. Open Startup.cs and add the following using statements to it:

   ```
   using Microsoft.AspNetCore.Authentication;
   using Microsoft.AspNetCore.Authentication.AzureAD.UI;
   using Microsoft.AspNetCore.Authentication.OAuth.Claims;
   using Microsoft.AspNetCore.Authentication.OpenIdConnect;
   using Microsoft.AspNetCore.Authorization;
   using Microsoft.AspNetCore.Mvc.Authorization;
   ```

4. The method AddAuthentication configures the service to add cookie-based authentication, which is used in browser scenarios, and to set the challenge to OpenID Connect.

   The line containing .AddAzureAd adds the Microsoft identity platform authentication to your application. It's then configured to sign in using the Microsoft identity platform endpoint. Add the following code to the ConfigureServices method, after Configur e<CookiePolicyOptions>, as follows:

   ```
   services.AddAuthentication(AzureADDefaults.AuthenticationScheme)
           .AddAzureAD(options => Configuration.Bind("AzureAd",
           options));
   services.Configure<OpenIdConnectOptions>(AzureADDefaults.
   OpenIdScheme, options =>
   ```

```
    {
        options.Authority = options.Authority + "/v2.0/";

        // Per the code below, this application signs in
            users in any Work and School
        // accounts and any Microsoft Personal Accounts.
        // If you want to direct Azure AD to restrict the
            users that can sign-in, change
        // the tenant value of the appsettings.json file
            in the following way:
        // - only Work and School accounts => 'organizations'
        // - only Microsoft Personal accounts => 'consumers'
        // - Work and School and Personal accounts =>
            'common'

        // If you want to restrict the users that can
            sign-in to only one tenant
        // set the tenant value in the appsettings.json
            file to the tenant ID of this
        // organization, and set ValidateIssuer below to true.

        // If you want to restrict the users that can
            sign-in to several organizations
        // Set the tenant value in the appsettings.json
            file to 'organizations', set
        // ValidateIssuer, above to 'true', and add the
            issuers you want to accept to the
        // options.TokenValidationParameters.ValidIssuers
            collection
        options.TokenValidationParameters.ValidateIssuer =
        false;
    });
```

5. Next, replace the `services.AddMvc` method with the following:

```
services.AddMvc(options =>
            {
                    var policy = new AuthorizationPolicyBuilder()
                        .RequireAuthenticatedUser()
                        .Build();
                    options.Filters.Add(new AuthorizeFilter(policy));
            }).SetCompatibilityVersion(CompatibilityVersion.
            Version_2_2);
```

6. Then open `appsettings.json` and add the following code to it:

```
"AzureAd": {
    "Instance": "https://login.microsoftonline.com/",
    "Domain": "[Enter the domain of your tenant, e.g. contoso.
    onmicrosoft.com]",
    "TenantId": "common",
    "ClientId": "Enter_the_Application_Id_here",
    "CallbackPath": "/signin-oidc"
  }
```

7. Next, open `_LoginPartial.cshtml` and replace the code with the following:

```
using System.Security.Claims

@if (User.Identity.IsAuthenticated)
{
    var identity = User.Identity as ClaimsIdentity; // Azure AD V2
endpoint specific
    string preferred_username = identity.Claims.FirstOrDefault(c
=> c.Type == "preferred_username")?.Value;
    <ul class="nav navbar-nav navbar-right">
        <li class="navbar-text">Hello @preferred_username!</li>
        <li><a asp-area="AzureAD" asp-controller="Account"
        asp-action="SignOut">Sign out</a></li>
    </ul>
}
```

```
else
{
    <ul class="nav navbar-nav navbar-right">
        <li><a asp-area="AzureAD" asp-controller="Account"
        asp-action="SignIn">Sign in</a></li>
    </ul>
}
```

8. Now that we have added the required code for authenticating to Azure, let's deploy the app to Azure. Note that we must make some further changes to `appsettings.json` later, but in order to retrieve a redirect URL, we are first going to deploy the app.

9. Deploy the application to Azure from Visual Studio.

10. After publishing the application, navigate to Web App in the Azure portal and copy the URL of the Web App to Notepad. We will use this in the next section for the reply URL.

Registering the CoffeeFix Web App in Azure AD

1. Go again to the Azure AD overview page in the Azure portal and select App Registrations in the left-hand menu.

2. Then click New registration in the top menu (Figure 7-7).

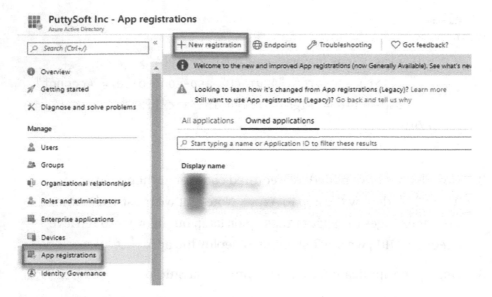

Figure 7-7. *Adding a new app registration*

3.   Add the following values to register the application:

- *Name*: CoffeeFix

- *Supported account types*: Accounts in any organizational directory (Any Azure AD directory - Multitenant)

- *Redirect URI*: Paste in the application URL that you copied (Figure 7-8).

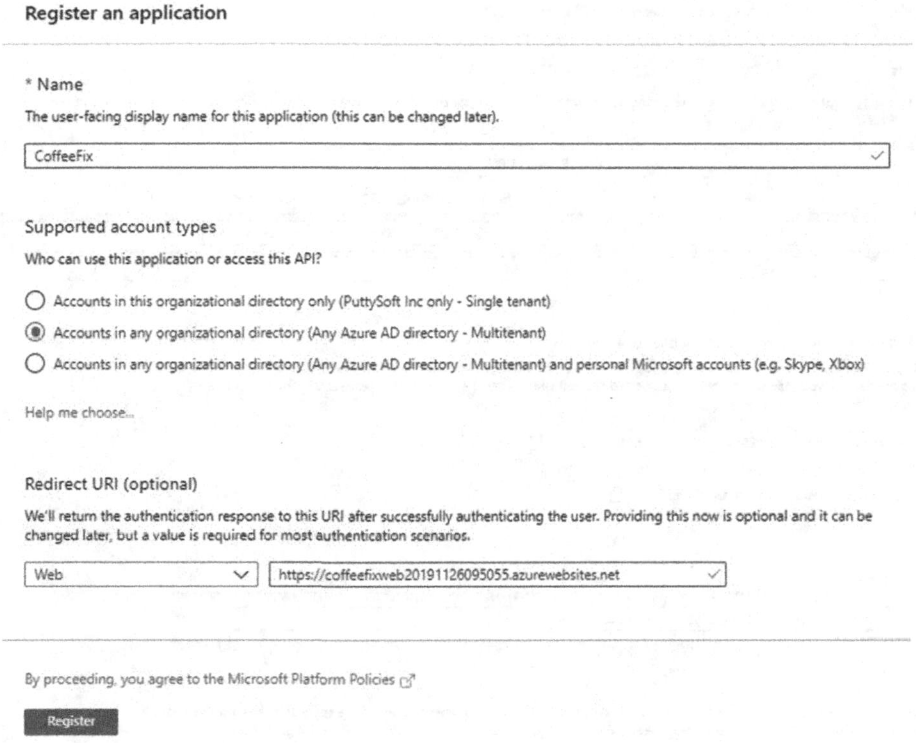

Register an application

* Name

The user-facing display name for this application (this can be changed later).

CoffeeFix	✓

Supported account types

Who can use this application or access this API?

○ Accounts in this organizational directory only (PuttySoft Inc only - Single tenant)

◉ Accounts in any organizational directory (Any Azure AD directory - Multitenant)

○ Accounts in any organizational directory (Any Azure AD directory - Multitenant) and personal Microsoft accounts (e.g. Skype, Xbox)

Help me choose...

Redirect URI (optional)

We'll return the authentication response to this URI after successfully authenticating the user. Providing this now is optional and it can be changed later, but a value is required for most authentication scenarios.

Web ⌄	https://coffeefixweb20191126095055.azurewebsites.net ✓

By proceeding, you agree to the Microsoft Platform Policies ⌐

Register

Figure 7-8. *Specifying the required values*

4. Click Register.

5. Once the application is registered, select the Authentication menu, and then add the following information:

    - *Redirect URI*: Add the URL for the Web App in Azure here, followed by /signin-oidc.

    - *Logout URL*: Add the URL for the Web App in Azure again, followed by /signout-oidc.

    - *Implicit grant*: Select ID tokens (Figure 7-9)

🖫 Save   ✕ Discard | ⇄ Try out the new experience | ♡ Got feedback?

Redirect URIs

The URIs that we will accept as destinations when returning authentication responses (tokens) after successfully authenticating users. Also referred to as reply URLs. Learn more about redirect URIs

Type		Redirect URI	
Web		https://coffeefixweb20191126095055.azurewebsites.net	🗑
Web ∨		https://coffeefixweb20191126095055.azurewebsites.net/signin-oidc ✓	🗑
Web ∨		e.g. https://myapp.com/auth	

Suggested Redirect URIs for public clients (mobile, desktop)

If you are using the Microsoft Authentication Library (MSAL) or the Active Directory Authentication Library (ADAL) to build applications for desktop or mobile devices, you may select from the suggested Redirect URIs below or enter a custom redirect URI above. For more information, refer to the library documentation.

☐ msal33143508-bb5f-40ad-a17c-b955987b727e://auth (MSAL only) ⧉
☐ https://login.microsoftonline.com/common/oauth2/nativeclient ⧉
☐ https://login.live.com/oauth20_desktop.srf (LiveSDK) ⧉

Advanced settings

Logout URL ⓘ | https://coffeefixweb20191126095055.azurewebsites.net/signout-oidc ✓ |

Implicit grant

Allows an application to request a token directly from the authorization endpoint. Recommended only if the application has a single page architecture (SPA), has no backend components, or invokes a Web API via JavaScript. Learn more about the implicit grant flow

To enable the implicit grant flow, select the tokens you would like to be issued by the authorization endpoint:

☐ Access tokens

☑ ID tokens

Figure 7-9. *Specifying authentication values*

6. Click Save.

7. Once the application is registered, copy the application ID from the overview page to Notepad. Also, copy the Azure AD directory URL (which is the name of the Azure AD tenant, followed by `onmicrosoft.com`) to Notepad as well.

We have now registered the application in Azure AD. The next step is to update the CoffeeFix `appsetings.json` using the registration values. The last step is to update the `appsettings.json` file. Follow these steps:

1. Open this file in Visual Studio again.

2. Inside the following code, replace the domain with the name of the Azure AD domain, followed by `.microsoft.com`. Replace the ClientID with the application ID we copied earlier:

```
"AzureAd": {
    "Instance": "https://login.microsoftonline.com/",
    "Domain": "[Enter the domain of your tenant, e.g. contoso.
    onmicrosoft.com]",
    "TenantId": "common",
    "ClientId": "Enter_the_Application_Id_here",
    "CallbackPath": "/signin-oidc"
}
```

3. Deploy the application to Azure again.

4. Once it is deployed, the browser automatically navigates to the application in Azure. You are redirected to the Azure login page. Sign in using credentials that are in the Azure AD tenant, such as the user credentials from the first demo.

5. Once you sign in, you are redirected to the home page. Your username is displayed in the top menu (Figure 7-10).

Figure 7-10. Signing in to the CoffeeFix web app

We have now secured our application and are able to sign in using an account that is registered in Azure AD. In the next sections, we are going to look at reporting and monitoring in Azure AD.

Azure Active Directory Reports

Azure AD reports offer a view of the activity in your Azure AD environment. This gives you the ability to determine how your apps and services are used. You can also troubleshoot issues users have signing up, signing in, using MFA, and more. There are two main reports provided by Azure AD: security reports and activity reports. Those are covered in the next sections.

Security Reports

Security reports are aimed at protecting identities of users in your organization. There is a *Users flagged for risks* security report, which gives you an overview of the user accounts that might have been compromised. There is also a *Risky sign in* report. This report indicates sign-in attempts that might have been performed by someone who is not the legitimate owner of a user account. All Azure AD licenses offer security reports; however, the level of report granularity varies between editions.

Activity Reports

Activity reports help you understand the behavior of users in your organization. Azure AD offers Audit logs that provide an overview and history of every task performed in your Azure AD tenant. It can give you information about which users have access to the admin group in Azure. It can also offer an overview of the amount of password resets in the tenant. Azure also offers sign-in reports that help determine who has performed the tasks reported by the audit logs report. This can give you insights into the sign-in pattern of a user and how many users have signed in during a week.

Next, we are going to look at audit logs in the Azure portal.

Auditing Logs in Azure AD

To look at the audit logs in Azure AD, you must take the following steps:

1. Open the Azure portal, by navigating to `https://portal.azure.com/`.

2. In the left-hand menu, click Azure Active Directory. Then, under Monitoring, select Audit Logs.

3. Here, you can get an overview of all the users that have signed in to your Azure AD tenant. You can filter on different values, such as the date, category, and more (Figure 7-11).

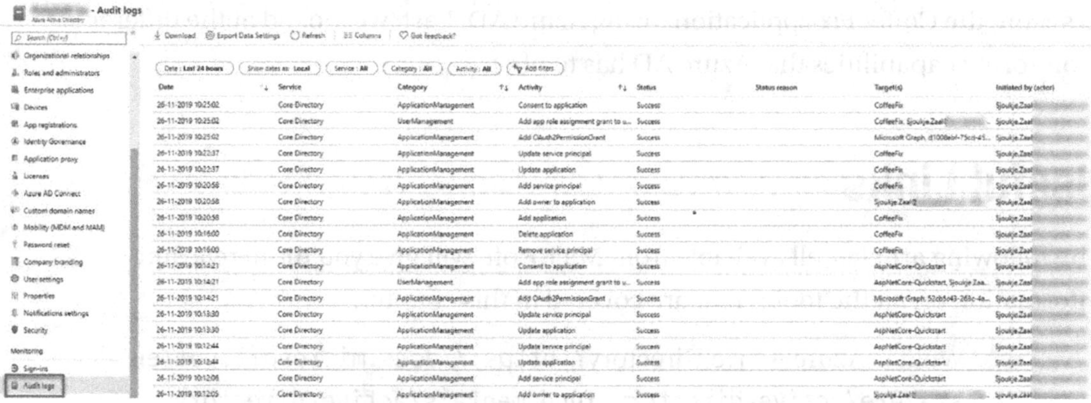

Figure 7-11. *Audit logs in Azure AD*

Azure Active Directory Monitoring

With Azure AD monitoring, which is part of Azure Monitor, you can route your Azure AD activity logs to different endpoints. This way, you can retain them for a longer time or integrate them with third-party security information and event management (SIEM) tools, to gain insights into your environment.

Currently, you can route the logs to the following:

- An Azure Storage account

- An Azure event hub, so that you can integrate it with third-party SIEM tools, such as Splunk

- An Azure Log Analytics workspace, where you can analyze the data and create dashboards and alerts on specific events

- Azure Monitor Logs, in which you can combine monitoring data from different sources. This provides a query language and analytics engine that give you insights into the operation of your applications and resources.

Summary

In this chapter, we covered the various aspects of Azure Active Directory. We performed some basic actions by adding a user and a group to Azure AD. Next, we covered how to secure the CoffeeFix application, using Azure AD. Last, we looked at the different monitoring capabilities that Azure AD has to offer.

Useful Links

The following articles, all available from Microsoft, will give you more relevant information on all the topics that are covered in this chapter:

- "What is Azure Active Directory?" `https://docs.microsoft.com/en-us/azure/active-directory/fundamentals/active-directory-whatis`, July 30, 2019.

- "Quickstart: Add sign-in with Microsoft to an ASP.NET Core web app," `https://docs.microsoft.com/en-us/azure/active-directory/develop/quickstart-v2-aspnet-core-webapp`, April 10, 2019.

- "Auditing and reporting a B2B collaboration user," `https://docs.microsoft.com/en-us/azure/active-directory/b2b/auditing-and-reporting`, December 13, 2018.

- "What is Azure Active Directory B2C?" `https://docs.microsoft.com/en-us/azure/active-directory-b2c/active-directory-b2c-overview`, September 18, 2019.

- "What are Azure Active Directory reports?" `https://docs.microsoft.com/en-us/azure/active-directory/reports-monitoring/overview-reports`, November 12, 2018.

- "What is Azure Active Directory monitoring?" `https://docs.microsoft.com/en-us/azure/active-directory/reports-monitoring/overview-monitoring`, April 17, 2019.

CHAPTER 8

Build and Release Automation

The previous chapters have focused on specific Azure technologies and Azure Portal features, including Application Insights and Azure Analytics. By exploring Azure Function as a Service (FaaS), Platform as a Service (PaaS), Infrastructure as a Service (IaaS), and Software as a Service (SaaS), you have gained an understanding of how these services run in the cloud.

This chapter will look at automating the build and release process, otherwise known as a pipeline. Continuous delivery and release automation (CDRA) is a modern software development technique that automates many of the tasks involved in building and releasing software. Azure has a wide range of support for CDRA, and in general, can be split into two categories: continuous integration (CI) and continuous delivery (CD). Typically, CI focuses on the building of an application, whereas CD focuses more on the release or delivery of software.

As the range of potential technologies involved is vast, we will focus on automating the build and release of a Docker application, with the goal of providing enough depth and context to be applicable to other scenarios.

There is a range of potential ways to implement CI/CD in Azure, and this chapter will use Azure DevOps. Azure DevOps is a collection suite of services and tools for managing a software project, including tools for team coordination, source control, CI/CD, and test automation. We will focus on Azure DevOps support for CI/CD.

© Jeffrey Chilberto, Sjoukje Zaal, Gaurav Aroraa and Ed Price 2020
J. Chilberto et al., *Cloud Debugging and Profiling in Microsoft Azure*,
https://doi.org/10.1007/978-1-4842-5437-0_8

Azure DevOps

Azure DevOps is a Microsoft product that provides a wide range of services for the software development life cycle (SDLC). These services include source control, project management, build management, test management, and product documentation. Azure DevOps shown in this chapter is an SaaS offering, but it is important to note that it is possible for organizations to run their own Azure DevOps server.

This chapter begins with the creation of an Azure DevOps project. If you don't already have an Azure DevOps subscription, acquiring one is simple. We suggest one with the same identity that you used for your Azure subscription. It is not a requirement, but it will make following this chapter easier.

Getting Started

On the DevOps page, `https://azure.microsoft.com/services/devops/`, you will find the free subscription option (Figure 8-1).

Azure DevOps

Plan smarter, collaborate better, and ship faster with a set of modern dev services.

Figure 8-1. *The Start free option*

After signing in and agreeing to the Terms of Service, you will have an empty DevOps environment.

To create an empty project, select the New organization option. You will then be asked to agree to some terms and conditions (Figure 8-2).

Figure 8-2. *Terms and conditions for using Azure DevOps*

For our example, we will use CoffeeFix as the name for our new organization (Figure 8-3).

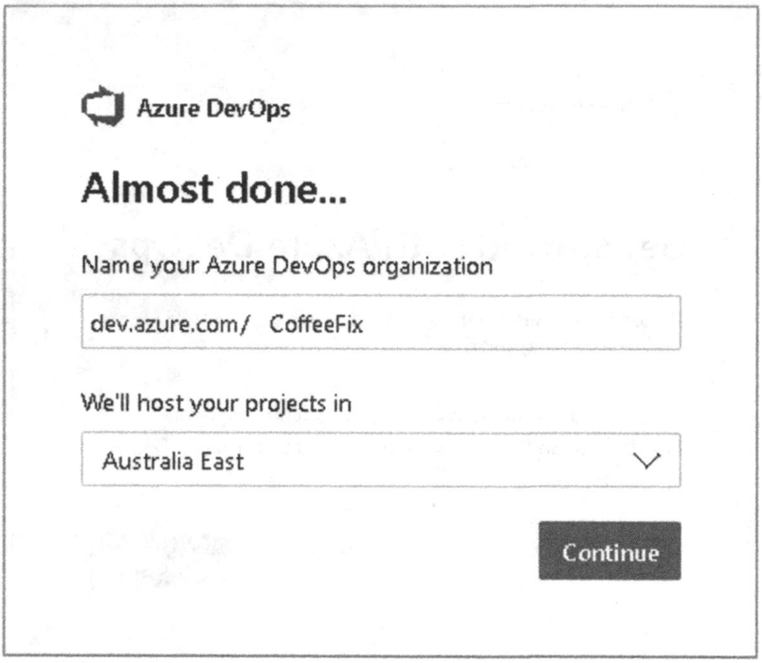

Figure 8-3. Naming the DevOps organization

A DevOps organization allows you to collaborate with other users in developing an application and managing shared features used by the different projects managed under the organization. An organization can have multiple projects. A DevOps project is a collection of tools and features that allows for the components of a project to be managed.

For CoffeeFix, we will create a new project that will manage the use of container technology to improve the current build, release, and deployment process. The following image (Figure 8-4) shows the initial creation of the project.

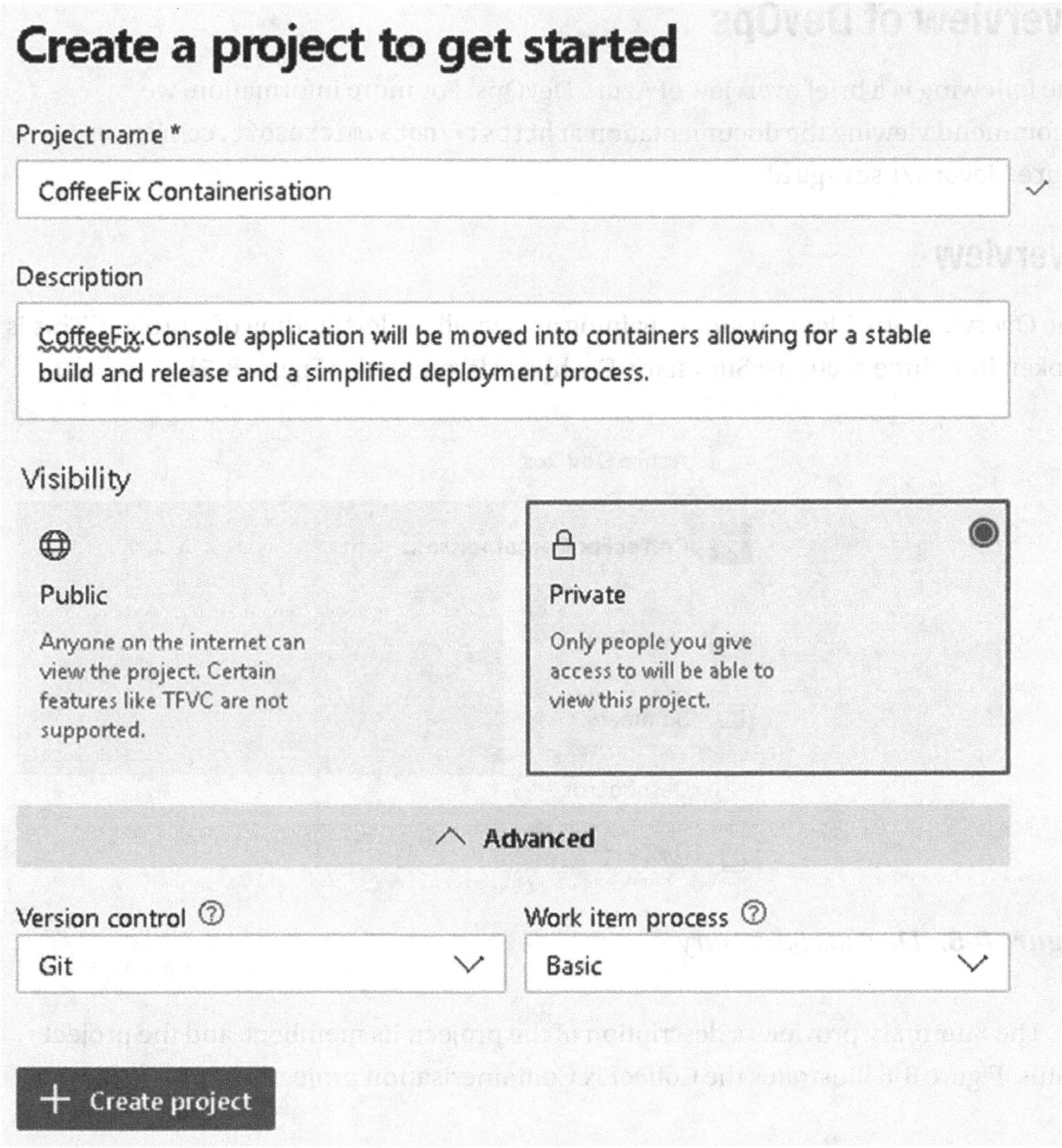

Create a project to get started

Project name *

CoffeeFix Containerisation ✓

Description

CoffeeFix.Console application will be moved into containers allowing for a stable
build and release and a simplified deployment process.

Visibility

🌐

Public

Anyone on the internet can
view the project. Certain
features like TFVC are not
supported.

🔒

Private   ◉

Only people you give
access to will be able to
view this project.

∧ **Advanced**

Version control ⑦   Work item process ⑦

Git   ∨   Basic   ∨

+ Create project

Figure 8-4. *Creating a DevOps project*

Let's highlight a couple of things about the creation of a project. First, the project can
be made public or private. In this scenario, CoffeeFix has chosen to make the project
private, as it is a corporate project. Also, the type of version control can be chosen
between Git and Team Foundation Server Control, as well as the process for handling
work items. For our purposes, Git was chosen for version control and Basic for handling
work items (Figure 8-4).

Overview of DevOps

The following is a brief overview of Azure DevOps. For more information, we recommend viewing the documentation at https://docs.microsoft.com/en-us/ azure/devops/user-guide.

Overview

The Overview provides a means of gaining an overall understanding of a project. This is broken into three sections: Summary, Dashboards, and Wiki (Figure 8-5).

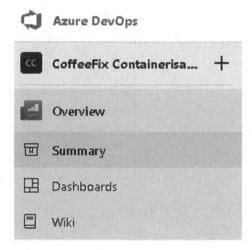

Figure 8-5. *DevOps Summary*

The Summary provides a description of the project, its members, and the project status. Figure 8-6 illustrates the CoffeeFix Containerisation project.

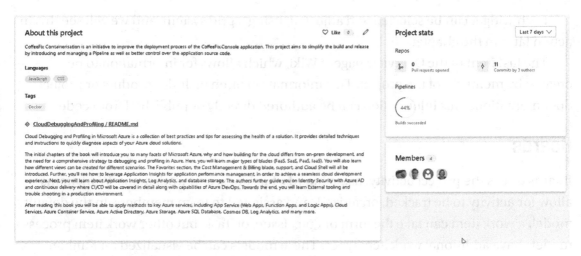

Figure 8-6. *About this project*

The Dashboards page allows for a customized view of the project and has a similar interface as the Azure portal dashboards, in which widgets are selected and added (Figure 8-7).

This dashboard doesn't have widgets just yet!

Add one or more widgets to gain visibility into your team's progress.

Add a widget

Figure 8-7. *A dashboard without widgets*

Each widget can be selected and adjusted, using a grid system, and we will see this in action later in the chapter.

The last item of the Overview page is Wiki, which allows for information to be created by members of the project. This information often includes product or project documentation. This information can be authored directly or published from code.

Boards

Boards tracks the project activity, using boards, backlogs, and work items. Work items allow for activity to be tracked, organized, and assigned to team members. In the default model, a work item can take the form of Epic, Issue, or Task, but other work item process models have additional work item types. These models can be visualized on Kanban boards and backlogs and can be organized into sprints (Figure 8-8).

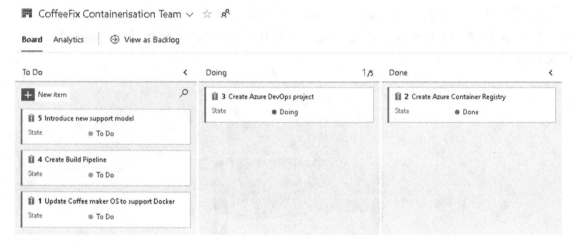

Figure 8-8. *The CoffeeFix Board*

In short, Boards allows for the project's business process to be managed and customized to fit an organization's project methodology.

Repos

Repos provides a view of the project source files. The type of version control was selected when the project was first created, and if Git was chosen, there are views available for Files, Commits, Pushes, Branches, Tags, and Pull requests.

Pipelines

Pipelines allows for a CI/CD process to be defined and maintained. In this chapter, Pipelines is where we will spend our time defining a build and release pipeline for the CoffeeFix.Console application.

Test Plans

Test plans allows for the manual, automated, and load tests to be managed and visualized. For this chapter, the status of the automated test runs performed during the build pipeline can be viewed using the Runs view (Figure 8-9).

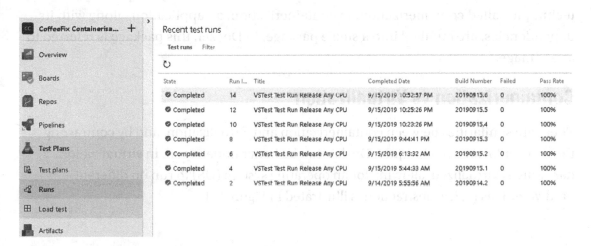

Figure 8-9. *Test plans*

Artifacts

Artifacts allows for package management to be integrated in the CI/CD pipelines, allowing for packages to be shared efficiently across the team.

Putting CoffeeFix in a Container

To illustrate the Azure DevOps Pipeline, we will use the console application used by the coffeemakers to submit back status telemetry. In this scenario, the console application is built on a server in the main office and then distributed globally, to different representatives in the different regions. This has had several failures in the past, in which the coffeemakers were not updated correctly or some were not updated at all. By introducing Azure DevOps, we hope to improve the process of building a new version of the application and to make updating the coffeemakers more reliable.

Docker

This section will provide a brief overview of Docker, for those who are not familiar with this technology. Docker is a popular container platform that allows applications to be packaged and run in a secure and reliable manner, by using a deployment technique called containerization. In containerization, an application, along with its dependencies, are bundled into a single package. In Docker, this package is referred to as an image.

Containerization vs Virtualization

There are similarities between containerization and virtualization, and by contrasting the two deployment techniques, Docker can be better understood. In virtualization, hardware is virtualized, allowing for an operating system (OS) to run on different hardware. This logical abstraction is illustrated in Figure 8-10.

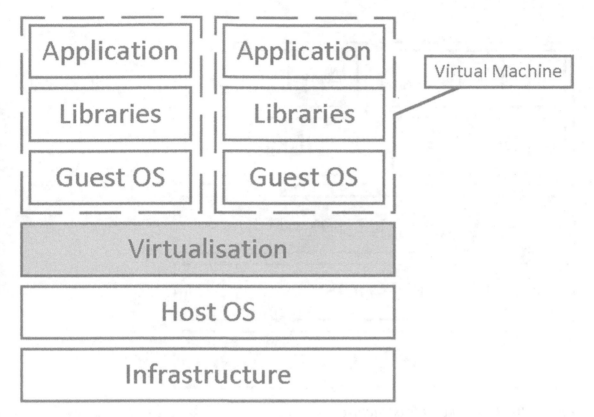

Figure 8-10. *Virtual machine infrastructure*

The preceding figure illustrates how multiple virtual machines can be run on the same infrastructure. This allows for logical abstractions to function like full systems, providing many benefits, including a better utilization of hardware and improved disaster recovery.

Containerization provides a different level of abstraction. Instead of abstracting the infrastructure, the operating system is abstracted, as shown in Figure 8-11.

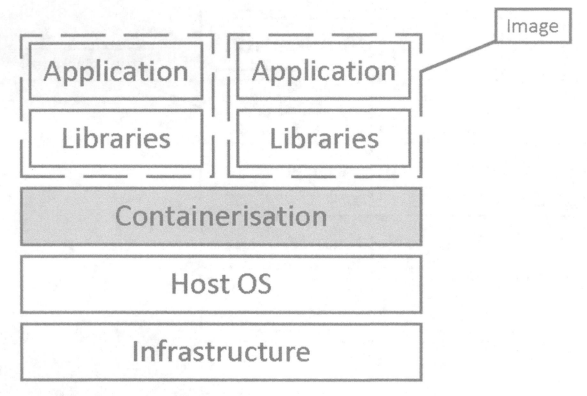

Figure 8-11. *Docker infrastructure*

This level of abstraction allows for the container to be smaller in size and, in many circumstances, to outperform a similar virtualized application. In general, containers make better use of hardware than virtualization and have faster starting and stopping times. A container gains these benefits by using the underlying hardware and operating system directly, instead of creating a level of abstraction in between, as a virtualized environment does. Because of the smaller file sizes, easier configuration and management, and cloud native support, DevOps support is generally better with containers.

As with all technologies, there are some disadvantages with containers, compared to virtualization. Containers tend to have less choice in operating system configurations and tend to promote a model best suited for a single application. Virtualization tends to support situations in which multiple applications are hosted in the same virtualized machine.

Adding Docker Support

The first step in this example is to add Docker support to the CoffeeMaker.Console application. There are many ways to accomplish this, but in this example, let's start with our console application project. We use the Add menu to add Docker Support, as shown in Figure 8-12.

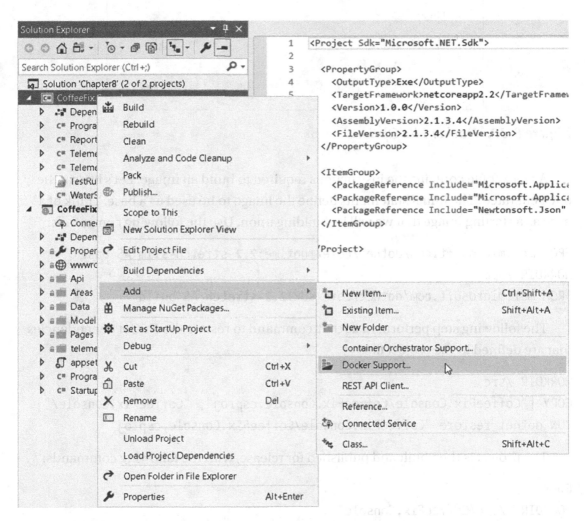

Figure 8-12. *Adding Docker support to a project*

Because we have created CoffeeFix.Console as a .NET Core application, we have the option of running the container in a Linux or Windows container. In general, there is an advantage to using Linux containers, as they are more lightweight than Windows containers and so have smaller image sizes and startup times.

In the CoffeeFix scenario, the coffeemakers run on a Linux operating system, so we will set the target OS to Linux (Figure 8-13).

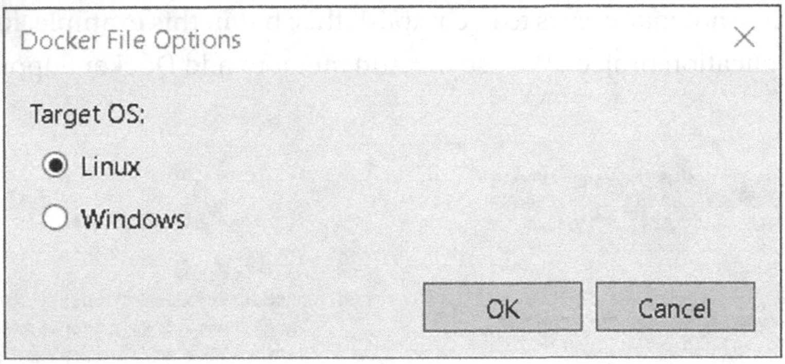

Figure 8-13. *Docker File Options*

A Docker file contains the instructions required to build an image. Let's look at the one generated. The initial statements define the image to be used as a base. Think of a base as a starting image that we will be building upon. Use the following commands:

```
FROM mcr.microsoft.com/dotnet/core/runtime:2.2-stretch-slim AS base
WORKDIR /app
FROM mcr.microsoft.com/dotnet/core/sdk:2.2-stretch AS build
```

The following step performs a dotnet command to restore the NuGet dependencies that are defined in the project file:

```
WORKDIR /src
COPY ["CoffeeFix.Console/CoffeeFix.Console.csproj", "CoffeeFix.Console/"]
RUN dotnet restore "CoffeeFix.Console/CoffeeFix.Console.csproj"
```

The project is then built and published for release, with the following commands:

```
COPY . .
WORKDIR "/src/CoffeeFix.Console"
RUN dotnet build "CoffeeFix.Console.csproj" -c Release -o /app

FROM build AS publish
RUN dotnet publish "CoffeeFix.Console.csproj" -c Release -o /app
```

The following final step copies the executables into the app folder and defines the dotnet core library to run:

```
FROM base AS final
WORKDIR /app
COPY --from=publish /app .
ENTRYPOINT ["dotnet", "CoffeeFix.Console.dll"]
```

The easiest way to test the build of the Docker file is to select this as the debug output and run the project (Figure 8-14).

Figure 8-14. Debugging Docker

When this is done, review the Build Output window and draw your attention to the build command used (Figure 8-15).

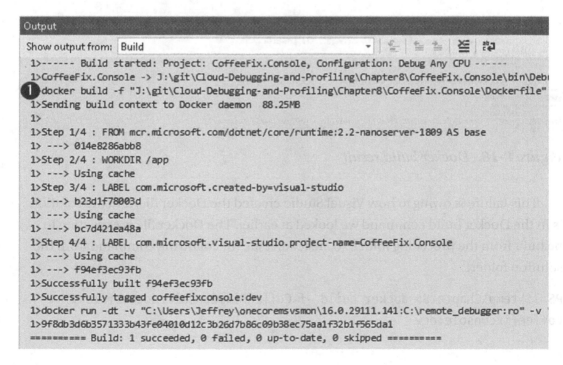

Figure 8-15. Build output

The Docker build shows the following command used to build the image:

```
docker build -f "J:\git\Cloud-Debugging-and-Profiling\Chapter8\CoffeeFix.
Console\Dockerfile" -t coffeefixconsole:dev --target base --label "com.
microsoft.created-by=visual-studio" --label "com.microsoft.visual-studio.
project-name=CoffeeFix.Console" "J:\git\Cloud-Debugging-and-Profiling\
Chapter8"
```

Being able to view the command is useful, as this allows us to both run this command from consoles, such as Git Bash or PowerShell, and to know that the details of the command will help when we create the CI/CD pipeline later in this project.

Let's run through the commands at the console, as this will help us when we add these to the CI/CD pipeline in Azure DevOps. First, in a PowerShell console (or Git Bash, if you prefer), navigate to the folder in which the Docker file is located, and then run the following Docker build command:

```
PS J:\temp\Chapter8\CoffeeFix.Console> docker build .
```

Note that this command fails during the build (Figure 8-16).

```
$ docker build .
Sending build context to Docker daemon    641kB
Step 1/15 : FROM mcr.microsoft.com/dotnet/core/runtime:2.2-stretch-slim AS base
 ---> b938a3374c58
Step 2/15 : WORKDIR /app
 ---> Using cache
 ---> 5e5853a4afb0
Step 3/15 : FROM mcr.microsoft.com/dotnet/core/sdk:2.2-stretch AS build
 ---> 08657316a4cd
Step 4/15 : WORKDIR /src
 ---> Using cache
 ---> 012ad303d9d0
Step 5/15 : COPY ["CoffeeFix.Console/CoffeeFix.Console.csproj", "CoffeeFix.Console/"]
COPY failed: stat /var/lib/docker/tmp/docker-builder132122456/CoffeeFix.Console/CoffeeFix.Console.csproj: no such file or directory
```

Figure 8-16. *Docker build result*

This failure is owing to how Visual Studio created the Docker file, and the solution is in the Docker build command we looked at earlier. The Docker file is expecting to be built from the preceding folder, so, instead, issue the following command from the solution folder:

```
PS J:\temp\Chapter8> docker build -f CoffeeFix.Console/dockerfile . -t
coffeefixconsole:dev
```

This will then build the image. Also, note the use of the tag parameter (-t) to name and version the image (Figure 8-17).

```
Removing intermediate container 404e388ee244
 ---> f36b7525cea7
Successfully built f36b7525cea7
Successfully tagged coffeefixconsole:dev
```

Figure 8-17. *Tagging Docker image*

From a console, let's view the images created, by running Docker images. Note the image ID (Figure 8-18).

```
$ docker images
REPOSITORY                          TAG              IMAGE ID           CREATED          SIZE
coffeefixconsole                    dev              f36b7525cea7       8 weeks ago      186MB
```

Figure 8-18. *Docker images*

The image can then be run with the following command, which includes the image ID as well as the option to remove the container once it has completed (be sure to use your generated image ID):

```
PS J:\temp\Chapter8> docker run --rm f36b7525cea7
```

Fortunately, the console application provides us with some guidance, so we know that we must supply two parameters, including the web site API address, as well as the ID of the coffeemaker (Figure 8-19).

```
CoffeeFix Console started with 1 parameters.
CoffeeFix Console requires two parameters: base url and the id of the coffee maker.
Example:
CoffeeFix.Console https://coffeefix.com/ CB81F3C2-1182-4A5D-A941-52A80CEBE1D1
```

Figure 8-19. *Docker run*

The application can then be run by supplying the following two parameters (substitute the URL of your hosted web site):

```
docker run --rm f36b7525cea7 https://coffeefix20190903060142.azurewebsites.
net CB81F3C2-1182-4A5D-A941-52A80CEBE1D1
```

The application should complete with a message, indicating that the telemetry was submitted successfully (Figure 8-20).

```
CoffeeFix Console started with 2 parameters.
CoffeeFix Console successfully submitted telemetry.
CoffeeFix Console completed.
```

Figure 8-20. *Completed CoffeeFix console app*

As an improvement to our image, let's modify the Docker file to include the URL of the web site, so that we don't have to specify this every time (be sure to change the URL to your hosted CoffeeFix web site). Use the following command:

```
ENTRYPOINT ["dotnet", "CoffeeFix.Console.dll", "https://coffeefix.com/"]
```

Go ahead and repeat the build and run of the container, but this time, only use one parameter (Figure 8-21).

```
PS J:\git\Cloud-Debugging-and-Profiling\Chapter8> docker run --rm f36b7525cea7 CB81F3C2-1182-4A5D-A941-52A80CEBE1D1
CoffeeFix Console started with 2 parameters.
CoffeeFix Console successfully submitted telemetry.
CoffeeFix Console completed.
```

Figure 8-21. *Using parameters in the build*

One last thing to note is the use of the - -rm flag, which removes the instance of the image after the application completes.

Using a Container Registry

Now that we have a working image, let's explore another aspect of Docker—the container registry. A container registry is a repository for storing container images. We have already used a container registry to retrieve the images during our build process. These were public images. In this section, we will create a private container registry in Azure and use this to store our private images for CoffeeFix. The important concept here is that by using a container registry, we will simplify the distribution of the CoffeeFix.Console application. This allows our coffeemakers to pull new versions of the application, instead of requiring them to be manually updated. We will illustrate this more later in the section.

The first step is to create a container registry in the Azure portal. There is only a small amount of information required to create a registry (Figure 8-22).

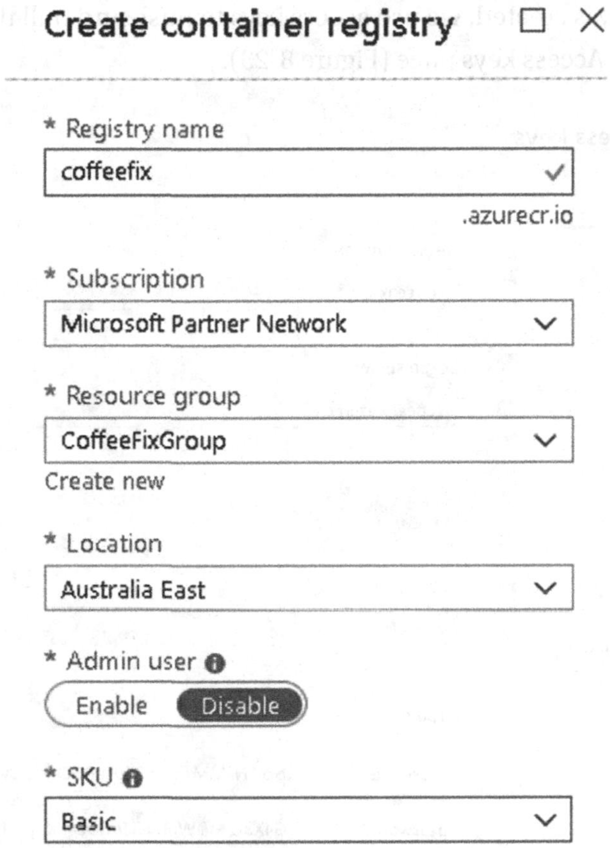

Create container registry □ ✕

* Registry name

coffeefix   ✓

.azurecr.io

* Subscription

Microsoft Partner Network   ⌄

* Resource group

CoffeeFixGroup   ⌄

Create new

* Location

Australia East   ⌄

* Admin user ❶

(Enable   Disable)

* SKU ❶

Basic   ⌄

Figure 8-22. *Create container registry*

In the example, we used "coffeefix" for the registry name, but you will have to create your own unique name.

Once the registry is created, we use access keys to push and pull the images. These can be found on the Access keys page (Figure 8-23).

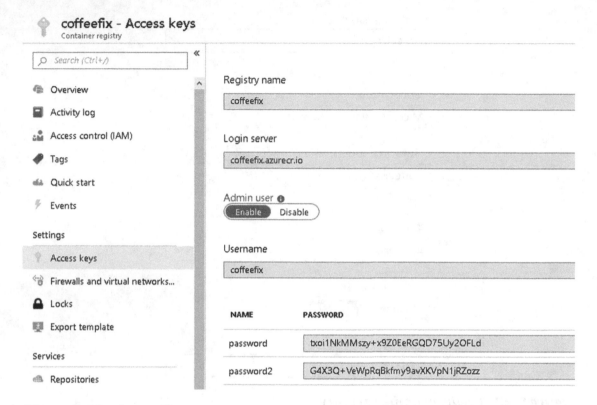

Figure 8-23. *Access Keys page*

Back in the console, use the password key to log in, using the following Docker login command (don't forget to substitute your registry name and login server):

```
PS J:\temp\Chapter8> docker login coffeefix.azurecr.io --username coffeefix
```

After entering the password, you are authenticated to the container registry. Now, let's create an alias of our image with the fully qualified path to the coffeefix container registry, using the following Docker tag command:

```
docker tag a1397fae89c0 coffeefix.azurecr.io/coffeefixconsole:v1.0
```

The next step is to take the image that we created and push it onto the container. Use the following command:

```
docker push coffeefix.azurecr.io/coffeefixconsole:v1.0
```

Back in the portal, in the Repositories page, we can see the images we pushed (Figure 8-24).

Figure 8-24. *CoffeeFix Repositories*

The preceding image shows three tags for the image of the CoffeeFix.Console application.

Let's take the example one step further and create another tag, release, by issuing the following two commands again:

```
docker tag a1397fae89c0 coffeefix.azurecr.io/coffeefixconsole:release
docker push coffeefix.azurecr.io/coffeefixconsole:release
```

And then let's remove our local copy of our image, by issuing the following remove command, which includes the force flag, because we have multiple tagged images:

```
docker image rm a1397fae89c0 -f
```

Using the docker image command, you can verify that the image was removed.

To finish this example of the power of Docker, let's issue the following command (be sure to update the command for your registry):

```
docker pull coffeefix.azurecr.io/coffeefixconsole:release
```

This then pulls the image down from the Azure container registry (Figure 8-25).

```
85bcf813f547: Already exists
be9897837a2f: Already exists
7c0677578daf: Already exists
eedfc8e9a5f2: Already exists
5a1312280005: Already exists
8a4cd2883a29: Already exists
dc71bedd4787: Already exists
a5a620d89713: Pull complete
cb0c1fb153a3: Pull complete
f60db81da49a: Pull complete
Digest: sha256:ac2174f4b995cd27bad43b32d12c7d3ec5c21f6ce234c72c2d1d01a123ee8b15
Status: Downloaded newer image for coffeefix.azurecr.io/coffeefixconsole:release
coffeefix.azurecr.io/coffeefixconsole:release
```

Figure 8-25. *Pulling a Docker image*

As shown above, the image of the CoffeeFix.Console application is composed of layers of images. The ones that have already been downloaded are not re-downloaded. Instead, only the missing images are downloaded.

Releasing CoffeeFix.Console

The CoffeeFix team must now update the coffeemakers to use the CoffeeFix.Console application in a container that takes advantage of the Azure container registry.

To help illustrate this, go ahead and remove all the downloaded images of the CoffeeFix.Console application. Issue the following command:

```
docker image rm -f coffeefix.azurecr.io/coffeefixconsole:release
```

With all the images removed, now issue the following run command, using the fully qualified name of the release version of the container:

```
docker run --rm coffeefix.azurecr.io/coffeefixconsole:release CB81F3C2-
1182-4A5D-A941-52A80CEBE1D1
```

This should result in a failure, as the image no longer exists (Figure 8-26).

```
Unable to find image 'coffeefix.azurecr.io/coffeefixconsole:release' locally
release: Pulling from coffeefixconsole
85bcf813f547: Already exists
be9897837a2f: Already exists
7c0677578daf: Already exists
eedfc8e9a5f2: Already exists
5a1312280005: Already exists
8a4cd2883a29: Already exists
dc71bedd4787: Already exists
a5a620d89713: Already exists
cb0c1fb153a3: Already exists
f60db81da49a: Already exists
Digest: sha256:ac2174f4b995cd27bad43b32d12c7d3ec5c21f6ce234c72c2d1d01a123ee8b15
Status: Downloaded newer image for coffeefix.azurecr.io/coffeefixconsole:release
CoffeeFix Console started with 2 parameters.
CoffeeFix Console successfully submitted telemetry.
CoffeeFix Console completed.
```

Figure 8-26. *The error showing the Docker image does not exist*

Docker identifies that the release image is not held locally, so it downloads the image from the container registry. By taking advantage of the Docker functionality, the CoffeeFix team has greatly simplified the deployment process.

In the next section, we will illustrate how Azure DevOps can be used to manage the CI/CD pipeline, by creating build and release pipelines.

Release and Latest Tag

Those familiar with Docker may recognize that there is a difference between the Docker run and the Docker pull commands. The Docker run command identifies if the image is missing from the local images and then pulls the image from the registry, while the Docker pull command also checks if the image is the most recent version.

Adding CoffeeFix.Console to Azure DevOps

The CoffeeFix team now wants to take the simplicity of releasing the CoffeeFix.Console as a container and add the control and reliability of Azure DevOps.

To illustrate the Azure DevOps CI/CD pipeline, we start by adding a copy of the source code into our Azure DevOps project. First, we add a copy of the Chapter 8 source into a new folder. For example, the following command copies the Chapter 8 directory into a temporary folder:

```
xcopy J:\git\Cloud-Debugging-and-Profiling\Chapter8 j:\temp\Chapter8 /e
```

In the Chapter 8 folder, use the following command to initialize an empty Git repository:

```
PS J:\temp\Chapter8> git init
Initialized empty Git repository in J:/temp/Chapter8/.git/
```

Now that we have an empty repository, we must add the files in the folder into the repo, as follows:

```
PS J:\temp\Chapter8 > git add .
```

And, as a final step, we must commit the changes, as follows:

```
PS J:\temp\Chapter8 > git commit -m "Initial coffeefix.console repo"
```

To recap what was just done, we copied the CoffeeFix.Console application source to a temporary folder. Next, we initialized a new local repository and added the application source to it. This requires both adding the files and committing them to the repo.

Azure DevOps provides many nice shortcuts and hints for setting up a new repo. In the portal, select the Repos section. You are presented with a page that should look something like that shown in Figure 8-27.

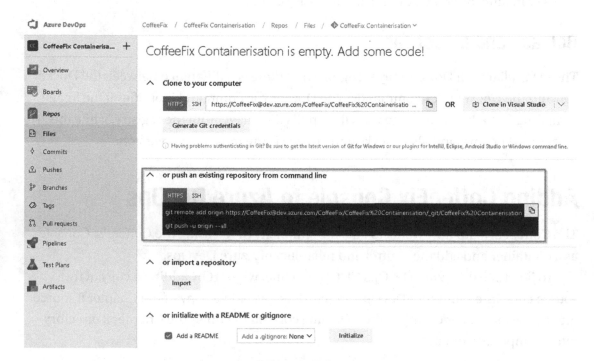

Figure 8-27. *Azure DevOps empty project*

On the page, you will notice a section for pushing an existing repo. Fortunately, DevOps provides the two commands required to push our local repo to Azure DevOps. First, the following command establishes a link between your local repo and the Azure DevOps repository:

```
PS J:\temp\Chapter8> git remote add origin https://CoffeeFix@dev.azure.com/
CoffeeFix/CoffeeFix%20Containerisation/_git/CoffeeFix%20Containerisation
```

This way, when we push from the local repo with the following command, Git will know where to send it:

```
PS J:\temp\Chapter8> git push -u origin --all
Counting objects: 13, done.
Delta compression using up to 8 threads.
Compressing objects: 100% (12/12), done.
Writing objects: 100% (13/13), 7.59 KiB | 1.90 MiB/s, done.
Total 13 (delta 0), reused 0 (delta 0)
remote: Analyzing objects... (13/13) (8 ms)
remote: Storing packfile... done (303 ms)
remote: Storing index... done (28 ms)
To https://dev.azure.com/CoffeeFix/CoffeeFix%20Containerisation/_git/
CoffeeFix%20Containerisation
 * [new branch]      master -> master
Branch 'master' set up to track remote branch 'master' from 'origin'.
```

Now, when we refresh the Azure DevOps Repos section, we see that our application source has been added (Figure 8-28).

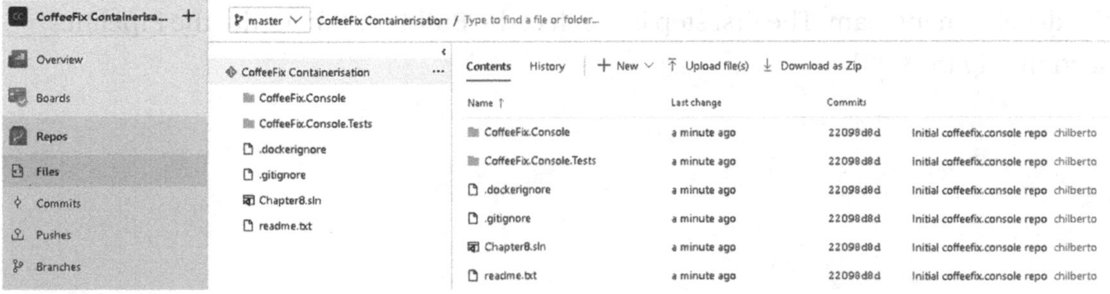

Figure 8-28. *Azure DevOps Repos view*

With the source added to our DevOps project, let's create some pipelines to help manage the release of new versions of the CoffeeFix.Console application.

Creating Pipelines

Now that we have our source code in DevOps, let's set up some build pipelines. Before we begin, we must spend some time planning our release process. The CoffeeFix team has decided on the following process. The development team will develop and test new enhancements locally, and when they believe the task is ready, they will push their changes to the main repo. The build server will then create a build for each commit to the main (that is, master) branch. This build will perform and compile the source and execute the unit tests included in the solution. Nightly, a Docker image will be created of the latest source for testing by the QA team the following day. Once a version has been reviewed by the QA team and the image has been approved for release, the Docker image will be tagged with release. The next time the coffeemakers are ready to send telemetry, a new release image will be identified, pulled to the coffeemaker, and then used to submit telemetry.

This process includes three pipelines: two build pipelines and one release pipeline. The first pipeline, Development Team Build, will create a build for each commit and verify that the unit tests run successfully. The second build pipeline, Docker Build, will build the image and push it to the Azure Container Registry. The release pipeline will be used to tag a specific image with the release tag.

Let's look at each one in more detail.

Development Team Build

The first pipeline we'll create will trigger with every commit to the master branch by the development team. The first step is to select the Builds option under the Pipelines section (Figure 8-29).

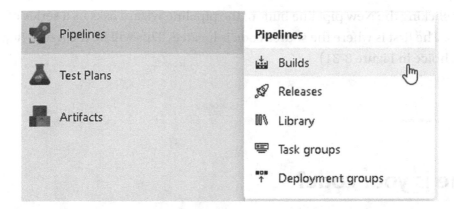

Figure 8-29. *Azure DevOps Builds*

Because this is our first pipeline, we are greeted by an image similar to that in Figure 8-30.

No build pipelines were found

Automate your build in a few easy steps with a new pipeline.

Figure 8-30. *Creating a new pipeline*

After clicking the New pipeline button, the pipeline wizard asks us a series of questions. The first is where the source code is located. This will be the Azure Repos Git (the top choice in Figure 8-31).

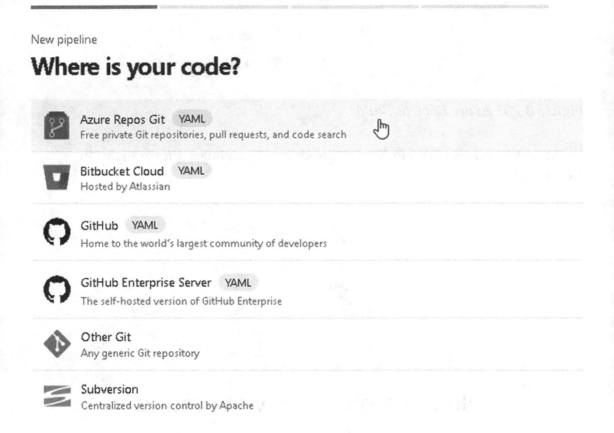

Use the classic editor to create a pipeline without YAML.

Figure 8-31. *Where is your code?*

As indicated in the preceding screenshot, many different types of source code providers are available.

Next, the specific repo is selected (Figure 8-32).

Figure 8-32. *Selecting a repository*

Now that the location of the source is selected, the next step is to configure the pipeline. A nice feature of Azure DevOps is the large number of templates available as a starting point for the pipeline.

In our case, we will build up the build pipeline using an existing YAML file (Figure 8-33).

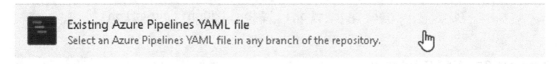

Figure 8-33. *Existing Azure Pipelines YAML file*

The file we will use is `developer.yml`, located in the Build Pipelines folder of our source (Figure 8-34).

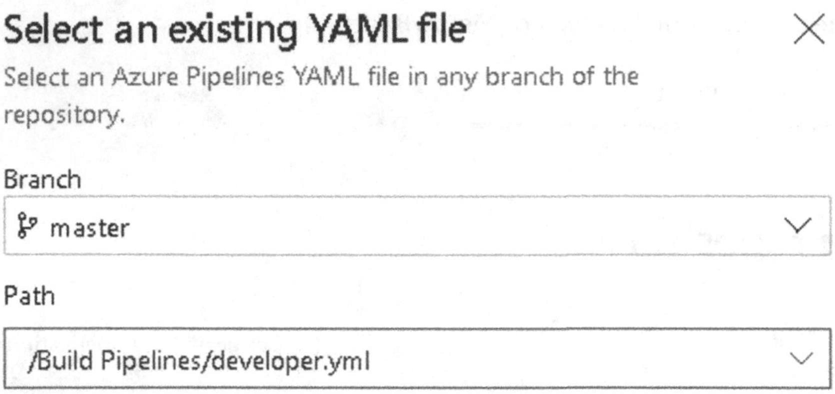

Select an existing YAML file   ✕

Select an Azure Pipelines YAML file in any branch of the
repository.

Branch

> ℔ master   ⌄

Path

> /Build Pipelines/developer.yml   ⌄

Figure 8-34. *Selecting an existing YAML file*

The Review tab provides a view of the YAML file. Let's take some time to review this file. An important thing to note, especially for those not used to YAML, is that indentation and spacing is significant. Fortunately, the online editor shows whitespace clearly. For example, note how the whitespace is indicated (Figure 8-35).

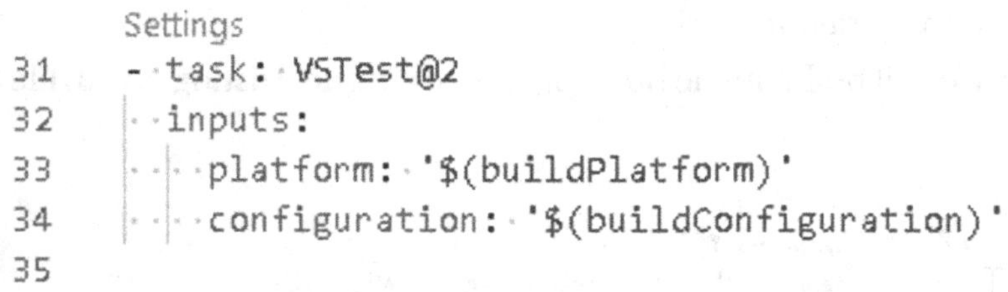

```
       Settings
31     --task:··VSTest@2
32     |··inputs:
33     |··|··platform:··'$(buildPlatform)'
34     |··|··configuration:··'$(buildConfiguration)'
35
```

Figure 8-35. *YAML whitespace*

First, the trigger statement identifies that this build will start with commits to the master branch, as follows:

```
trigger:
- master
```

The next statement sets up the virtual machine image of the agent that is used to perform the build. This image can range from virtual machines hosted by Azure DevOps to self-hosted agents. Depending on the build requirements, some pipelines might require special configuration or features available on a virtual machine.

```
pool:
  vmImage: 'ubuntu-latest'
```

Variables are then created, as follows, allowing for information to be passed into the different tasks and steps of the pipeline:

```
variables:
  buildConfiguration: 'Release'
```

Next, we have a series of steps defined. First, the following step installs .NET Core version 2.2:

```
- task: DotNetCoreInstaller@0
  inputs:
    version: '2.2.100'
```

Now that .NET Core is available on the build server, we then issue the following restore, which runs across our solution and restores any required packages:

```
- script: dotnet restore
```

With the required packages restored, the following statements perform a build of the projects in the solution:

```
- task: DotNetCoreCLI@2
  displayName: Build
  inputs:
    command: build
    projects: '**/*.csproj'
    arguments: '--configuration Release'
```

With the projects built, any unit tests are then performed, as follows. (Note the wildcard that will match all projects that end in Tests.csproj.)

```
- task: DotNetCoreCLI@2
  inputs:
    command: test
    projects: '**/*Tests.csproj'
    arguments: '--configuration $(buildConfiguration)'
```

The last two steps are included, in order to publish the build as an artifact. The following statements allow the development team to download the build, if they want to inspect the result of the build:

```
- task: DotNetCoreCLI@2
  inputs:
    command: publish
    publishWebProjects: false
    arguments: '--configuration $(BuildConfiguration) --output $(Build.
ArtifactStagingDirectory)'
    zipAfterPublish: True

- task: PublishBuildArtifacts@1
  inputs:
    pathtoPublish: '$(Build.ArtifactStagingDirectory)'
    artifactName: 'CoffeeFix.Console'
```

Now that the YAML file has been inspected, go ahead and click the Run button, to start a build (Figure 8-36).

Figure 8-36. *The Run button*

After the build completes, all the associated steps should have succeeded (Figure 8-37).

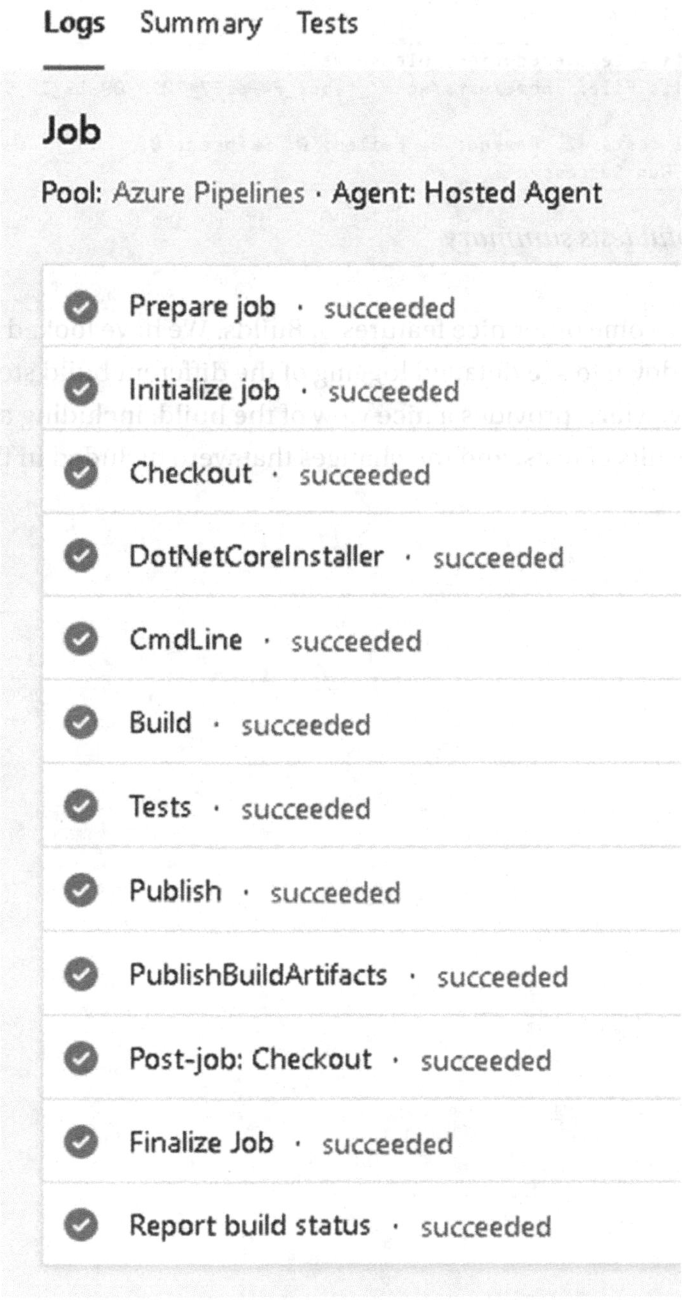

Logs   Summary   Tests

Job

Pool: Azure Pipelines · **Agent: Hosted Agent**

- ✅ **Prepare job** · succeeded
- ✅ **Initialize job** · succeeded
- ✅ **Checkout** · succeeded
- ✅ **DotNetCoreInstaller** · succeeded
- ✅ **CmdLine** · succeeded
- ✅ **Build** · succeeded
- ✅ **Tests** · succeeded
- ✅ **Publish** · succeeded
- ✅ **PublishBuildArtifacts** · succeeded
- ✅ **Post-job: Checkout** · succeeded
- ✅ **Finalize Job** · succeeded
- ✅ **Report build status** · succeeded

Figure 8-37. *A successful run*

Each step has detailed logs that can be used to view the activity. For example, if we expand the Tests step, we can see the number of unit tests that have successfully run (Figure 8-38).

```
17    Starting test execution, please wait...
18    Results File: /home/vsts/work/_temp/_fv-az77_2019-09-19_22_53_03.trx
19
20    Total tests: 2. Passed: 2. Failed: 0. Skipped: 0.
21    Test Run Successful.
```

Figure 8-38. *Total tests summary*

Also, there are some other nice features of Builds. We have looked at Logs, which allows us to drill down to see detailed logging of the different build steps. Next, let's inspect Summary, which provides a nice view of the build, including any artifacts published, the results of tests, and the changes that were included in this build (Figure 8-39).

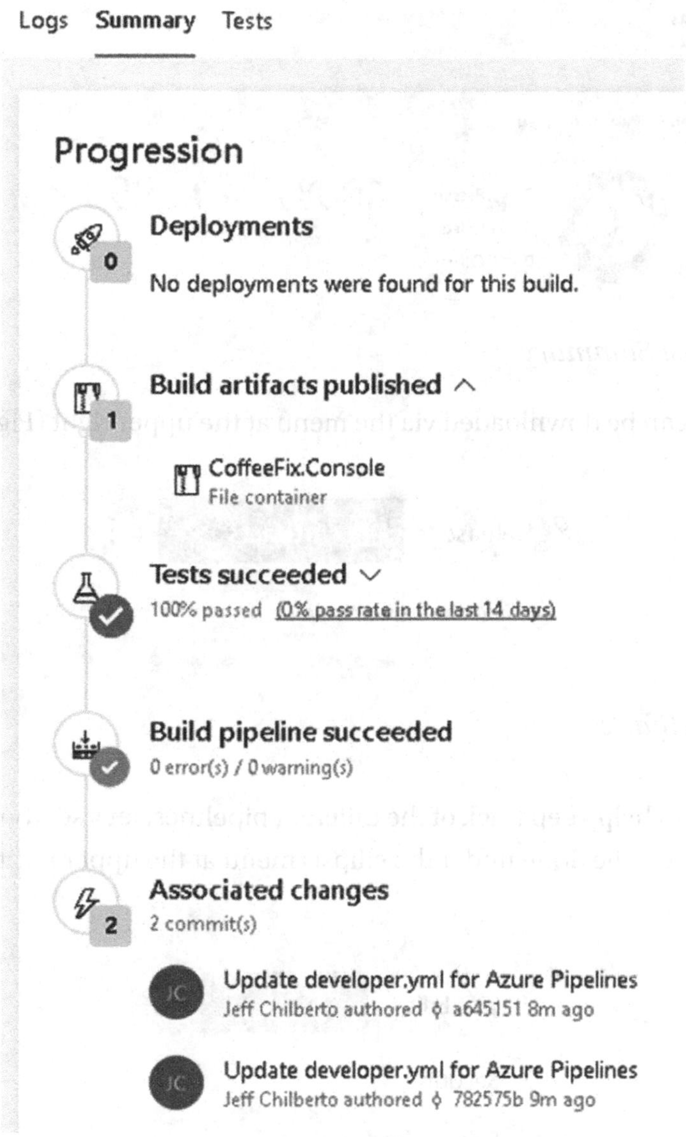

Logs   **Summary**   Tests

Progression

Deployments   0

No deployments were found for this build.

Build artifacts published ∧   1

CoffeeFix.Console
File container

Tests succeeded ∨

100% passed   (0% pass rate in the last 14 days)

Build pipeline succeeded

0 error(s) / 0 warning(s)

Associated changes   2

2 commit(s)

JC   Update developer.yml for Azure Pipelines
Jeff Chilberto authored ◊ a645151 8m ago

JC   Update developer.yml for Azure Pipelines
Jeff Chilberto authored ◊ 782575b 9m ago

Figure 8-39. *Associated changes in the build*

The last view is of the tests that were included. There are two tests (Figure 8-40).

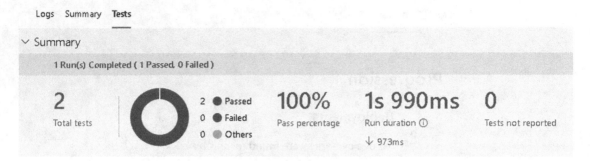

Figure 8-40. *Test Summary*

The artifacts can be downloaded via the menu at the upper right (Figure 8-41).

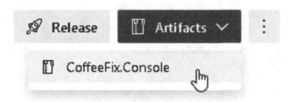

Figure 8-41. *Artifacts*

As a last step to help keep track of the different pipelines, let's set the name of the pipeline. This can be done under the ellipsis menu at the upper right of the page (Figure 8-42).

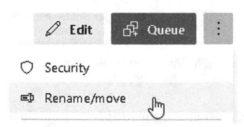

Figure 8-42. *Rename option*

Let's rename the build Development Build (Figure 8-43).

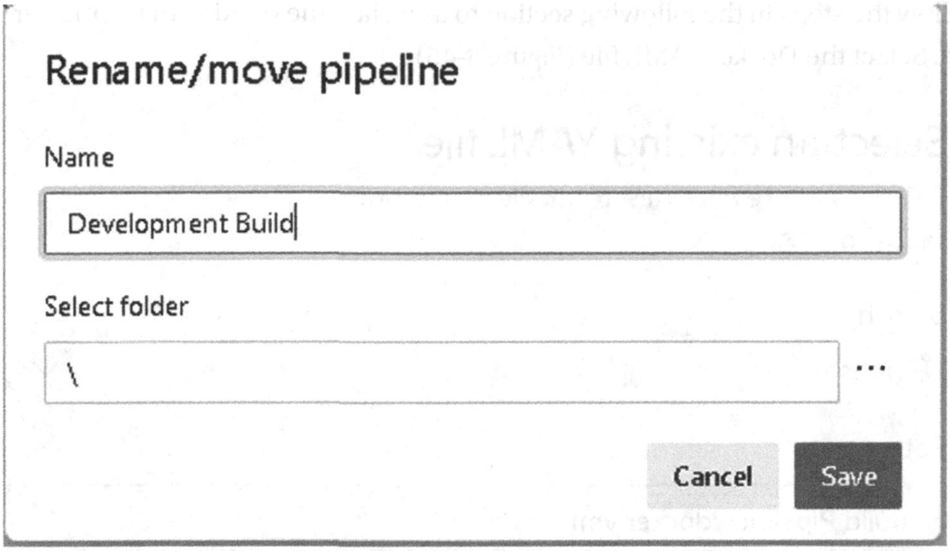

Rename/move pipeline
Name
Development Build
Select folder
\
...
Cancel
Save

Figure 8-43. *Renaming a pipeline*

This will help once we have more than one build pipeline.

Docker Build

This section will create a pipeline to generate the Docker image. This pipeline builds the image and publishes it to the Azure Container Registry. The CoffeeFix team has chosen to have this pipeline triggered, based on time and not on when commits are performed.

To begin, click the New option (Figure 8-44).

New
New build pipeline
Import a pipeline

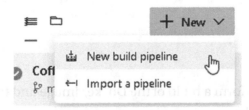

Figure 8-44. *New build pipeline*

Follow the steps in the following section to associate the build with the master branch. Select the Docker YAML file (Figure 8-45).

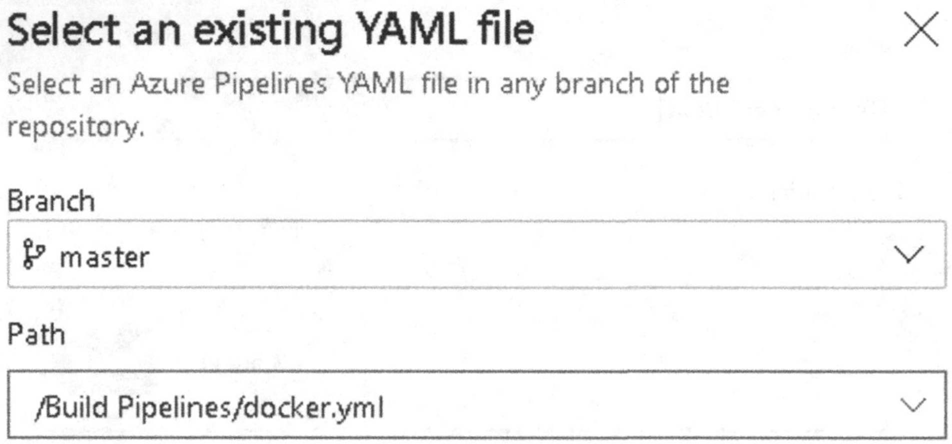

Select an existing YAML file   ✕

Select an Azure Pipelines YAML file in any branch of the repository.

Branch

> ⎇ master   ∨

Path

> /Build Pipelines/docker.yml   ∨

Figure 8-45. Selecting an existing YAML file

Let's review the YAML statements in this file. In the following step, the first thing to note is that instead of a trigger, there is a schedule setup using a `cron` syntax to specify a daily build:

```
trigger:
- none

schedules:
- cron: "0 0 * * *"
  displayName: Daily midnight build
  branches:
    include:
    - master
```

The next step is to perform a build of the Docker image and to push that to the Azure Container Registry, as follows:

```
- task: Docker@2
  displayName: Build and push image
  inputs:
    buildContext: '$(Build.SourcesDirectory)'
    containerRegistry: 'CoffeeFix Registry'
```

```
repository: 'coffeefixconsole'
command: 'buildAndPush'
Dockerfile: '**/Dockerfile'
tags: |
  $(tag)
```

Now, go ahead and run the pipeline, but don't worry if you receive an error message such as the following (Figure 8-46):

> ⊗ The pipeline is not valid. Job Build: Step Docker input containerRegistry references service connection CoffeeFix Registry which could not be found. The service connection does not exist or has not been authorized for use. For authorization details, refer to https://aka.ms/yamlauthz.
>
> **Authorize resources**

Figure 8-46. *Authorize resources error*

Now we must set up a service connection to the Azure Container Registry that we created earlier. First, in the lower-left corner, select Project settings (Figure 8-47).

Figure 8-47. *Project settings*

Then select the Service connections option in the Pipelines section (Figure 8-48).

Pipelines

Agent pools

Parallel jobs

Settings

Test management

Release retention

Service connections

Figure 8-48. *Service connections*

Next, select Docker Registry, to create a new connection (Figure 8-49).

Figure 8-49. *Docker Registry as a new service connection*

The final step is to complete the following dialog. Make sure to use the Connection name "CoffeeFix Registry" and to pick your subscription and container registry (Figure 8-50).

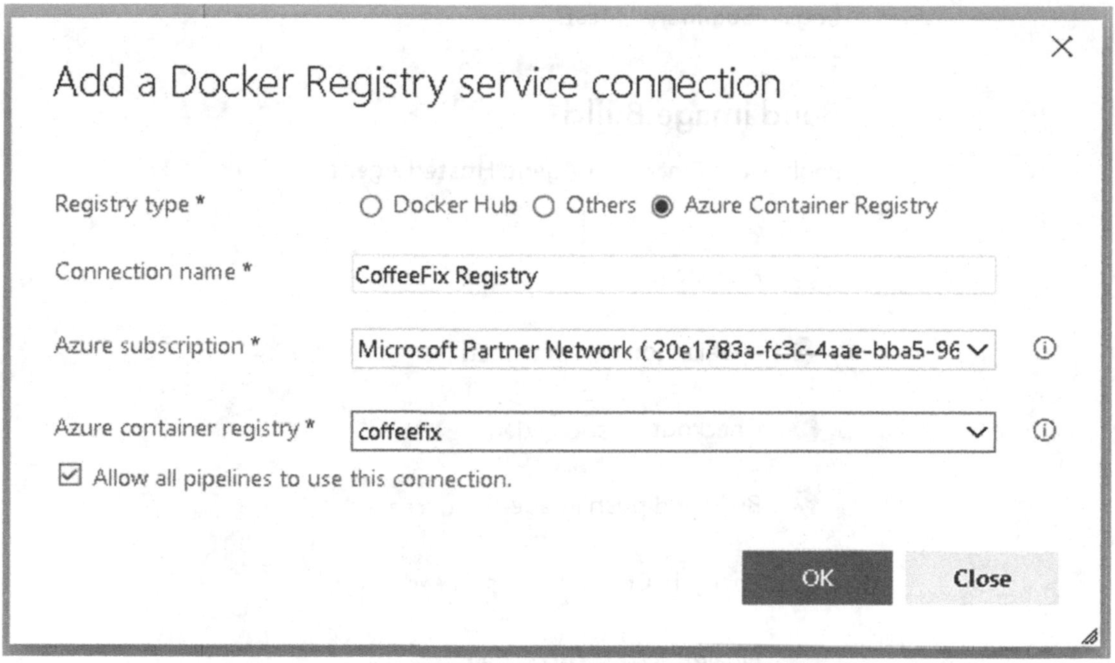

Add a Docker Registry service connection   ✕

Registry type *   ○ Docker Hub ○ Others ● Azure Container Registry

Connection name *   CoffeeFix Registry

Azure subscription *   Microsoft Partner Network (20e1783a-fc3c-4aae-bba5-96 ∨   ⓘ

Azure container registry *   coffeefix   ∨   ⓘ

☑ Allow all pipelines to use this connection.

                                                    OK   Close

Figure 8-50. *Adding a Docker Registry service connection*

Once that completes, navigate back to Builds, and either wait until the schedule kicks off, or queue a build, using the Queue button at the upper right of the screen (Figure 8-51).

Figure 8-51. *Queue new build*

Now that we have an authorized pipeline, the build and push of the image should succeed (Figure 8-52).

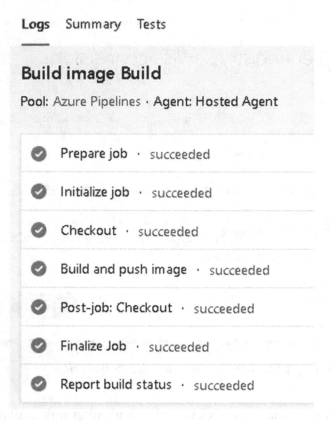

Figure 8-52. *Build image logs*

To check if the push was successful, you can navigate to the Azure Container Registry in the Azure portal and check the Repositories option in the Services section (Figure 8-53).

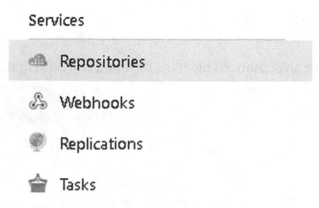

Figure 8-53. *Services Repositories*

Selecting the repository, you should see a new tag that has been updated recently (Figure 8-54).

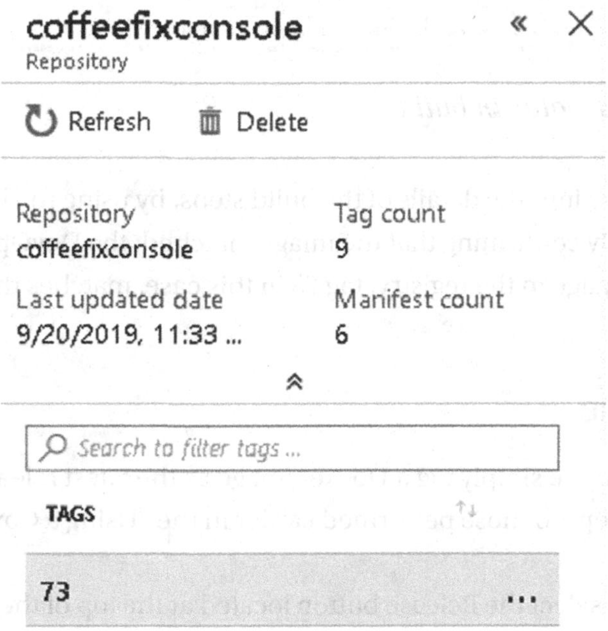

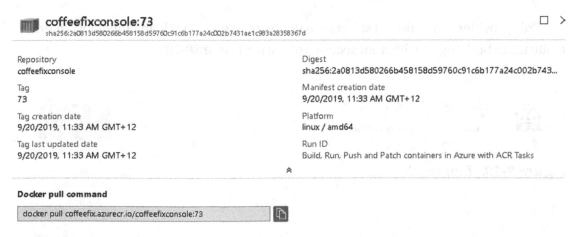

Figure 8-54. *Repository Tags*

Let's take a moment to double-check that everything matches up as we expect. Select the tag and view its properties, taking special note of the Digest value (Figure 8-55).

Figure 8-55. *Docker registry Digest value*

Now, navigate back to Builds, expand the Build and push image step, and look through the log. You will find the value toward the end of the log (Figure 8-56).

```
182    2285f8661ee8: Pushed
183    73: digest: sha256:2a0813d580266b458158d59760c91c6b177a24c002b7431ae1c983a28358367d size: 1581
184    [command]/usr/bin/docker history --format createdAt:{{.CreatedAt}}; layerSize:{{.Size}}; createdBy:{{.CreatedBy}} --no-trunc ***/coffeefixconsole:73
```

Figure 8-56. *Digest value in build*

Being able to dive into the details of the build steps, by using the logs, is essential when issues occur. By confirming that the image matched, the DevOps team can be confident that the image in the registry, tag 73 in this case, matches the build from Azure DevOps.

Release Pipeline

For the final pipeline, we simply tag a Docker image as the latest release version. We will follow similar steps to those performed earlier in the "Using a Container Registry" section.

To start, you can select the Release button located at the top of the build (Figure 8-57).

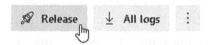

Figure 8-57. *The Release button*

This provides the option of selecting a template. We start with an empty job, in order to illustrate building the different sections of the job (Figure 8-58).

Figure 8-58. *Empty job*

278

At this point, take the time to provide a more meaningful name (Figure 8-59).

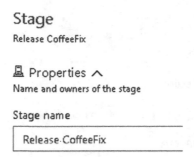

Figure 8-59. *Naming Stage in the DevOps release*

In the Stages section, click the job and task link, which takes you to where you can view and set the different stage tasks (Figure 8-60).

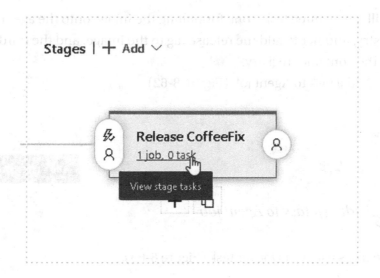

Figure 8-60. *View stage tasks*

Make sure the Agent job uses the correct agent. Set it to use the Ubuntu agent (Figure 8-61).

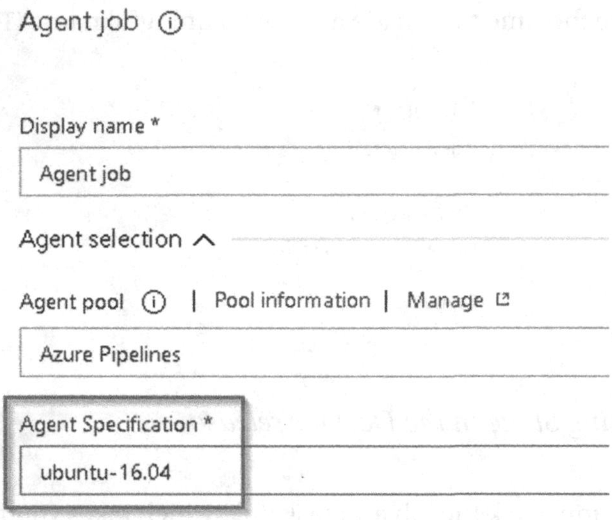

Agent job ⓘ

Display name *

Agent job

Agent selection ∧ ─────────────────────────────

Agent pool ⓘ | Pool information | Manage ⬀

Azure Pipelines

Agent Specification *

ubuntu-16.04

Figure 8-61. *Agent specification*

Now we will create three tasks: one for pulling the image onto the agent from the container registry, another to add the release tag to the image, and the third to push the image back to the container registry.

First select Add a task to Agent job (Figure 8-62).

Agent job
🖥 Run on agent

+ ⤵
Add a task to Agent job

Figure 8-62. *Adding a task to Agent job*

Each of the tasks will be a Docker task (Figure 8-63).

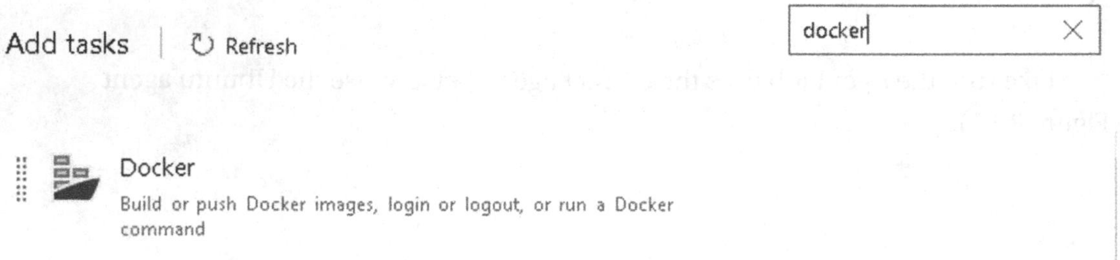

Add tasks | ↻ Refresh

docker   ✕

⠿ 🐳 Docker
        Build or push Docker images, login or logout, or run a Docker
        command

Figure 8-63. *Adding a Docker task*

For the first task, we use the task version of 0. This is because we want to issue an action, Run a Docker command, that is not available in the other versions (Figure 8-64).

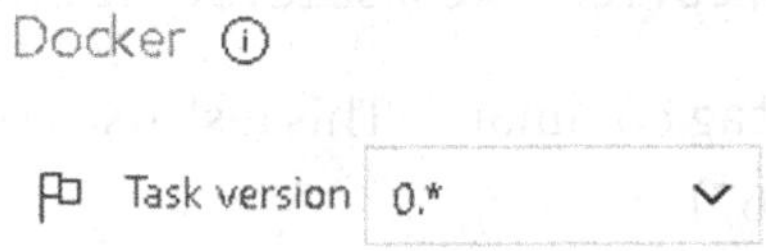

Docker ⓘ

🏳 Task version   0.*   ⌄

Figure 8-64. *Docker Task version*

We provide a Display name and select our Container Registry Type, so that the agent is authenticated to the registry, in order to pull the image (Figure 8-65).

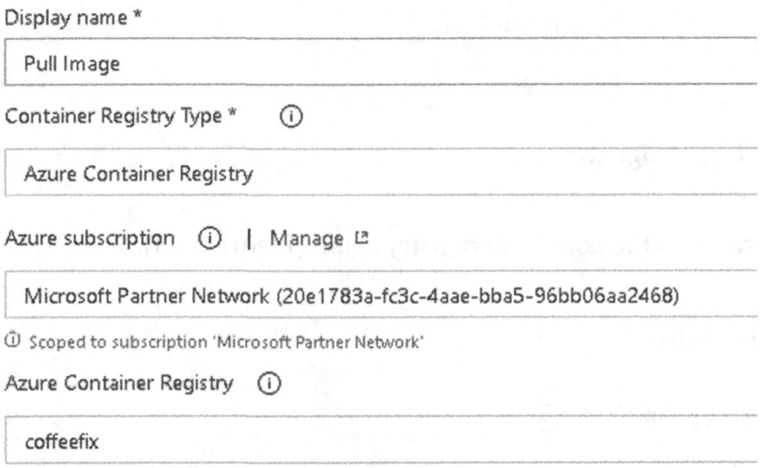

Display name *

Pull Image

Container Registry Type *   ⓘ

Azure Container Registry

Azure subscription   ⓘ | Manage ↗

Microsoft Partner Network (20e1783a-fc3c-4aae-bba5-96bb06aa2468)

ⓘ Scoped to subscription 'Microsoft Partner Network'

Azure Container Registry   ⓘ

coffeefix

Figure 8-65. *Docker Pull image task*

The final step is to issue our command. Note that the command contains the build ID that is associated with this release (Figure 8-66).

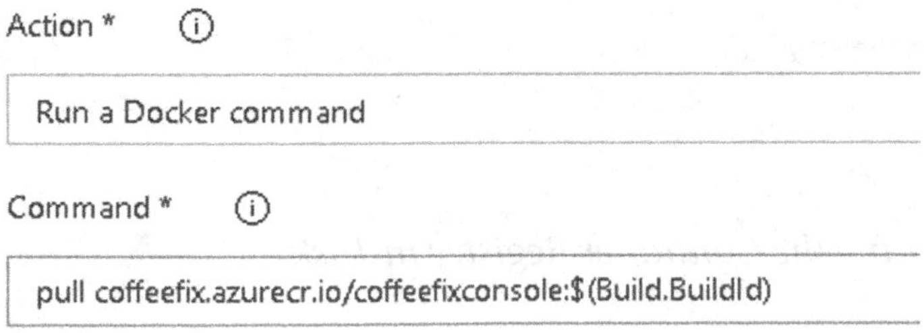

Action *   ⓘ

Run a Docker command

Command *   ⓘ

pull coffeefix.azurecr.io/coffeefixconsole:$(Build.BuildId)

Figure 8-66. *Pull command*

The following command should be familiar, as it is like the one we used in the "Using a Container Registry" section:

```
pull coffeefix.azurecr.io/coffeefixconsole:$(Build.BuildId)
```

The next task performs a `tag` command. This task uses version 1 and sets the Display name to Tag Image (Figure 8-67).

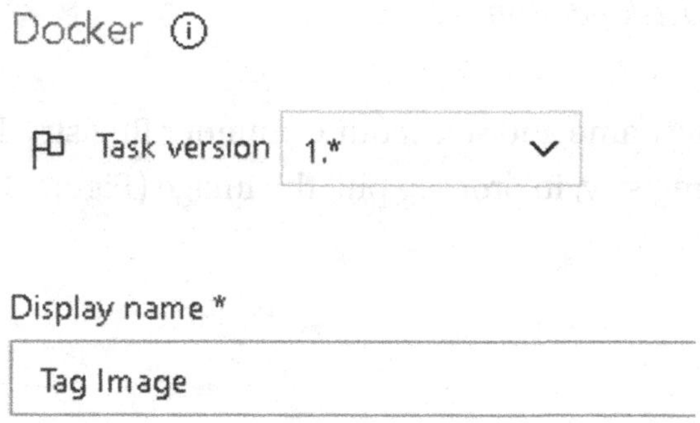

Docker ⓘ

⊡ Task version 1.* ⌄

Display name *

Tag Image

Figure 8-67. *Tag Image task*

Also, be sure to set the container registry again (Figure 8-68).

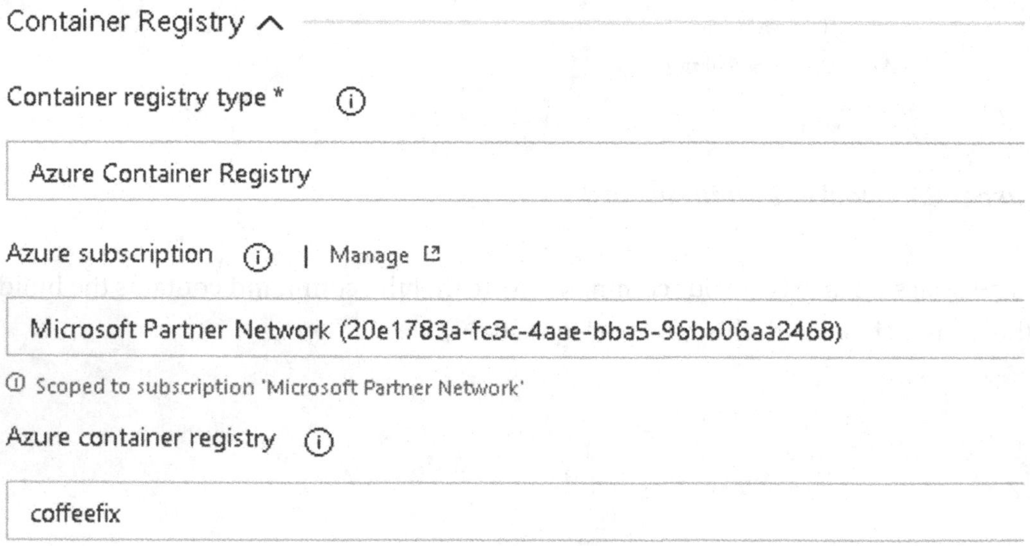

Container Registry ⌃

Container registry type * ⓘ

Azure Container Registry

Azure subscription ⓘ | Manage ↗

Microsoft Partner Network (20e1783a-fc3c-4aae-bba5-96bb06aa2468)

ⓘ Scoped to subscription 'Microsoft Partner Network'

Azure container registry ⓘ

coffeefix

Figure 8-68. *Setting the Container Registry in Task*

The tag command supplies the release tag in the argument (Figure 8-69).

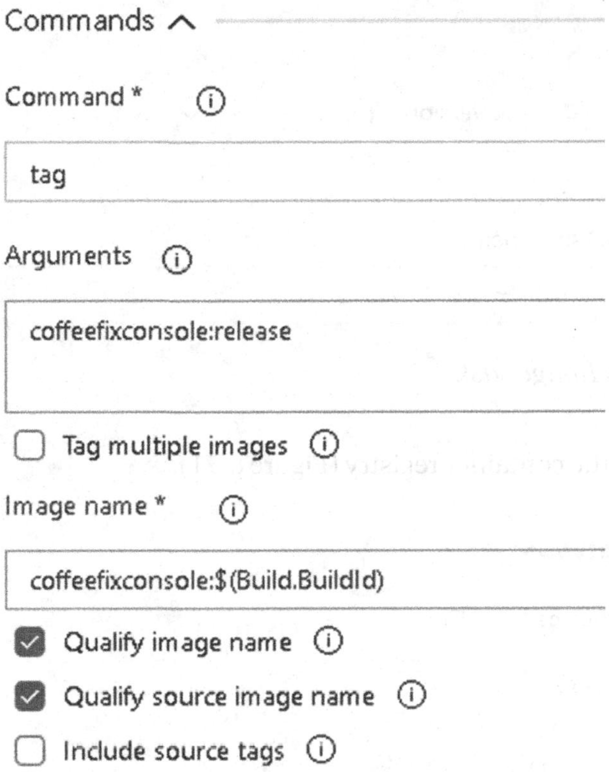

Figure 8-69. Docker tag *command*

Also notice that Qualify is enabled, to apply the container registry to both the source and target images.

The last task is also version 1 and has the Display name *Push Image* (Figure 8-70).

Docker ⓘ

🏳 Task version   1.*   ⌄

Display name *

Push Image

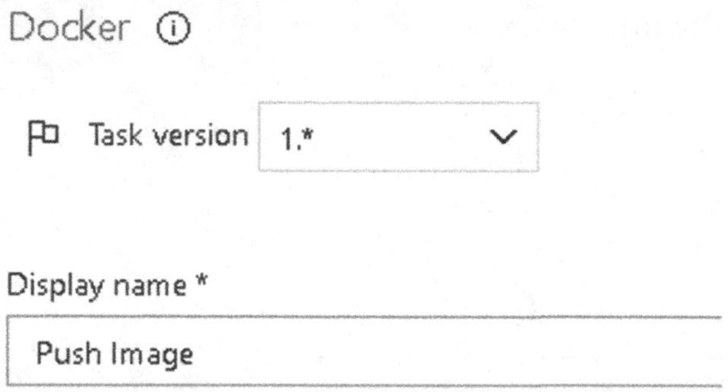

Figure 8-70. *Push Image task*

Again, we enter the container registry (Figure 8-71).

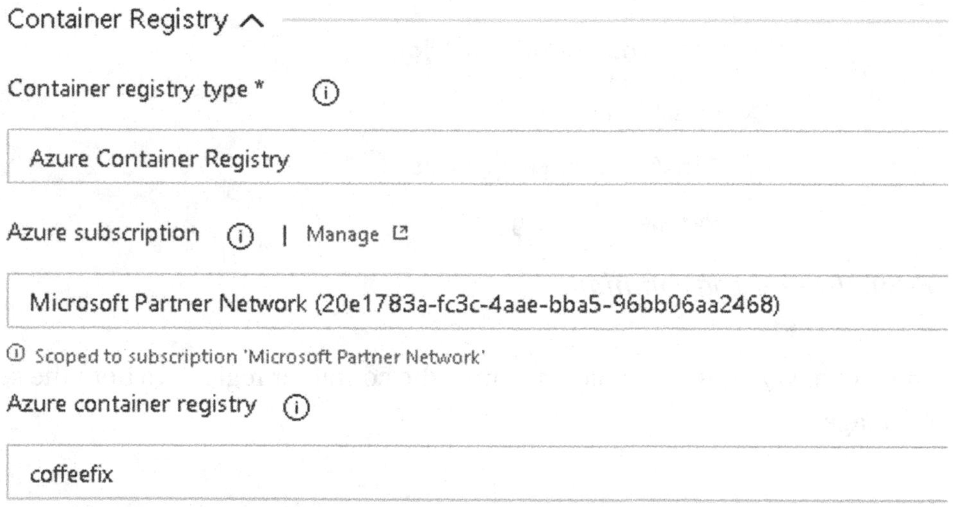

Container Registry ⌃ ────────────────

Container registry type *   ⓘ

Azure Container Registry

Azure subscription   ⓘ | Manage ⌞⌝

Microsoft Partner Network (20e1783a-fc3c-4aae-bba5-96bb06aa2468)

ⓘ Scoped to subscription 'Microsoft Partner Network'

Azure container registry   ⓘ

coffeefix

Figure 8-71. *Container registry selection*

The command is set to push and specifies the release tag (Figure 8-72).

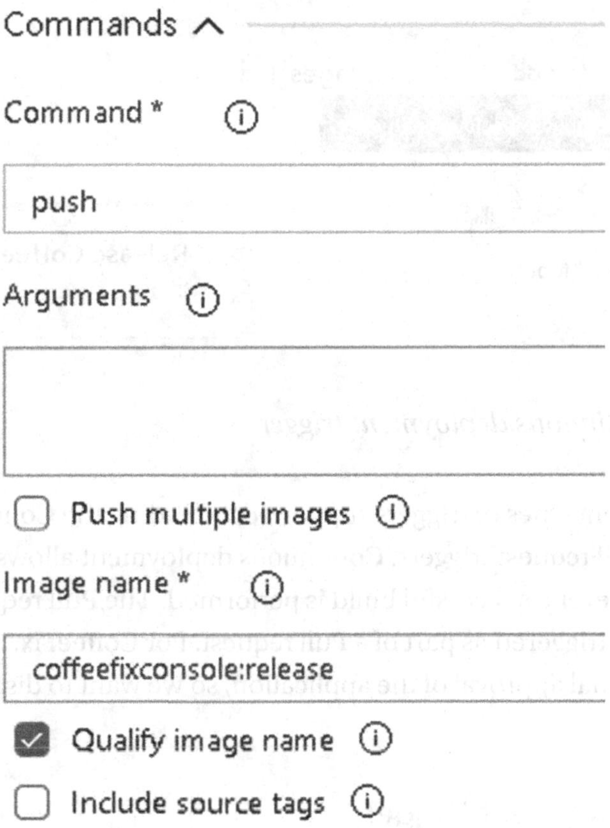

Figure 8-72. *The push command*

Now navigate back to the Pipeline view, as we want to set up a trigger to start the pipeline (Figure 8-73).

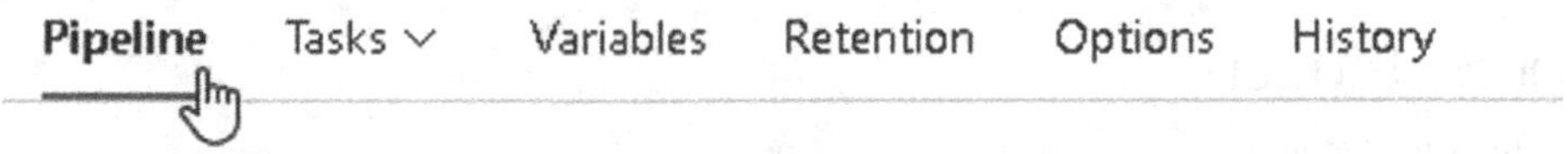

Figure 8-73. *The Pipeline tab*

The trigger can be accessed by clicking the button indicated in Figure 8-74.

Artifacts | + Add
Stages | + Add
Continuous deployment trigger
CoffeFixFinalHopef
ully (1)
Release CoffeeFix
1 job, 3 tasks

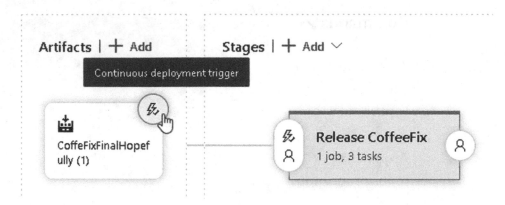

Figure 8-74. *Continuous deployment trigger*

There are different types of triggers supported, including the Continuous deployment and Pull request triggers. Continuous deployment allows for the release to be performed whenever a successful build is performed. The Pull request trigger allows for the release to be triggered as part of a Pull request. For CoffeeFix, the release will be controlled by a manual approval of the application, so we want to disable both options (Figure 8-75).

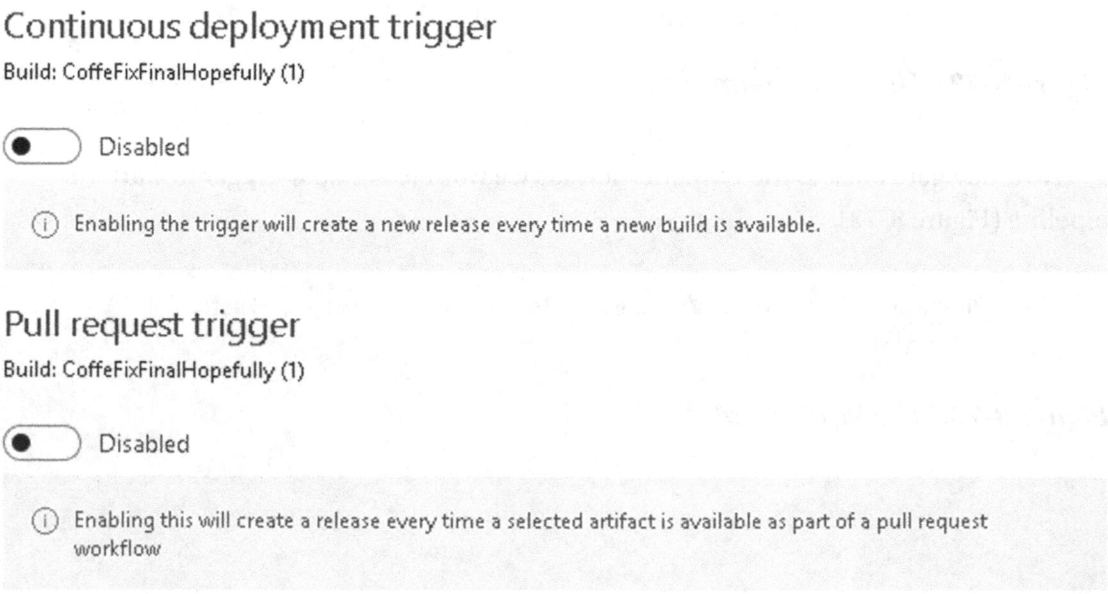

Continuous deployment trigger
Build: CoffeFixFinalHopefully (1)
Disabled
Enabling the trigger will create a new release every time a new build is available.
Pull request trigger
Build: CoffeFixFinalHopefully (1)
Disabled
Enabling this will create a release every time a selected artifact is available as part of a pull request workflow

Figure 8-75. *Continuous deployment trigger*

Click the Save button at the top of the page, and then click OK (Figure 8-76).

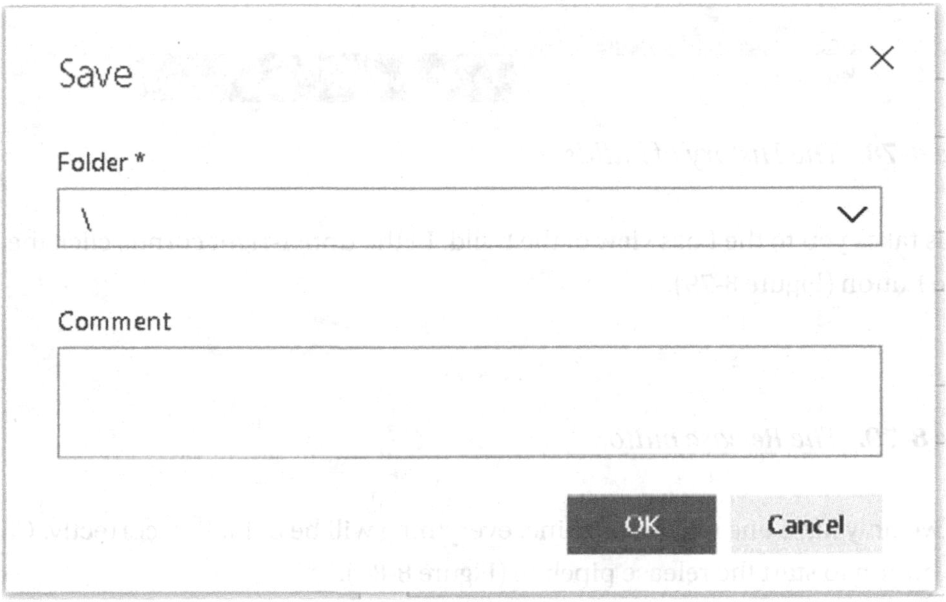

Figure 8-76. *Save*

Let's go back to our successful build. Select the Builds option (Figure 8-77), and then click the name of the successful build (Figure 8-78).

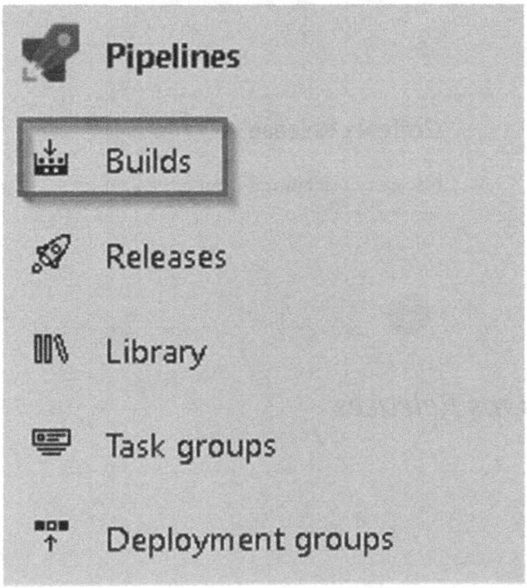

Figure 8-77. *Builds option*

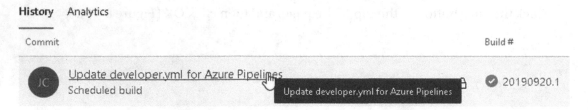

Figure 8-78. *The History of builds*

This takes you to the Logs view of the build. In the upper-right corner, click the Release button (Figure 8-79).

Figure 8-79. *The Release button*

As we only have one release pipeline, everything will be defaulted correctly. Click the Create button to start the release pipeline (Figure 8-80).

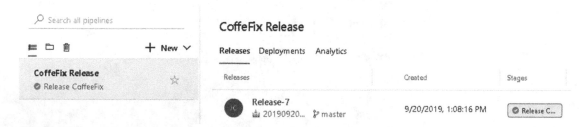

Figure 8-80. *The Create button*

Back under Releases, select the release that either is building or has completed (Figure 8-81).

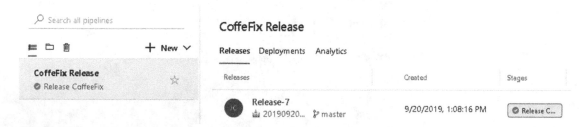

Figure 8-81. *Azure DevOps Releases*

This takes you to a summary view of the release (Figure 8-82).

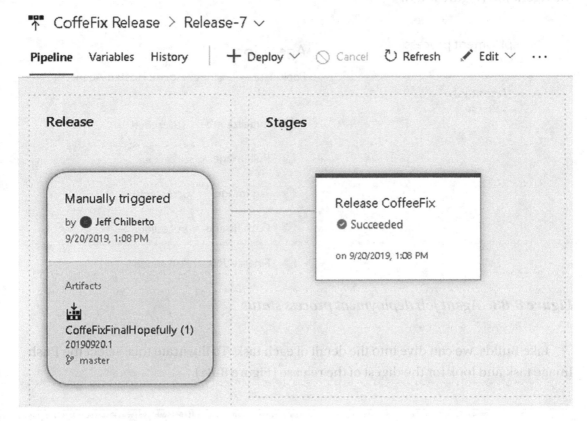

Figure 8-82.   Release pipeline view

Let's review the stages. Click the Succeeded link, which takes you to a summary of the Agent Job (Figure 8-83).

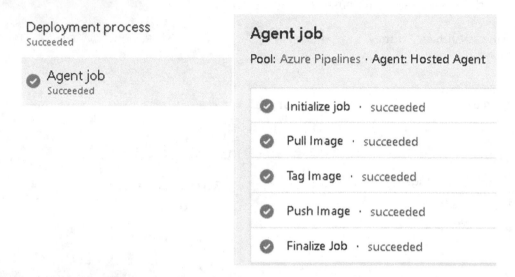

Figure 8-83. *Agent job deployment process status*

Like Builds, we can dive into the detail of each task. To illustrate this, select the Push Image task and look for the digest of the release (Figure 8-84).

```
24    2019-09-20T01:08:42.8272272Z release: digest: sha256:ae70ac38b8287ced416de1e058f45067681f0f460ab169eeafd695a5ccbc9c02 size: 1581
25    2019-09-20T01:08:42.8453491Z ##[section]Finishing: Push Image
```

Figure 8-84. *The digest of the release*

If we look at the Azure Container Registry, we will be able to see that the release tag has been updated with this version (Figure 8-85).

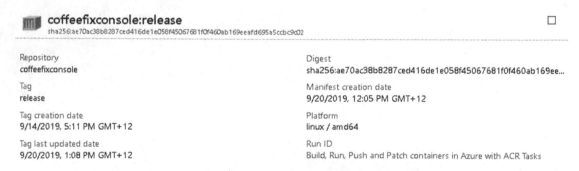

Figure 8-85. *Azure Container Registry release details*

CoffeeFix now has a build and release pipeline established, and now we can look at ways to improve the development workflow in a controlled and consistent way. The team might decide to completely automate the release process by tying the release to another branch of the Repos. Or the team might want greater visibility to the changes in the application and the success rate of the unit tests. The important thing here is now that the team is using DevOps, it has many options available to improve its CI/CD process.

Profiling and Debugging in Azure DevOps

This section will use the Azure DevOps project created in the previous section to illustrate some common scenarios. Azure DevOps provides an enormous number of features, especially considering the extensions that can be brought into the product. This section will explore the following scenarios: setting up dashboards, sending notifications—e-mail, sending notifications—webhook, build conditions, and auditing.

Sending Notifications—E-mail

To illustrate sending an e-mail notification, we will use the scenario of a broken build. Let's perform a commit that breaks the build. In the Repos section, select the Files option (Figure 8-86).

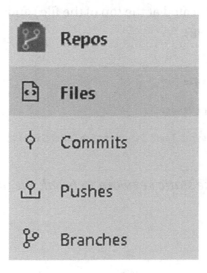

Figure 8-86. *Repos Files option*

Then navigate to the ReportSender.cs file (Figure 8-87).

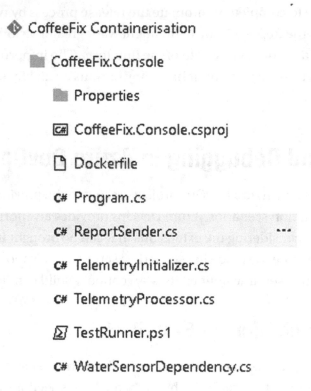

Figure 8-87. *The ReportSender.cs file*

Next, edit the file (✎ Edit is located at the top of the file) and change the file, by removing the static keyword (Figure 8-88).

```
12  namespace CoffeeFix.Console
13  {
14      internal class ReportSender
15      {
16          public static async Task SendMessageToWebSite(string baseurl, Guid makerId)
17          {
```

Figure 8-88. *Removing the static keyword to break the build*

Commit the changes by using the Commit button (Figure 8-89).

Commit...
Discard

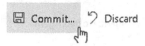

Figure 8-89. *Commit button*

Save the changes, as the defaults are fine for this example. This starts a build, as a commit to the master branch will trigger Development Build (Figure 8-90).

Development Build
History
Analytics
Commit
Build #
JC
Updated ReportSender.cs
CI build for Jeff Chilberto
20190920.2

Figure 8-90. *Development Build*

The build will break at the Build step, which compiles the source (Figure 8-91).

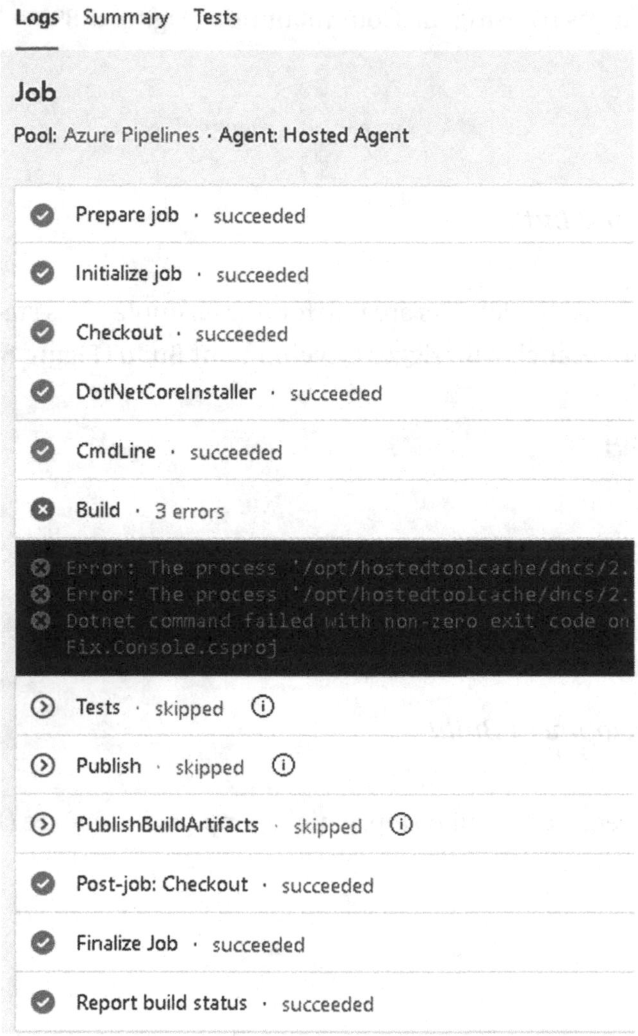

Logs Summary Tests

Job
Pool: Azure Pipelines · **Agent: Hosted Agent**

✅ **Prepare job** · succeeded

✅ **Initialize job** · succeeded

✅ **Checkout** · succeeded

✅ **DotNetCoreInstaller** · succeeded

✅ **CmdLine** · succeeded

❌ **Build** · 3 errors

❌ Error: The process '/opt/hostedtoolcache/dncs/2.
❌ Error: The process '/opt/hostedtoolcache/dncs/2.
❌ Dotnet command failed with non-zero exit code on
Fix.Console.csproj

▶ **Tests** · skipped ⓘ

▶ **Publish** · skipped ⓘ

▶ **PublishBuildArtifacts** · skipped ⓘ

✅ **Post-job: Checkout** · succeeded

✅ **Finalize Job** · succeeded

✅ **Report build status** · succeeded

Figure 8-91. *The broken build step*

We can dive into the logs, to see that the problem was removing *static* (Figure 8-92).

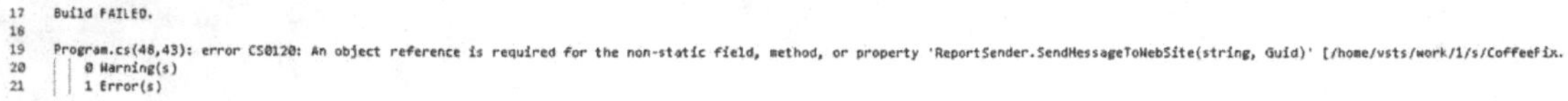

```
17    Build FAILED.
18
19    Program.cs(48,43): error CS0120: An object reference is required for the non-static field, method, or property 'ReportSender.SendMessageToWebSite(string, Guid)' [/home/vsts/work/1/s/CoffeeFix.
20    |   0 Warning(s)
21    |   1 Error(s)
```

Figure 8-92. *Object reference error*

This is fine, and we can see the failure on the dashboard. The CoffeeFix team also is notified when there are build failures, but this does not seem to be doing the trick. The team lead has decided to be alerted when this happens and decides that a simple e-mail will suffice. Fortunately, this can be done with some basic configuration.

The first step is to navigate to the Project settings, by clicking the link at the lower-left corner (Figure 8-93).

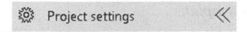

Figure 8-93. *The Project settings link*

In the General section, the different notifications can be found under the Notifications option (Figure 8-94).

Figure 8-94. *The Notifications option*

Because we want to create a new notification, we select the New subscription button in the menu (Figure 8-95).

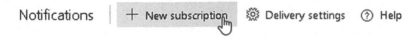

Figure 8-95. *New subscription*

The template we want to use is called *A build fails*, in the Build category (Figure 8-96).

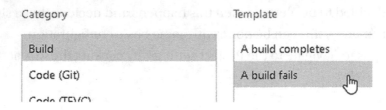

Figure 8-96. *Build fails template*

This template allows us to send a notification to an e-mail address, either for the existing members of the team or to any other e-mail address. In the following image, you can see how we deliver the build failure notification to a custom e-mail address (Figure 8-97).

New subscription

Description		Subscriber
A build fails		CoffeFixFinalHopefully Team

Deliver to	Address
Custom email address	wolf@watchingyou.com

Filter
○ Any team project   ● A specific team project   CoffeFix Containerisation

Filter criteria

And/Or	Field	Operator	Value
+ × □	Status	=	Failed

Figure 8-97. *New subscription with custom e-mail address*

This new notification is added to the list of notifications. Take a moment to review the other notifications that are automatically enabled.

As an example, let's say the team decides that it doesn't want to be notified when a Build completes successfully. This notification can be removed by setting the state to disabled (Figure 8-98).

Figure 8-98. *Stopping build e-mails*

After taking a moment to explore the other options in Project Settings, be sure to go back and set the `ReportSender.cs` file back to what it was before, by making the method static.

The next section will perform something similar but will require the build not to be broken. Instead, it will use a failure of the unit test to illustrate a webhook notification.

Sending Notifications—Webhook

A webhook is a convenient web service API that many applications provide, to allow for incoming messages. Many of the team collaboration tools, such as Microsoft Teams, Slack, Trello, and Jira, support webhooks for posting messages from external applications and services. In this example, we will use Slack to illustrate a webhook message when there is a failure with the release. In this situation, it will be a break during the tag of the Docker image.

Before we break our pipeline, let's integrate our Azure DevOps with Slack. If you don't have an existing Slack account, signing up for Slack is a simple process. We will not go into detail on some of this, as Slack has done a good job of documenting the process. So, for further information, please search for any specific details on Slack at `https://slack.com`.

With a Slack account, we will use a new slack channel to receive messages about our CoffeeFix builds (Figure 8-99).

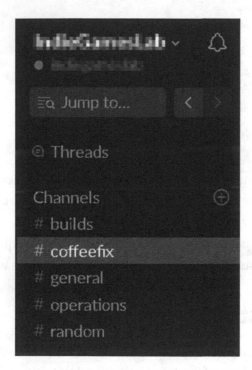

Figure 8-99. *Slack channels*

The first step is to get the URL of the webhook of the Slack channel. This can be retrieved by clicking the channel title and selecting the *Add an app* link (Figure 8-100).

#coffeefix

Jump to date...
Add people to channel
View channel details
Additional options...

Notification preferences...
Mute #coffeefix

Add an app

Leave #coffeefix

Figure 8-100. *Adding an app to a Slack channel*

Next, use the search box to find the Visual Studio Team Services entry and click the Install button (Figure 8-101).

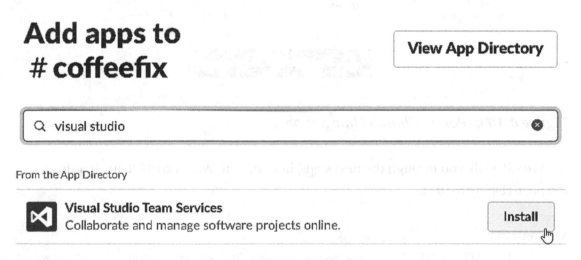

Add apps to
coffeefix

View App Directory

Q visual studio

From the App Directory

Visual Studio Team Services
Collaborate and manage software projects online.

Install

Figure 8-101. *Adding an app to the CoffeeFix channel*

This opens a web browser, which allows you to set up the integration. Use the Set Up button located under the Visual Studio Team Services logo (Figure 8-102).

Figure 8-102. *Visual Studio Team Services*

Select a channel and click the Add Visual Studio Integration button (Figure 8-103).

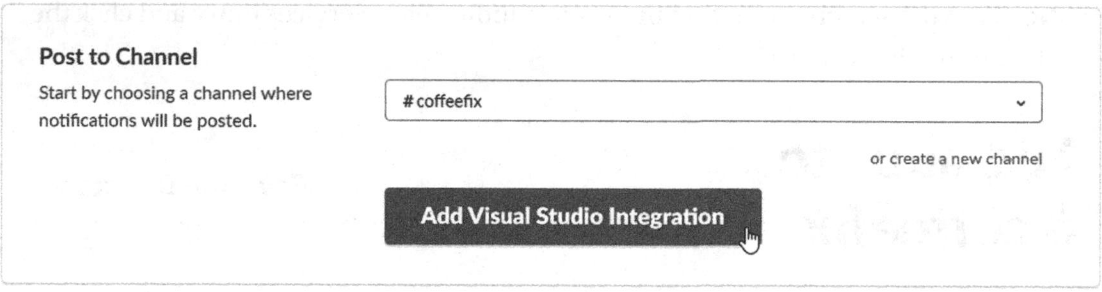

Post to Channel

Start by choosing a channel where notifications will be posted.

coffeefix

or create a new channel

Add Visual Studio Integration

Figure 8-103. *Post to Channel integration*

We will walk you through the next steps, but note the Webhook URL further down the page (Figure 8-104).

Webhook URL

When setting up this integration, this is the URL that you will paste into Visual Studio Team Services.
Show setup instructions

https://hooks.slack.com/services/T301JE3PD/BNNTRA95L/aUpxXxBcwhk9II9Tr

Regenerate

Figure 8-104. *Webhook URL*

In addition, be sure to click the Save Integration button before proceeding.

Back in Azure DevOps, in order to send messages to the channel, we must set up integration. In Azure DevOps, navigate to Project Settings (Figure 8-105).

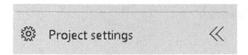

Figure 8-105. *The Project settings link*

Select the Service hooks option in the General section (Figure 8-106).

Figure 8-106. *Sevice hooks*

Here, we use the Create subscription button (Figure 8-107).

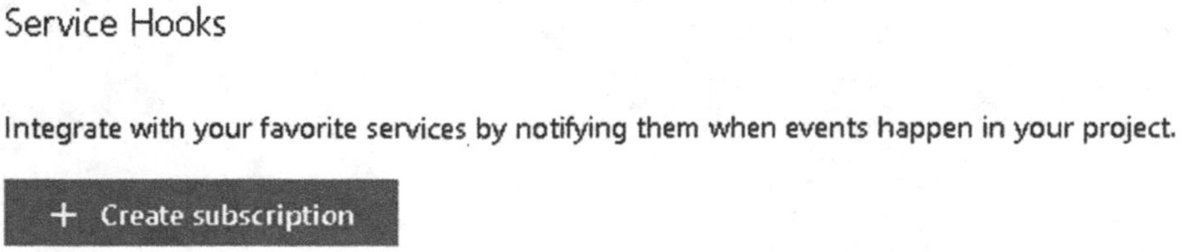

Service Hooks

Integrate with your favorite services by notifying them when events happen in your project.

+ Create subscription

Figure 8-107. *The Create subscription button*

Take a moment to scan the list of integrations. There are many services that have webhook support, including Jenkins, Microsoft Teams, Office 365, and others. Select the Slack service to continue (Figure 8-108).

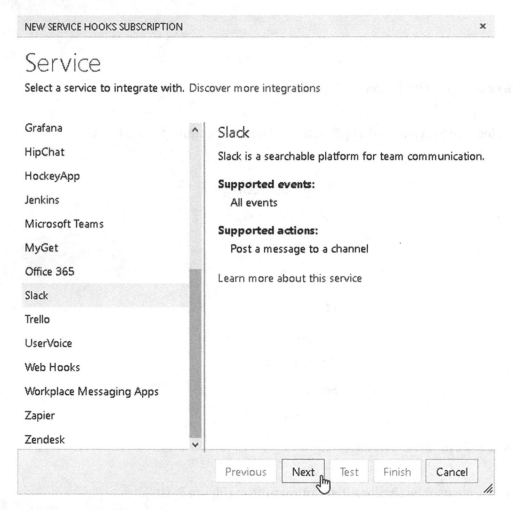

Figure 8-108. *A new service hook*

On the next page, we select the Release deployment trigger completed for the CoffeeFix Release pipeline, and then we set the Status to Failed. This will trigger when the Docker release fails (Figure 8-109).

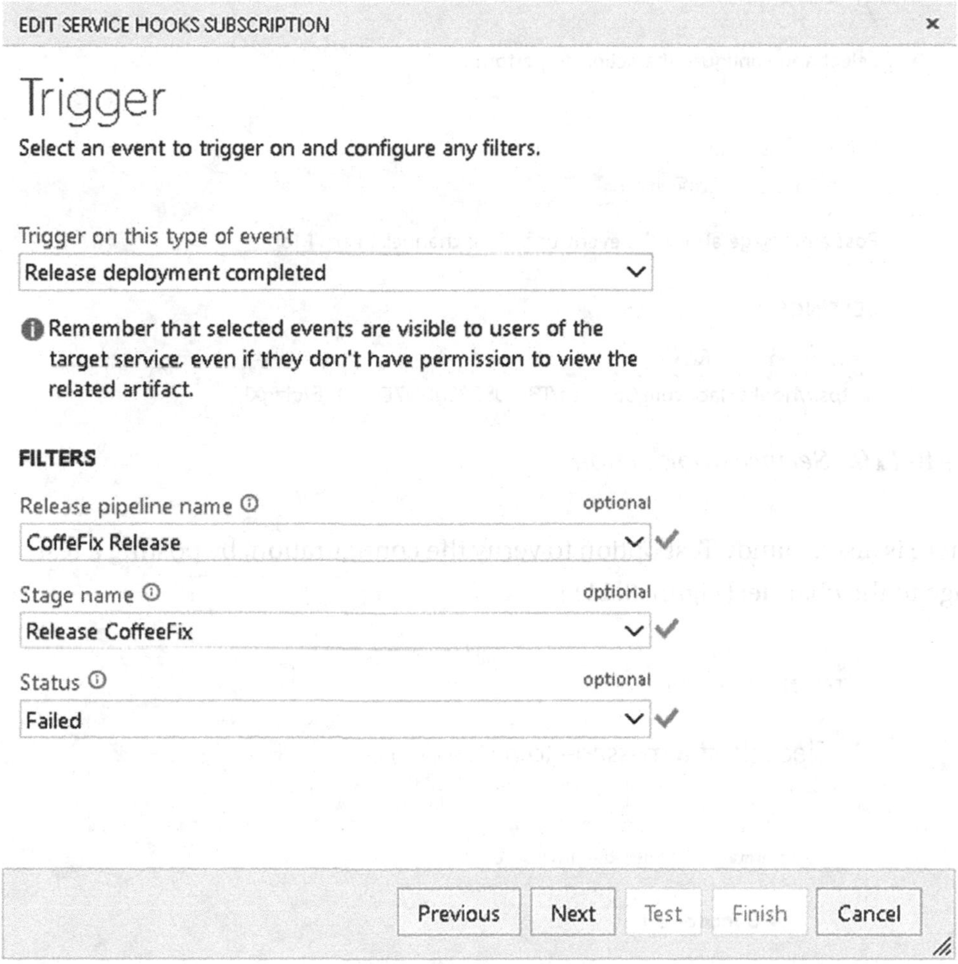

Figure 8-109. Service hook trigger

The next page requires you to enter the Slack webhook URL (Figure 8-110).

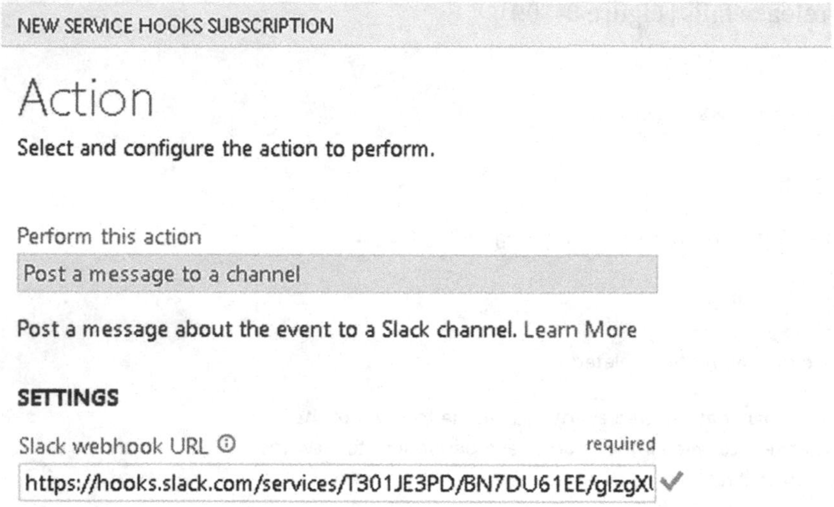

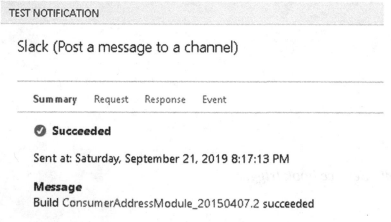

NEW SERVICE HOOKS SUBSCRIPTION

Action

Select and configure the action to perform.

Perform this action

Post a message to a channel

Post a message about the event to a Slack channel. Learn More

SETTINGS

Slack webhook URL ⓘ   required

https://hooks.slack.com/services/T301JE3PD/BN7DU61EE/glzgXl ✔

Figure 8-110. *Service hook action*

There is also a handy Test option to verify the configuration, by posting a test message to the channel (Figure 8-111).

TEST NOTIFICATION

Slack (Post a message to a channel)

Summary   Request   Response   Event

✅ **Succeeded**

Sent at: Saturday, September 21, 2019 8:17:13 PM

Message
Build ConsumerAddressModule_20150407.2 succeeded

Figure 8-111. *Test notification*

Back in the Slack channel, you can view the activity, including the test message (Figure 8-112).

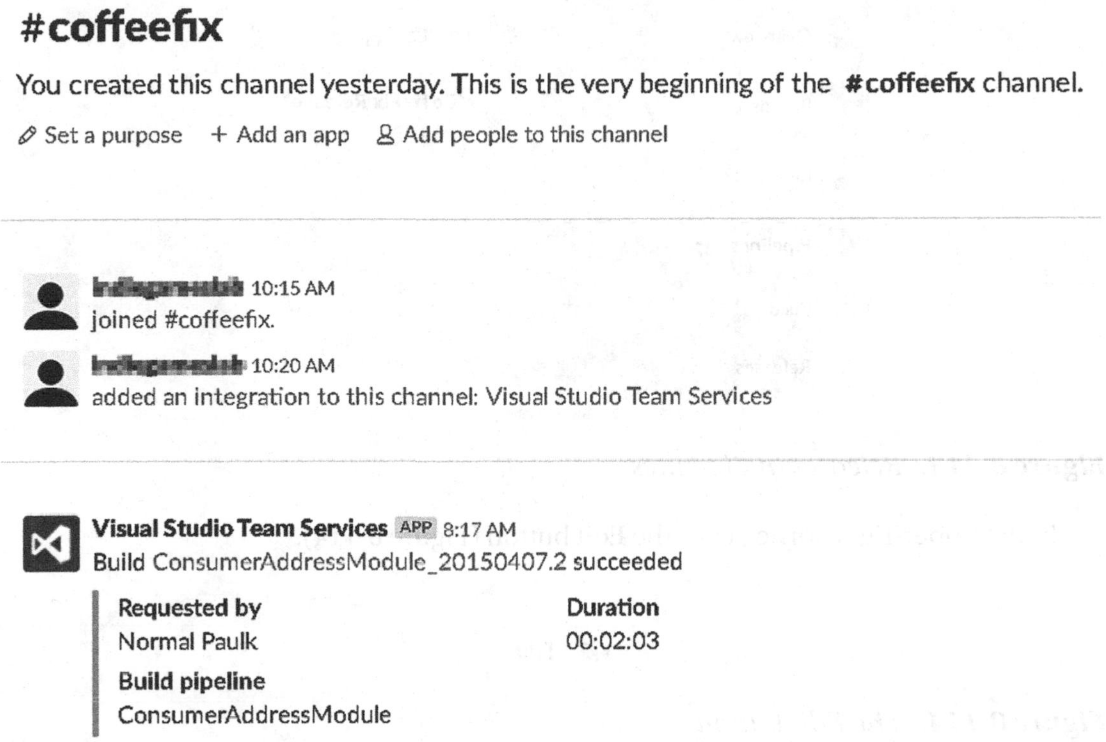

#coffeefix

You created this channel yesterday. This is the very beginning of the **#coffeefix** channel.

⌀ Set a purpose   + Add an app   & Add people to this channel

---

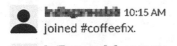 10:15 AM
joined #coffeefix.

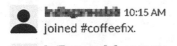 10:20 AM
added an integration to this channel: Visual Studio Team Services

---

 **Visual Studio Team Services** APP 8:17 AM
Build ConsumerAddressModule_20150407.2 succeeded

Requested by	**Duration**
Normal Paulk	00:02:03
Build pipeline	
ConsumerAddressModule	

Figure 8-112. *Channel notification*

Now that we have the webhook set up, let's alter the release pipeline. In Azure DevOps, navigate to Releases and select the CoffeeFix Release pipeline (Figure 8-113).

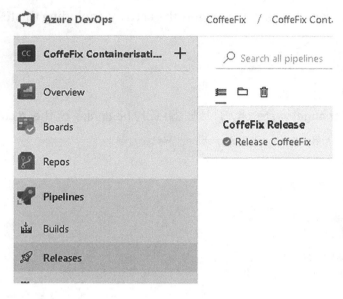

Figure 8-113. *Releases in Pipelines*

In the upper-right corner, click the Edit button (Figure 8-114).

Figure 8-114. *The Edit button*

We are going to break the release by using a Windows agent instead of a Unix agent. To change the agent, on the Tasks tab, select Agent job (Figure 8-115).

Figure 8-115. *Release Tasks*

Switch the Agent Specification from ubuntu-16.04 to another agent, and then save the changes (Figure 8-116).

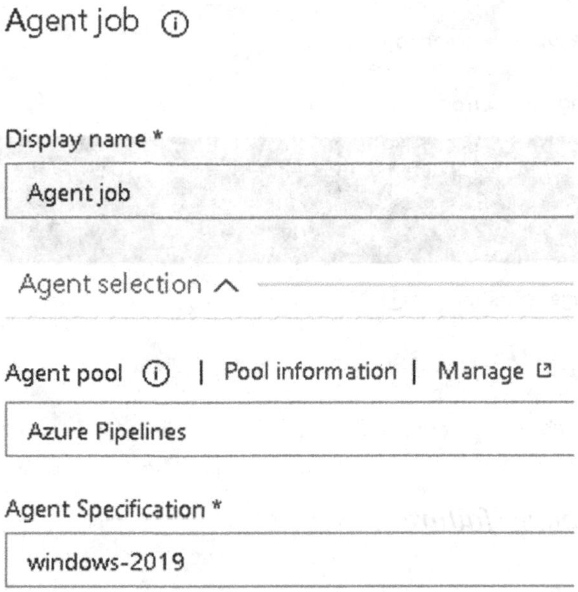

Agent job ⓘ

Display name *

Agent job

Agent selection ∧ ─────────────────

Agent pool ⓘ | Pool information | Manage ⎘

Azure Pipelines

Agent Specification *

windows-2019

Figure 8-116. *Agent specification*

With the changes saved, start a release, by clicking the Create release button (Figure 8-117).

🖫 Save   🚀 **Create release**   ☰ **View releases**

Figure 8-117. *The Create release button*

This will result in a failure in the Pull Image step (Figure 8-118).

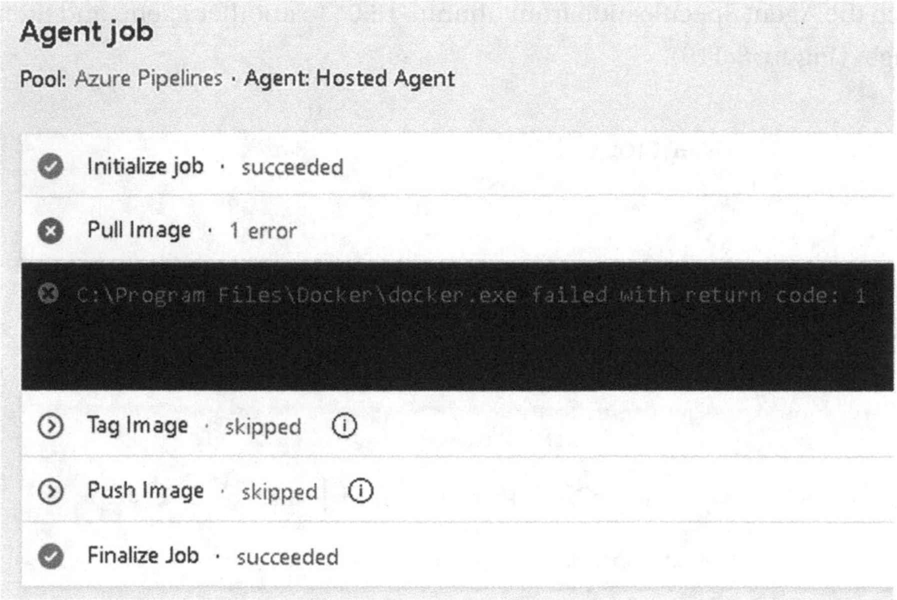

Agent job

Pool: Azure Pipelines · Agent: Hosted Agent

✅ Initialize job · succeeded

❌ Pull Image · 1 error

❌ C:\Program Files\Docker\docker.exe failed with return code: 1

▷ Tag Image · skipped ⓘ

▷ Push Image · skipped ⓘ

✅ Finalize Job · succeeded

Figure 8-118. *Pull image failure*

If we expand the task, we can see that the reason for the failure is clearly stated (Figure 8-119).

```
 9   2019-09-22T02:42:03.3622969Z [command]"C:\Program Files\Docker\docker.exe" pull coffeefix.azurecr.io/coffeefixconsole:83
10   2019-09-22T02:42:08.6843776Z 83: Pulling from coffeefixconsole
11   2019-09-22T02:42:09.1531388Z image operating system "linux" cannot be used on this platform
12   2019-09-22T02:42:09.1812244Z ##[error]C:\Program Files\Docker\docker.exe failed with return code: 1
```

Figure 8-119. *Docker image failure*

We should also see that a notification has been sent to Slack (Figure 8-120).

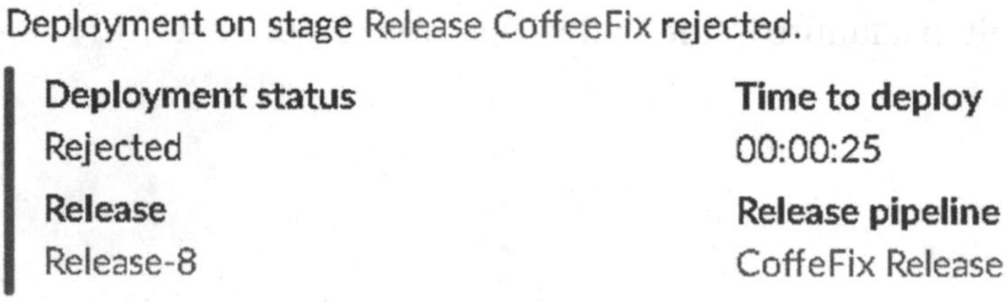

Deployment on stage Release CoffeeFix rejected.

Deployment status	**Time to deploy**
Rejected	00:00:25
Release	**Release pipeline**
Release-8	CoffeFix Release

Figure 8-120. *Release notification of failure*

Take a moment to revert the changes, by setting the agent back to the Ubuntu agent.

Many teams find webhooks a more effective way of receiving alerts than e-mails. This section should give you some ideas as to how to integrate more effective measures into your existing collaboration tools.

Build Conditions

So far, we have illustrated pipelines in which a failure in a task stops the subsequent tasks from running. In some situations, you might want tasks to run despite a failure in a previous task. For example, the CoffeeFix team has decided that when unit tests fail, it still would like the artifacts to be produced. This means it would like the publish steps to run nonetheless. In this situation, we will use a build condition to indicate that we always want these tasks to run.

First, let's break the code, by changing one of the unit test asserts. In the Files section of Azure DevOps, select the `TelemetryProcessorTests.cs` file in the CoffeeFix.Console. Tests project (Figure 8-121).

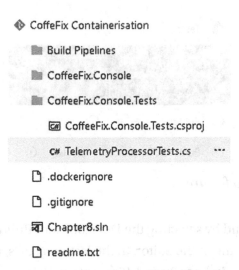

Figure 8-121. The `TelemetryProcessorTests.cs` file

Alter the `Assert.IsTrue` statement to `Assert.IsFalse`, in the `ProcessRemoval_NoMatch` test method (Figure 8-122).

```
[TestMethod]
public void ProcessRemoval_NoMatch()
{
    var telemetry = new EventTelemetry("This does not Match");

    var next = new NextProcessor();
    var sut = new MyTelemetryProcessor(next);

    sut.Process(telemetry);

    Assert.IsTrue(next.WasTriggered, "The next processor should be triggered!");
}
```

Figure 8-122. *Changing the test assert*

After saving the file, the build automatically starts, as the file is in the master branch, and we have this build set to trigger whenever a file is committed.

The build will fail. Note that the Publish and PublishBuildArtifacts tasks have been skipped (Figure 8-123).

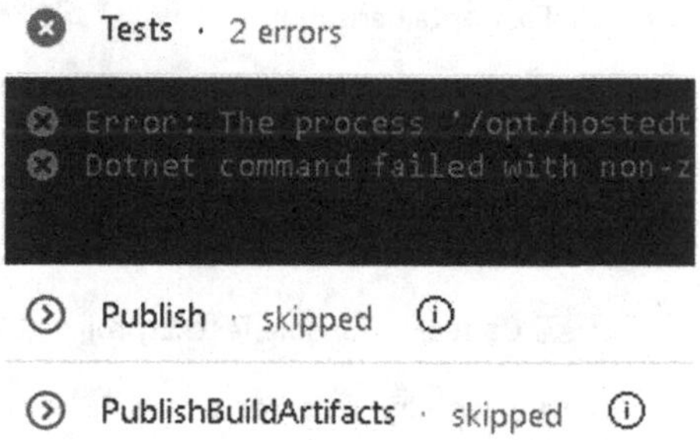

Figure 8-123. *Tests step failure*

Now let's alter our build by selecting the Development Build and selecting edit, which will load the YAML file in the editor. In the last two tasks, add the `condition: always()` option, as shown in lines 38 and 46 (Figure 8-124).

```
     Settings
36   - task: DotNetCoreCLI@2
37     displayName: Publish
38     condition: always()
39     inputs:
40       command: publish
41       publishWebProjects: false
42       arguments: '--configuration $(BuildConfiguration) --output $(Build.ArtifactStagingDirectory)'
43       zipAfterPublish: True
44
     Settings
45   - task: PublishBuildArtifacts@1
46     condition: always()
47     inputs:
48       pathtoPublish: '$(Build.ArtifactStagingDirectory)'
49       artifactName: 'CoffeeFix.Console'
```

Figure 8-124. *Condition settings*

Saving the YAML file will also start a build, as this file is located in our master branch. This time, note that the build does fail, but the two tasks are still performed (Figure 8-125).

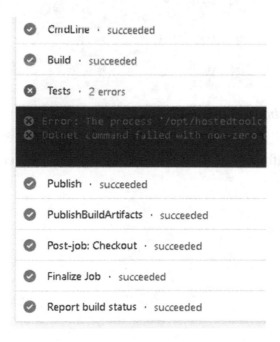

Figure 8-125. *Condition always for build steps*

This is useful to the CoffeeFix team, as it can retrieve the artifacts from both successful and failed builds.

Take the time now to reset the unit test to no longer fail.

Setting Up Dashboards

Dashboards are a great way of getting a quick view of the CI/CD pipelines. In the following example, we will set up dashboards to show the status of our build and release pipelines, as the outcome of the unit tests performed.

Under the Overview section, select Dashboards to begin (Figure 8-126).

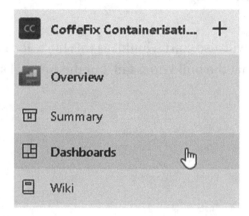

Figure 8-126. *Dashboards*

You are greeted with the following image (Figure 8-127). Select *Add a widget* to proceed.

This dashboard doesn't have widgets just yet!

Add one or more widgets to gain visibility into your team's progress.

Figure 8-127. *The Add a widget button*

The first widget you'll add will be one to show the outcome of the builds. Select the Build History widget and click the Add button twice (Figure 8-128).

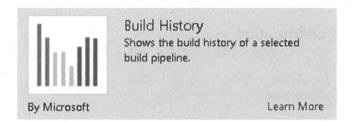

Figure 8-128. *The Build History widget*

You can then configure the widgets by selecting the settings (gear) button (Figure 8-129).

Figure 8-129. *Configure widget*

Now, select the Development Build pipeline, as shown in Figure 8-130, for one of the widgets.

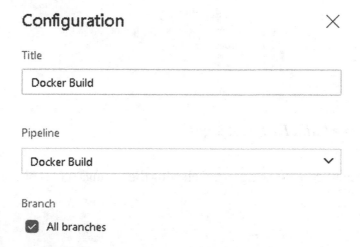

Figure 8-130. *The Configuration of the Development Build widget*

And select the Docker Build for the other widget (Figure 8-131).

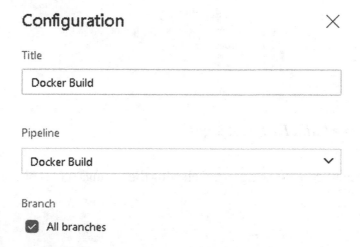

Figure 8-131. *The Configuration of the Docker Build widget*

The next widget we'll add will be for our Release pipeline. Select the Release Pipeline Overview widget (Figure 8-132).

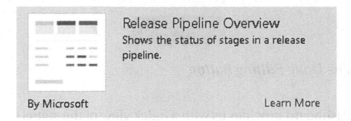

Figure 8-132. *Release Pipeline Overview*

Now, we configure the widget for our CoffeeFix Release pipeline (Figure 8-133).

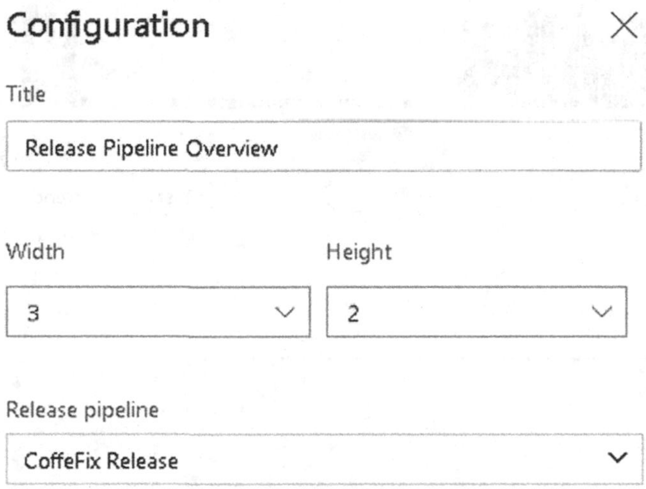

Configuration   ✕

Title

| Release Pipeline Overview |

Width   Height

| 3   ∨ | | 2   ∨ |

Release pipeline

| CoffeFix Release   ∨ |

Figure 8-133. *Configuration of Release Pipeline Overview*

The final widget will be for the unit tests, and we will use the Test Results Trend widget (Figure 8-134).

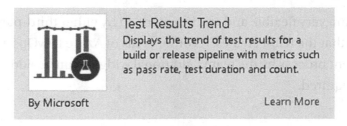

Figure 8-134. *The Test Results Trend widget*

315

On the grid, we can arrange the widget, and once we are satisfied with the layout, we will click Done Editing, to save our changes (Figure 8-135).

Done Editing

Figure 8-135. *The Done Editing button*

The created dashboard provides us with a quick view of the status of the project's CI/CD pipeline (Figure 8-136).

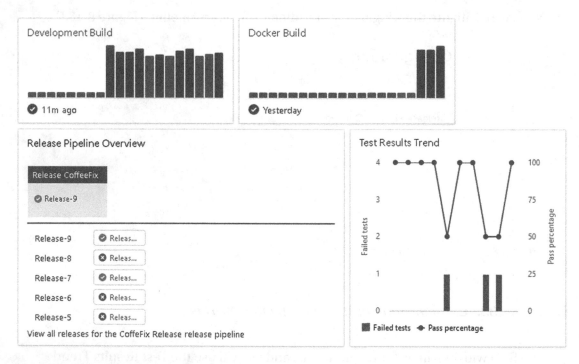

Figure 8-136. *A dashboard example*

Dashboards are very flexible and can be extended by either third-party widgets or bespoke widgets that the team creates. As other areas of Azure DevOps are incorporated in the development process by the team, additional widgets can be added to different dashboards, as required.

Summary

This chapter explored different aspects of Azure DevOps and used the CoffeeFix. Console application for a basic scenario in creating a CI/CD pipeline for the CoffeeFix team. We explored different aspects of Azure DevOps, but we mostly focused on CI/CD-related sections, namely Repos and Pipelines. We explored Docker in an example, to illustrate how this technology could simplify the release process of the application to the coffeemakers. This approach was then brought into Azure DevOps by creating Build and Release pipelines, in order to verify the integrity of the application, using automated builds and unit tests. The process of publishing the application into a container was automated to run nightly for the QA team. The release process was greatly simplified by automating the tag of an approved and verified Docker image as the latest CoffeeFix. Console release.

In the next chapter, we will look at external tooling and how the Azure portal and Azure DevOps can be extended. To illustrate the use of an external CI server, we will discuss Jenkins, and we will incorporate it into our DevOps pipeline.

CHAPTER 9

External Tooling

The previous chapter focused on automating the build and release process (also known as a pipeline). The current chapter aims to highlight the important and useful widgets of the Azure portal dashboard. It will also cover various build tools and extend the continuous integration (CI) and continuous delivery (CD) capabilities previously explored, followed by a discussion of Jenkins CI services.

The chapter's principal sections cover tiles and widgets in the Azure portal dashboard and plug-ins in Azure DevOps.

Technical Requirements

This chapter uses sample code to elaborate on the various topics presented. The following are prerequisites for working with this sample code:

- *Visual Studio 2019*: Visual Studio is available for both Windows and Mac. If you do not have Visual Studio 2019 installed on your machine, you can install it from here: `https://visualstudio.microsoft.com/downloads/`. In this chapter, we use Visual Studio 2019 Community edition for Windows (a free version). However, you can select an edition of your choice. Click Download and follow the instructions on your screen to install Visual Studio. Do not forget to install Azure SDK (select *Azure development* from the Workloads tab, as shown in Figure 9-1).

© Jeffrey Chilberto, Sjoukje Zaal, Gaurav Aroraa and Ed Price 2020
J. Chilberto et al., *Cloud Debugging and Profiling in Microsoft Azure*,
https://doi.org/10.1007/978-1-4842-5437-0_9

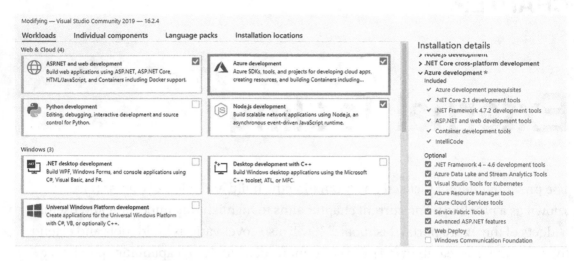

Figure 9-1. *Selecting Workloads*

- *A valid Azure account*: You will require login credentials for the Azure portal. If you don't have an Azure account, you can get a free account from here: `https://azure.microsoft.com/free/`.

Note   The source code for this chapter can be downloaded here: `https://apress.com/9781484254363`.

- *Jenkins server*: To use the code samples cited in this chapter, you should set up a Jenkins server. Download and install a Jenkins server from `https://jenkins.io/download`. To set up a Jenkins server on a Linux box, refer to the complete tutorial available at `https://docs.microsoft.com/en-us/azure/jenkins/install-jenkins-solution-template`.

Azure Portal Dashboard—Tiles/Widgets

The Azure portal dashboard is where you can find the resources, services, and more, which are available in your subscription (default or placed per your choice). The dashboard allows you to drag and drop various available widgets for information on the available page (a web page).

Note   If you are logging in for the first time, you will see a default Azure portal dashboard. The default name is Dashboard.

You can also create multiple dashboards. There are various advantages to setting up multiple dashboards, such as the ability to create separate dashboards for a development team, top management team, or infrastructure team. In this way, each dashboard provides the information related to a specific team. Figure 9-2 shows a sample dashboard.

Figure 9-2. *A sample dashboard*

In the preceding figure, you can see information about the available services, including billing information (the user is not set up with permission to view the information).

Note   In Chapter 2, we covered the Azure portal dashboard and its components.

The default dashboard is private and visible only to you. If you want to share this dashboard, you must publish it as an Azure resource. In Chapter 2, you saw how to create a new dashboard. This section will discuss various tiles that offer information about your resources. Figure 9-3 shows the tiles available in the Tile Gallery.

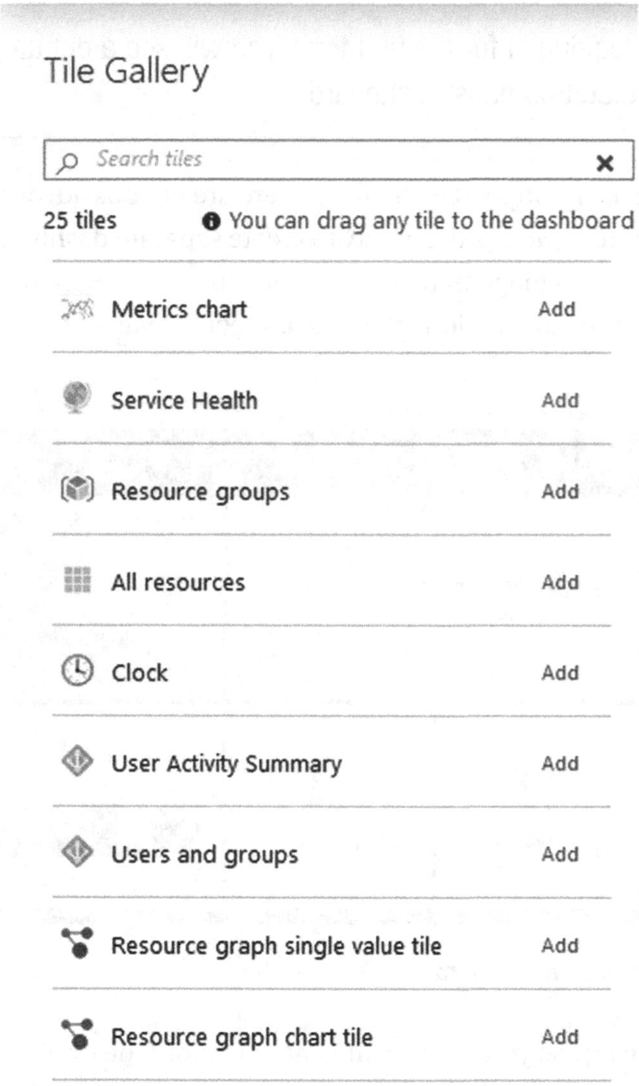

Tile Gallery

🔍 Search tiles	✕

25 tiles   ℹ You can drag any tile to the dashboard

🐾	Metrics chart	Add
🌐	Service Health	Add
📦	Resource groups	Add
▦	All resources	Add
🕐	Clock	Add
◈	User Activity Summary	Add
◈	Users and groups	Add
⦿	Resource graph single value tile	Add
⦿	Resource graph chart tile	Add

Figure 9-3. *The tiles available in the Tile Gallery*

You can add Metrics chart to show the metrics from Azure Monitor. By default, the data is from the previous 24 hours, but you can customize the time to show data from the period of your choice. Figure 9-4 illustrates customizing the Metrics chart data.

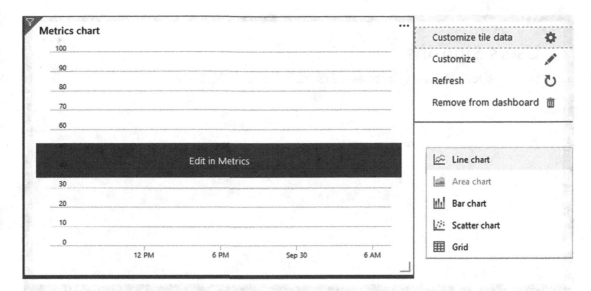

Figure 9-4. *Metrics chart customization*

The Clock tile can be set to show the time of the current time zone (Figure 9-5). Time zones can also be changed.

Figure 9-5. *The Clock showing the date and time*

The User Activity Summary tile can be set to show sign-in activities for all users belonging to Azure Active Directory (AD). Figure 9-6 shows user sign-in activities for "All Users" from 08/31/2019 to 09/30/2019.

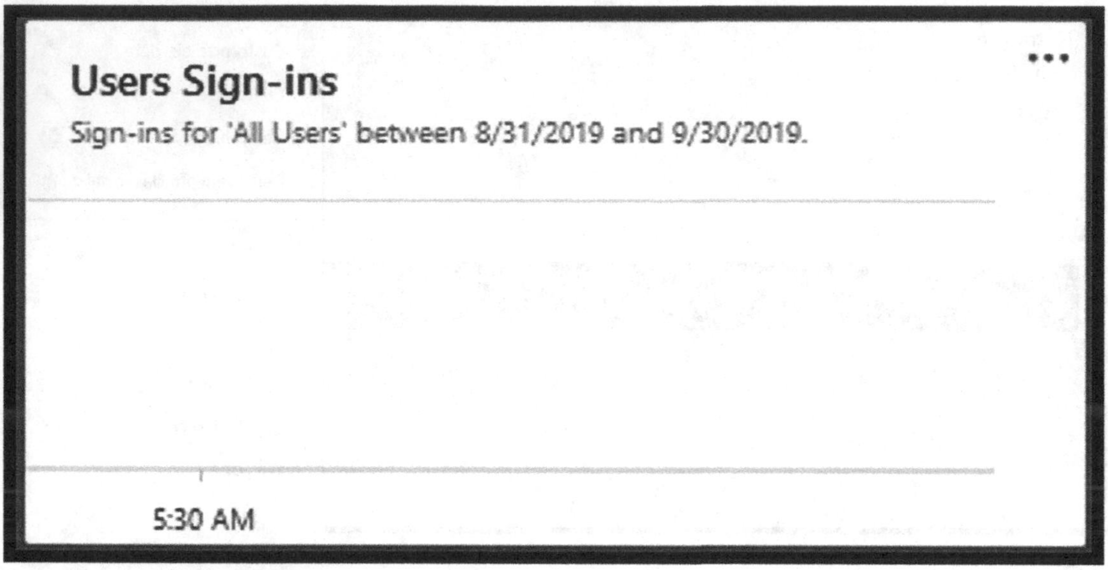

Users Sign-ins

Sign-ins for 'All Users' between 8/31/2019 and 9/30/2019.

5:30 AM

Figure 9-6. Users Sign-ins

You will only be able to use this tile if you have subscribed to the Premium plan of Azure AD. We've opted for a free Azure AD plan, which is why there is no data. Instead, you will see the following screen (Figure 9-7), if you click in this tile.

Access denied

You do not have access

To see sign-in data, upgrade your organization's subscription to include Azure AD P1 or P2. Your current license status: Azure AD Free

Start a free Premium Trial

? Get support

Figure 9-7. Access denied

The Users and groups tile can be set to show complete details of all the users and groups (Figure 9-8). You can use it to navigate individual user details and groups. Currently, we have a single user.

Figure 9-8. Users and groups

You can see complete information about the tile's specific use by clicking one of the icons. Figure 9-9 shows the information related to the selected user.

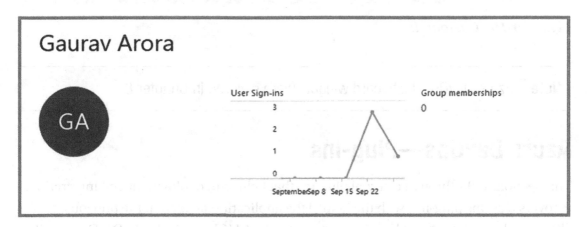

Figure 9-9. User Sign-ins info

The Markdown tile can be set to show custom static contents. This is very important if you want to provide instructions.

We have created a custom tile using Markdown text, as shown in Figure 9-10. You can find the markdown file for this widget in the source code for Chapter 9.

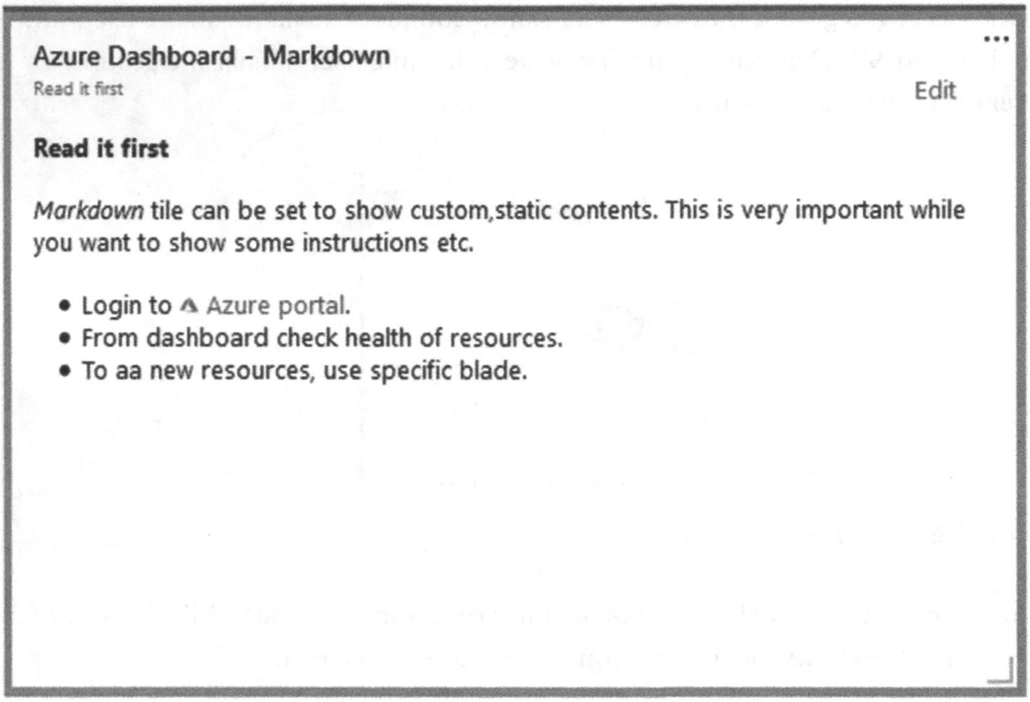

Figure 9-10.   *Custom tile*

Note   Azure DevOps dashboard widgets were covered in Chapter 8.

Azure DevOps—Plug-ins

This section walks through external plug-ins that help with deployment and integration. It covers DevOps plug-ins, with the help of the application created in the previous chapter, which discussed release management with CI/CD, using Azure DevOps and its built-in support for the tools used.

Note   Visual Studio Team Services is now Azure DevOps Services. This name change was announced in September 2018 (see `https://docs.microsoft.com/en-us/azure/devops/user-guide/what-is-azure-devops`).

Azure DevOps and Jenkins

Jenkins is a CI server that is open source and was developed using Java. Jenkins helps dev teams to continuously build applications across platforms.

This section highlights the Azure DevOps capabilities to work with Jenkins. We will not detail how to do a fresh install of the Jenkins server. You can obtain this information from the official Jenkins page (`https://jenkins.io/`) or from Microsoft (`https://docs.microsoft.com/en-us/azure/jenkins/install-jenkins-solution-template`).

Creating Pipelines

In the previous chapter, we set up the build pipelines of the CoffeeFix console application. The current section will pick the same application and set up CI using Jenkins server plug-ins for Azure DevOps.

Figure 9-11 shows a typical approach to building an application using Jenkins. Here, we have a source code hosted in the Azure Repos GitHub; we set up Azure Pipelines, and, with the help of Jenkins, we deploy the application over Azure.

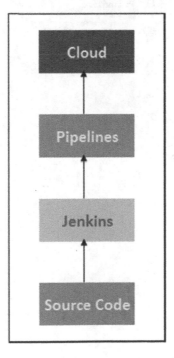

Figure 9-11. *Building an app using Jenkins*

Next, we must add the Jenkins service connection and the Azure Resource service connection.

To do so, we must add a Service connection. You can open the Service connection page by clicking Project settings from the left navigation bar (Figure 9-12).

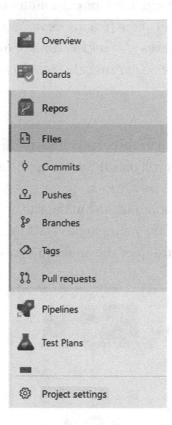

Figure 9-12. *Project settings*

From Figure 9-13, you can see that there are different services available, and you can select any service you need. Select Jenkins. In Figure 9-14, we add the Jenkins service connection.

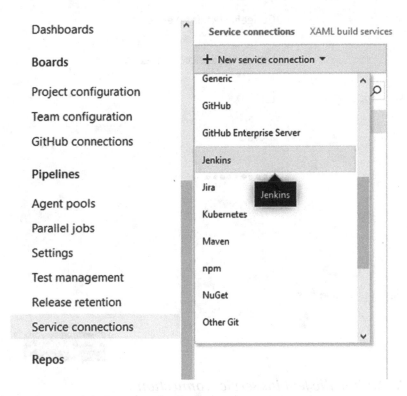

Figure 9-13. *Selecting Jenkins as the new service connection*

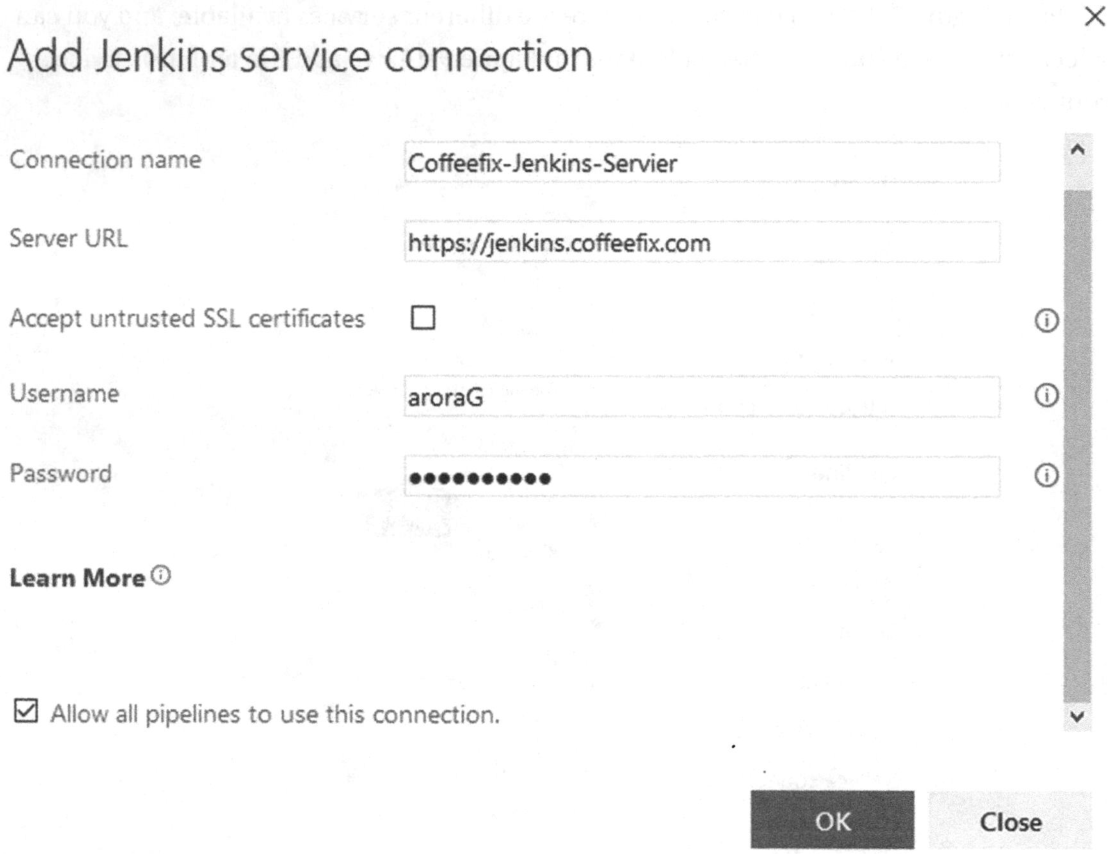

×

Add Jenkins service connection

Connection name	Coffeefix-Jenkins-Servier
Server URL	https://jenkins.coffeefix.com
Accept untrusted SSL certificates	☐ ⓘ
Username	aroraG ⓘ
Password	•••••••••• ⓘ

Learn More ⓘ

☑ Allow all pipelines to use this connection.

OK   Close

Figure 9-14. *Adding the Jenkins service connection*

We then create the Azure Resource Manager service connection for our example (Figure 9-15).

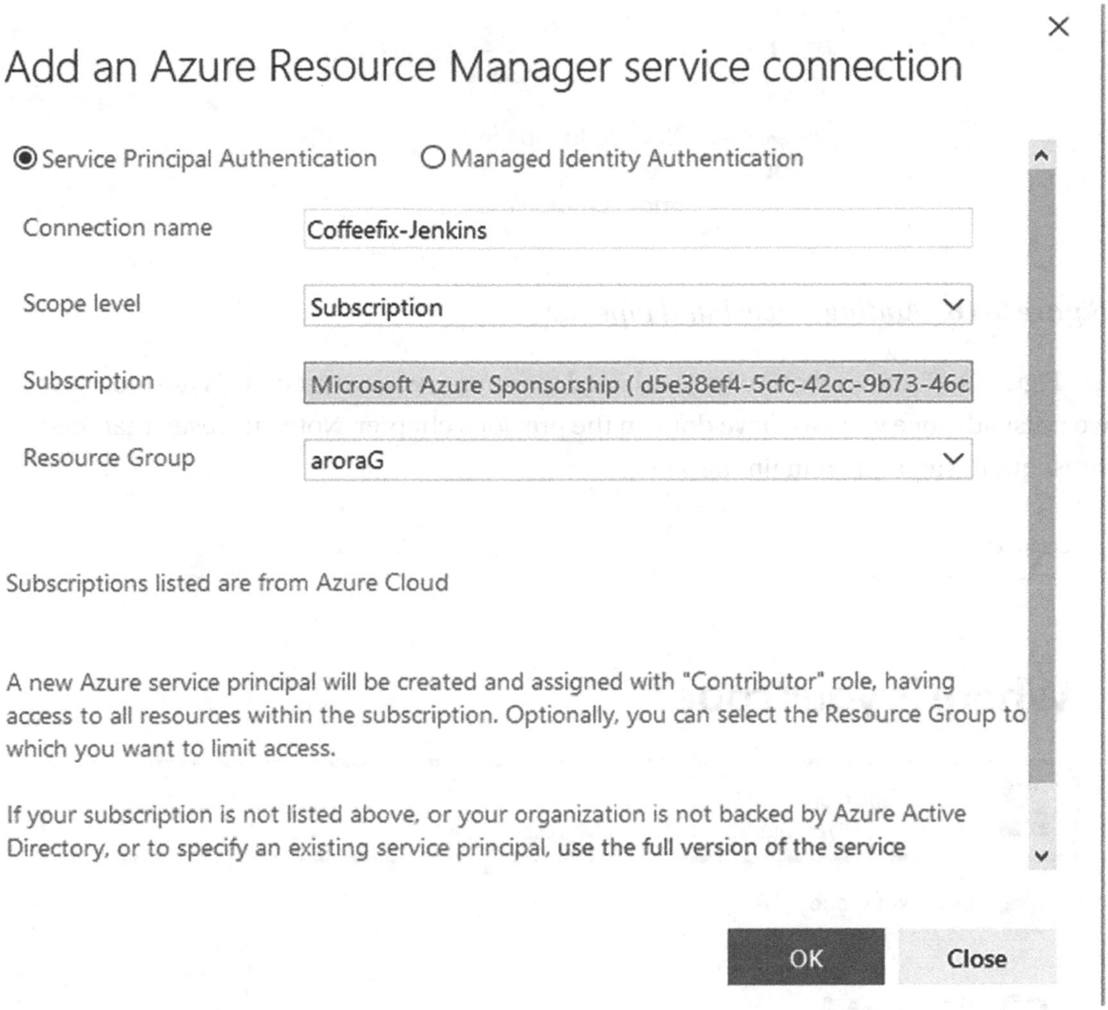

Add an Azure Resource Manager service connection

✕

◉ Service Principal Authentication   ○ Managed Identity Authentication

Connection name | Coffeefix-Jenkins |

Scope level | Subscription ∨ |

Subscription | Microsoft Azure Sponsorship (d5e38ef4-5cfc-42cc-9b73-46c |

Resource Group | aroraG ∨ |

Subscriptions listed are from Azure Cloud

A new Azure service principal will be created and assigned with "Contributor" role, having access to all resources within the subscription. Optionally, you can select the Resource Group to which you want to limit access.

If your subscription is not listed above, or your organization is not backed by Azure Active Directory, or to specify an existing service principal, use the full version of the service

`OK`   `Close`

Figure 9-15. *Adding an Azure Resource Manager service connection*

In Figure 9-15, you can see that we have defined a service connection for Azure Resource. This connection dialog may look different for different services.

Next, we must link Jenkins with Azure Pipelines. First, we will add a new build pipeline. In the previous chapter, we added a pipeline to our project. Here, we are adding a new pipeline. First, we must click *New build pipeline* under New (Figure 9-16).

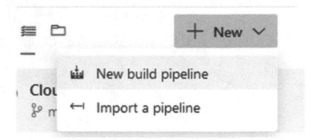

Figure 9-16. *Adding a new build pipeline*

Figure 9-17 shows that we have selected the source where our code is hosted. Now we must advance what we have done in the previous chapter. Note, however, that the subsequent steps will remain the same.

Connect	Select	Configure	Review

New pipeline

Where is your code?

Azure Repos Git   YAML
Free private Git repositories, pull requests, and code search

Bitbucket Cloud   YAML
Hosted by Atlassian

GitHub   YAML
Home to the world's largest community of developers

GitHub Enterprise Server   YAML
The self-hosted version of GitHub Enterprise

Other Git
Any generic Git repository

Subversion
Centralized version control by Apache

Use the classic editor to create a pipeline without YAML.

Figure 9-17. *Selecting the source of our code repository*

Note   By default, Jenkins deploys artifacts to the specified server path. You can also set these artifacts to be stored in Azure Blobs.

Next, we must add a release pipeline. To add a new release pipeline, click Pipelines ➤ Releases and then New pipeline (Figure 9-18).

No release pipelines found

Automate your release process in a few easy steps with a new pipeline

New pipeline

Figure 9-18. *Adding a new release pipeline*

Select Empty job (Figure 9-19) and name it "coffeefix jenkins Stage1" (Figure 9-20). You can, however, assign any name, per your requirement.

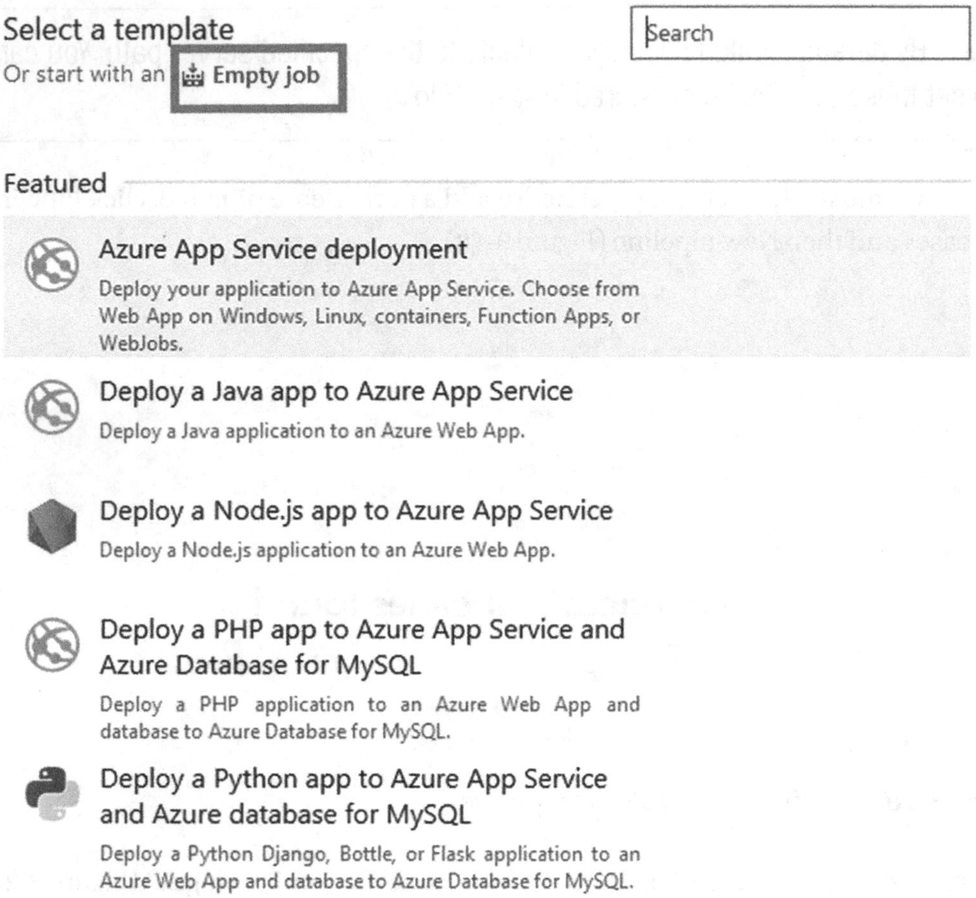

Select a template

Or start with an [icon] **Empty job**

Search

Featured

[icon] **Azure App Service deployment**
Deploy your application to Azure App Service. Choose from Web App on Windows, Linux, containers, Function Apps, or WebJobs.

[icon] **Deploy a Java app to Azure App Service**
Deploy a Java application to an Azure Web App.

[icon] **Deploy a Node.js app to Azure App Service**
Deploy a Node.js application to an Azure Web App.

[icon] **Deploy a PHP app to Azure App Service and Azure Database for MySQL**
Deploy a PHP application to an Azure Web App and database to Azure Database for MySQL.

[icon] **Deploy a Python app to Azure App Service and Azure database for MySQL**
Deploy a Python Django, Bottle, or Flask application to an Azure Web App and database to Azure Database for MySQL.

Figure 9-19. *Selecting a template*

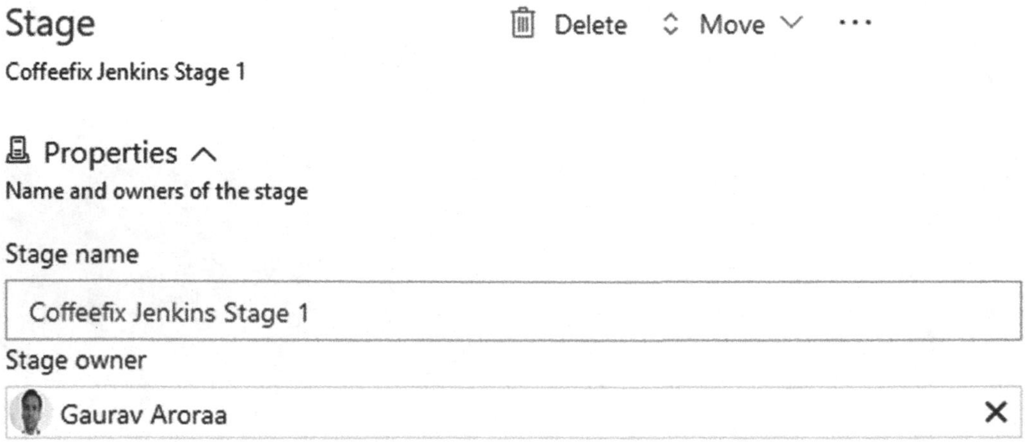

Stage

[trash] Delete   ⇕ Move ∨   ⋯

Coffeefix Jenkins Stage 1

[icon] **Properties** ∧
Name and owners of the stage

Stage name

Coffeefix Jenkins Stage 1

Stage owner

[avatar] Gaurav Aroraa   ✕

Figure 9-20. *Stage 1 properties*

Next, we must add an artifact (Figure 9-21).

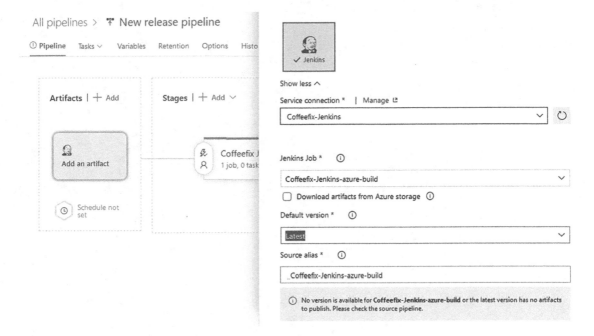

Figure 9-21. *Adding artifact*

As we have already added post-build actions to our Jenkins build job from our Jenkins server, there is no need to add any extra steps here. You can make any changes in the code repository, and they will work. You can also trigger a build manually.

In the preceding section, we set up the build and integration. Similarly, you can add continuous deployment from the Jenkins server.

Summary

This chapter explored different aspects of Azure DevOps and used the CoffeeFix. Console application for a basic scenario to create a CI/CD pipeline for the CoffeeFix team. We explored various tiles and widgets of the Azure dashboard. Also, we set up the Jenkins server to use with Azure DevOps services, as an external tool/plug-in. We set up CI with Jenkins. There are many other external plug-ins/tools related to CI/CD, including TeamCity, Octopus, Travis CI, CloudBees Core, Cruise Control, GitLab CI/CD, Spinnaker, and Atlassian Bamboo, among others. To streamline our approach, we limited the discussion to Azure DevOps and covered only Jenkins. The next chapter will cover troubleshooting in a production environment and will discuss enterprise reports.

CHAPTER 10

Visualizing the Health of a Solution

Up to this chapter, we have covered various topics related to Microsoft Azure, including Function as a Service (FaaS), Software as a Service (SaaS), Platform as a Service (PaaS), Infrastructure as a Service (IaaS), the Azure portal, implementation of Azure functions, Logic Apps, Azure SQL Database, Azure Cosmos DB and Azure Storage Tables, Azure Web Apps, Azure AD security, Azure DevOps, and Azure API Management services. In previous chapters, we created an application related to a fictitious company, CoffeeFix. We have seen that our CoffeeFix app is an implementation of the topics covered in the relevant chapters. Our CoffeeFix app has grown chapter by chapter and topic by topic, and now it has been deployed in production.

Now this chapter investigates various unforeseen issues and troubleshooting scenarios that can occur in the production environment. It discusses visualizing and analyzing virtual machine (VM) data, Azure Monitor, the health monitoring of CoffeeFix VMs, disaster recovery for CoffeeFixDev, and monitoring the CoffeeFixWeb application.

Technical Requirements

This chapter uses the sample code for the CoffeeFix application that was developed in previous chapters. The following are prerequisites for working with this sample code (note that these requirements are similar to those detailed in Chapter 9):

- *Visual Studio 2019*: Visual Studio is available for both Windows and Mac. If you do not have Visual Studio 2019 installed on your machine, you can install it from here: https://visualstudio.microsoft.com/downloads/. In this chapter, we used Visual Studio 2019 Community

© Jeffrey Chilberto, Sjoukje Zaal, Gaurav Aroraa and Ed Price 2020
J. Chilberto et al., *Cloud Debugging and Profiling in Microsoft Azure*,
https://doi.org/10.1007/978-1-4842-5437-0_10

edition for Windows (a free version). However, you can select the edition of your choice. Click Download and follow the instructions on your screen to install Visual Studio. Do not forget to install Azure SDK (select Azure development from the Workloads tab, as shown in Figure 10-1).

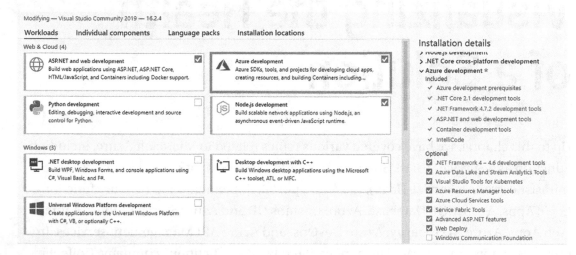

Figure 10-1. *Selecting Workloads*

- *A valid Azure Account*: You must have login credentials to access the Azure portal. If you don't have an Azure account, you can obtain a free account from `https://azure.microsoft.com/free/`.

Note   The source code for this chapter can be downloaded from GitHub via the book's product page, located at `www.apress.com/9781484254363`.

Before we start our discussion of production troubleshooting, you should consider the following points:

- The team released the CoffeeFix application in the production environment.

- Team challenges were introduced to manage and release new versions of the CoffeeFix app into the production environment.

- Visualizing various errors and issues occurred in the production environment.

There may be more scenarios or issues that might occur in an actual production-based application. We are discussing here a couple of scenarios, to understand how to handle and troubleshoot certain production issues. Note that this chapter attempts to mitigate and manage these production issues, but it cannot guarantee that these solutions are applicable to each and every troubleshooting scenario that can arise in a production environment.

To visualize your monitoring activities, you can show them on your Azure dashboard. Figure 10-2 shows the customized dashboard, which you can configure according to your needs. The statistics provided are only to showcase the various reports and may not be relevant to your activities related to our CoffeeFix sample application.

Note   You can revisit the "Azure Portal" section in Chapter 2, to see how to create a customized Azure dashboard.

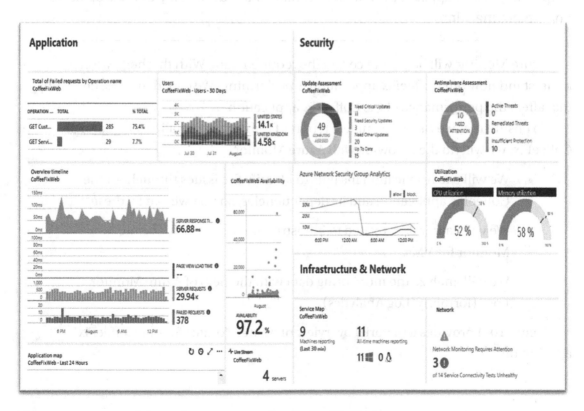

Figure 10-2. Dashboard to monitor the CoffeeFixWeb app

Visualizing and Analyzing the Virtual Machine Data

To visualize the health of the CoffeeFix application, we need data. This data is related to application performance, issues, exceptions, and other factors that may cause the application to fail.

This section covers how to collect data, analyze it, and prepare reports to visually display facts related to the CoffeeFix application, based on the following considerations:

- Performance of the application

- Application uptime

- Various resources that affect the performance of the application

- Logs related to application activities

Tip   In general, application uptime depends on the availability of the web server or remote machine.

Azure Monitor will help us to collect the required data. With this help, we can understand how our CoffeeFix application is performing. We can identify issues, if any, that affect the performance of the CoffeeFix application.

To ensure that we issue a complete report of the data to visualize the health of CoffeeFix, we will do the following with Azure Monitor:

- We will use Application Insights to identify the issues throughout the CoffeeFix application and its dependencies, so that we can fix these.

- We will gather data related to infrastructure issues, using Azure Monitor for VMs.

- We will analyze the monitoring data with the help of Azure Monitor Logs (formerly, Log Analytics).

Figure 10-3 provides a pictorial overview of Azure Monitor for our CoffeeFix application.

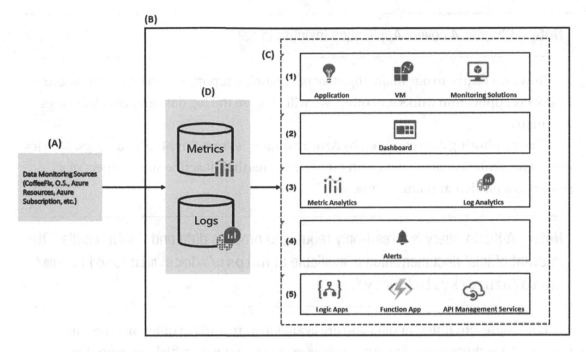

Figure 10-3. *Pictorial overview of Azure Monitor for the CoffeeFix app*

The preceding figure shows the following four main parts of the Azure Monitor related to our application:

- Part (A) shows the sources of the data monitored. The CoffeeFix application is included as a source of the monitoring data. Additional resources include an on-premises operating system, Azure Resources, and an Azure subscription.

- Part (B) shows Azure Monitor components.

- Part (C) shows the different operations/functions that can help to determine and analyze the cause of an issue. Each numbered row in Part (C) corresponds to its function. These functions are as follows:

  1. Insights

  2. Visualize

  3. Analyze

  4. Respond

  5. Integrate

- Part (D) is the data store that contains various metrics and logs.

Note   Chapter 4 covers Application Insights in detail.

Now let's return to our main objective of creating a report, which ensures that our CoffeeFix application works smoothly. We will analyze the log data and check the logs and metrics.

The monitoring data captured by Azure Monitor is stored in Metrics or Logs. Metrics are a representation of the data with numeric values that describe some aspect of a system at a particular point in time.

Note   A Kusto query is a read-only request to process data and return results. The relevant official documentation is available at `https://docs.microsoft.com/ en-us/azure/kusto/query/`.

Logs represent different data and are available as records of different types. In Chapter 2, we discussed telemetry, such as events and traces, which are stored as logs. The performance data is also stored in logs. From the logs, we can combine the data, analyze it, and prepare a health report for our CoffeeFix application.

Internally, Azure Monitor uses the Kusto query language to query logs. If required, we can write and use our custom queries to query log data. An extensive discussion of the implementation of query log data is beyond the scope of this book. For further information, you can review the official documentation from this link: `https://docs. microsoft.com/en-us/azure/azure-monitor/log-query/get-started-queries`.

Health Monitoring of CoffeeFix Virtual Machines

The development team decided to deploy CoffeeFix by commissioning a VM. The main concern of the team is to monitor the VM. In this section, we will discuss the steps to monitor Azure VM.

To create a Virtual Machine, follow these steps you took previously to create an Azure VM:

1. Log in to the Azure portal: `https://portal.azure.com`.

2. After successfully logging in, you see your homepage, which should look like Figure 10-4.

Figure 10-4. *The Azure portal landing page*

3. Search "Virtual machines" in the search text box (Figure 10-5).

Figure 10-5. *Searching "Virtual machines"*

4. Or select *Virtual machines* from All services ➤ Compute ➤ Virtual machines (Figure 10-6).

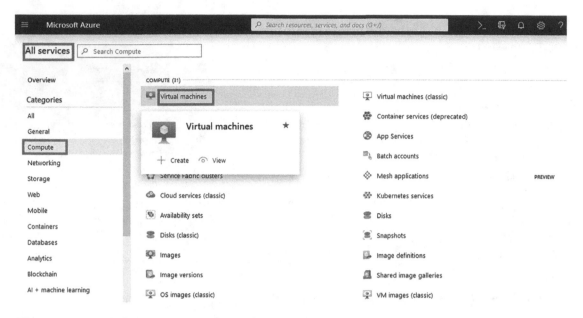

Figure 10-6. *Selecting Virtual machines*

5.   From the Virtual machines screen, click *Create virtual machine*
       (Figure 10-7).

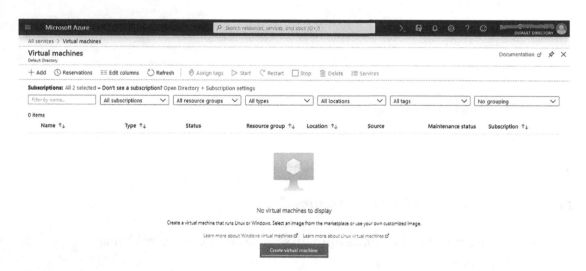

Figure 10-7. *Virtual machines*

6.   From the Basics tab of the Create a virtual machine screen,
       fill in all the required fields. In our example, we created a new
       Resource group and named it CoffeeFix (Figure 10-8).

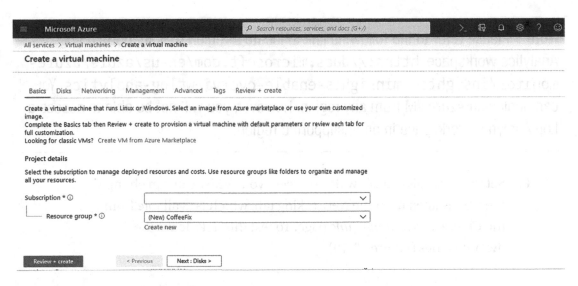

Figure 10-8. *Project details*

7.   Under Instance details, we set the name of our VM to
     CoffeeFixDev and select (US) East US as the Region. Next, we
     select an image and add an Administrator account (Figure 10-9).

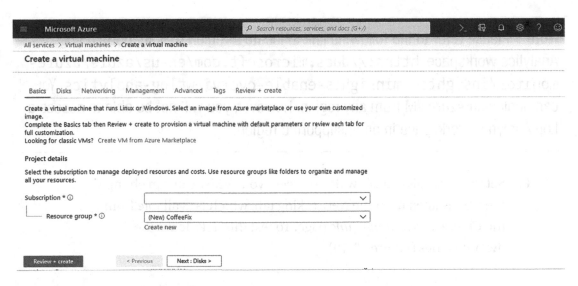

Figure 10-9. *Instance details, Administrator account*

> **Note**   Please refer to the following link to locate a region that supports a Log Analytics workspace: `https://docs.microsoft.com/en-us/azure/azure-monitor/insights/vminsights-enable-overview#log-analytics`. You can deploy an Azure VM from any region. However, you will not be able to access a Log Analytics workspace in an unsupported region.

8. Set the port rules to allow IPs to access your VMs. You can change the values later, from the Networking tab, which is available from the *Create a virtual machine* page. To test this, let's leave the default values (Figure 10-10).

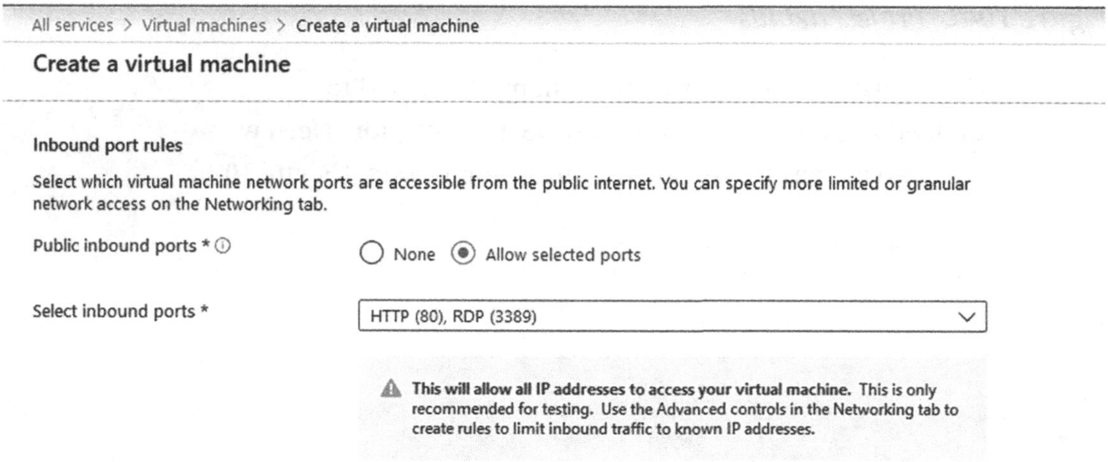

All services > Virtual machines > Create a virtual machine

Create a virtual machine

Inbound port rules

Select which virtual machine network ports are accessible from the public internet. You can specify more limited or granular network access on the Networking tab.

Public inbound ports * ⓘ   ◯ None ⦿ Allow selected ports

Select inbound ports * | HTTP (80), RDP (3389)   ∨ |

⚠ This will allow all IP addresses to access your virtual machine. This is only recommended for testing. Use the Advanced controls in the Networking tab to create rules to limit inbound traffic to known IP addresses.

Figure 10-10. *Inbound port rules*

9. Next, you can either click the Review + create button or the last tab, Review + create (Figure 10-11).

Basics   Disks   Networking   Management   Advanced   Tags   Review + create

Figure 10-11. *Available tabs in Create a virtual machine*

10. From the Create + Review tab, review the details of your VM, and then click Create. We have selected HTTP (80), so ignore any warning related to Internet access (Figure 10-12).

⚠ **You have set RDP port(s) open to the internet.** This is only recommended for testing. If you want to change this setting, go back to Basics tab.

Figure 10-12. *RDP port(s) warning*

Note   You can also download the VM Template (from the Review + create tab), to perform automation-related activities. We have created one template for our CoffeeFixDev VM and a related file (`template.zip`) is available in the source code for Chapter 10 at `www.apress.com/9781484254363`.

Now go to the CoffeeFixDev VM, click Connect, and download the RDP file. Log in to the Virtual Machine and verify that it is working well. From the Overview tab of the CoffeeFixDev VM screen, you can see a simple usage snapshot of the various resources of the Virtual Machine (Figure 10-13).

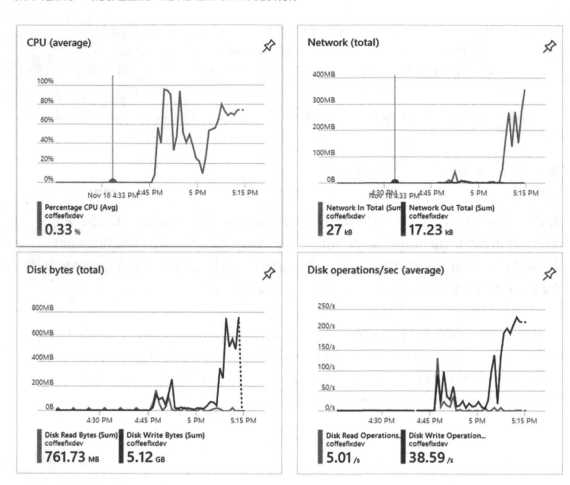

Figure 10-13. *Usage snapshot*

You can also commission Azure VMs using Azure PowerShell commands. To do so, you must go to Azure Cloud Shell, via the following link: `https://shell.azure.com/powershell`.

Note   To simplify our example, we used Azure Cloud Shell, which is a free interactive shell that can be used to run Azure PowerShell commands. However, we are not going to delve into the topic of creating Azure VMs using PowerShell, as this is out of scope for the book.

Please use your existing Microsoft Azure account to access Azure Cloud Shell. If you're new to using it, you will see the welcome screen. Click PowerShell (Figure 10-14).

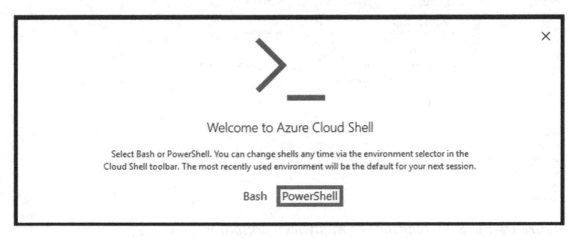

Figure 10-14. *The Azure Cloud Shell welcome screen*

Note   You can find the Azure PowerShell commands (file name: `CreateVM_PowerShell.md`) in the source code for Chapter 10 at `www.apress.com/9781484254363`.

The goal is to obtain more data, so that we can include it in the report to visualize the health of our VM. To make sure that all the resources are working as expected, we need to create a Log Analytics workspace. To do this, take the following steps:

1. From the Azure portal, go to All services.

2. From the Search text box, type "Log Analytics" and select *Log Analytics workspaces* from among the search results (Figure 10-15).

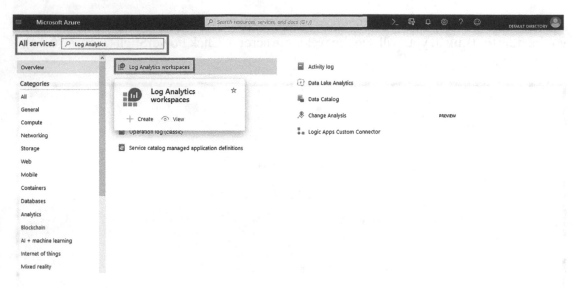

Figure 10-15. *Searching for Log Analytics workspaces*

3. Click Create log analytics workspace from the Log Analytics
    workspaces screen (Figure 10-16).

Figure 10-16. *The Create log analytics workspace button*

4. Now provide a valid name and select a resource. Note that you
    must select the location from which you have deployed your
    VM. In our case, we have deployed our VM in the East US region,
    so we select East US as our Location (Figure 10-17).

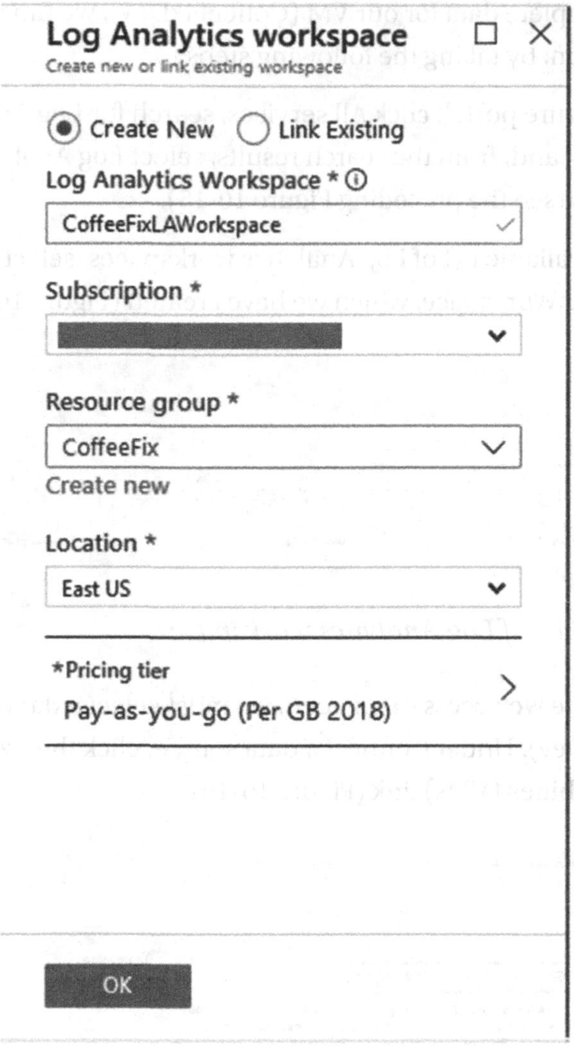

Log Analytics workspace   □ ✕
Create new or link existing workspace

◉ Create New   ○ Link Existing

Log Analytics Workspace * ⓘ

CoffeeFixLAWorkspace   ✓

Subscription *

████████████████████   ⌄

Resource group *

CoffeeFix   ⌄
Create new

Location *

East US   ⌄

*Pricing tier   ›
Pay-as-you-go (Per GB 2018)

OK

Figure 10-17. *Log Analytics workspace*

Note   If you have installed the Linux VM, the Log Analytics agent can only be configured for one Log Analytics workspace.

To collect the complete data for our VM (CoffeeFixDev), we must enable the Log Analytics VM extension, by taking the following steps:

1. From the Azure portal, click All services, search for Log Analytics workspaces, and, from the search results, select Log Analytics workspaces (see the preceding Figure 10-15).

2. From the available list of Log Analytics workspaces, select CoffeeFoxLAWorkspace, which we have created (Figure 10-18).

Figure 10-18. *The List of Log Analytics workspaces*

3. The first time we access this screen, we must select a data source (CoffeeFixDev). Under Connect a data source, click the Azure virtual machines (VMs) link (Figure 10-19).

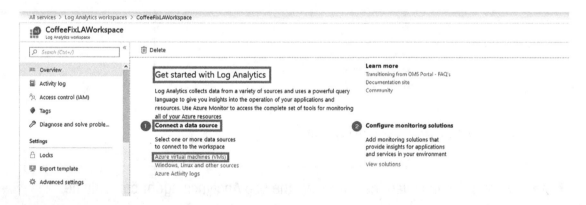

Figure 10-19. *Connecting a data source*

4. From the available list under Virtual machines, select CoffeeFixDev. The status of the Log Analytics connection is "Not connected" (Figure 10-20).

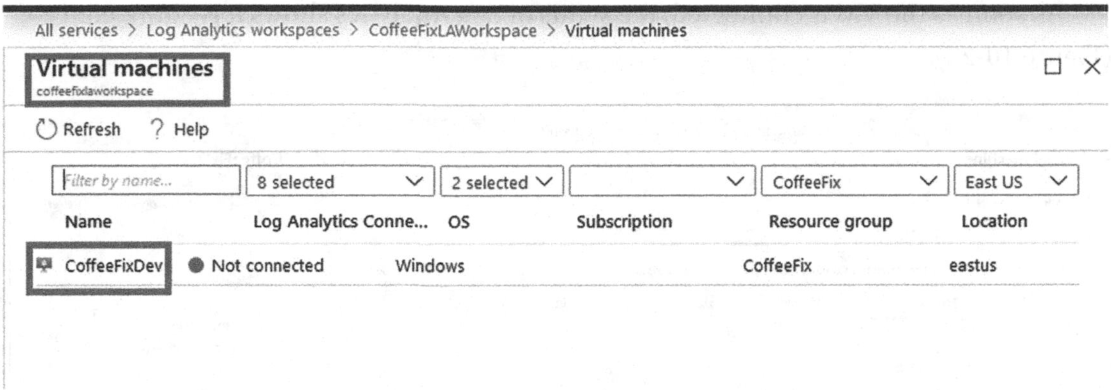

All services > Log Analytics workspaces > CoffeeFixLAWorkspace > Virtual machines

Virtual machines
coffeefixlaworkspace   □ ✕

○ Refresh   ? Help

Filter by name...	8 selected ∨	2 selected ∨		CoffeeFix ∨	East US ∨
Name	Log Analytics Conne...	OS	Subscription	Resource group	Location
🖵 CoffeeFixDev	● Not connected	Windows		CoffeeFix	eastus

Figure 10-20. *The list of available virtual machines for CoffeeFixLAWorkspace*

5. Click Connect (Figure 10-21).

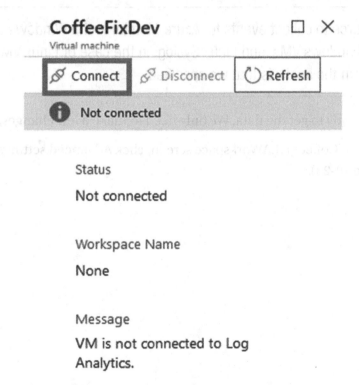

Figure 10-21. *Connecting CoffeeFixDev to Log Analytics*

As soon as the VM is connected, the status of Log Analytics shows it is connected (Figure 10-22).

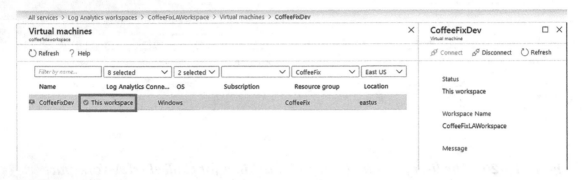

Figure 10-22. *CoffeeFixDev VM—The Log Analytics connection status*

Note   The source to collect events for Azure Monitor is the Windows event logs, in the case of Windows VMs, and Linux Syslog, in the case of Linux VMs. This data can then perform the analysis that we specified.

Now we are ready to get the data. We only need to make a few changes, as follows:

1.   From the CoffeeFixLAWorkspace screen, click Advanced settings (Figure 10-23).

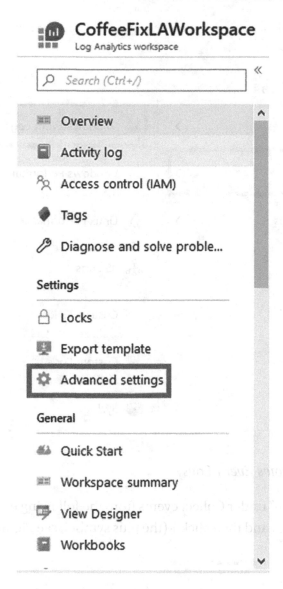

Figure 10-23. *CoffeeFixLAWorkspace—Advanced settings*

2. From the Advanced settings screen, click Data ➤ Windows Event
   Logs (Figure 10-24).

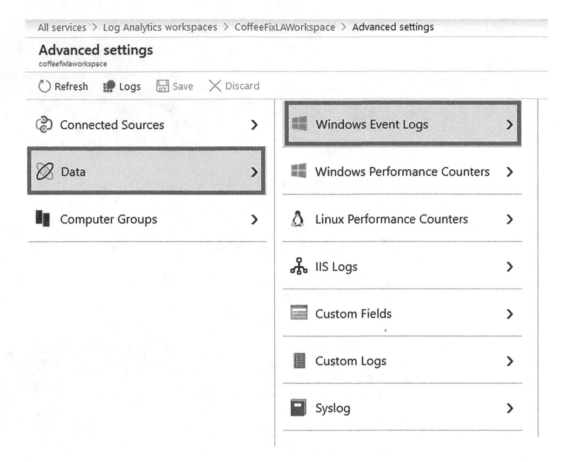

Figure 10-24. *Windows Event Logs*

3. Type "System" under Collect events from the following event logs, select System, and then click + (the plus symbol; see Figure 10-25).

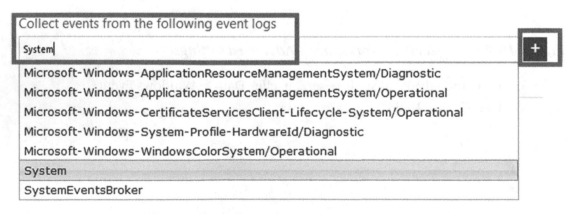

Figure 10-25. *Selecting event logs*

4. Finally, click Save (Figure 10-26).

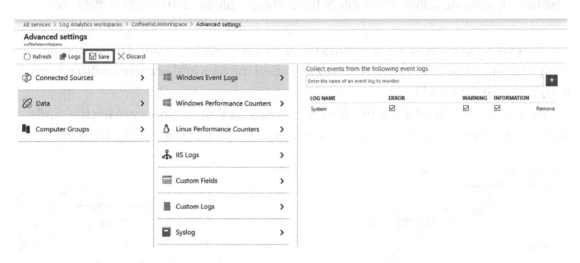

Figure 10-26. *Saving the settings*

5. Now, select Windows Performance Counters. This will enable the performance counters (see preceding Figure 10-24) from our CoffeeFixDev Windows VM. As this is the first time that we will be selecting Windows Performance Counters, we will see all the available options. Select all the counters you want (Figure 10-27).

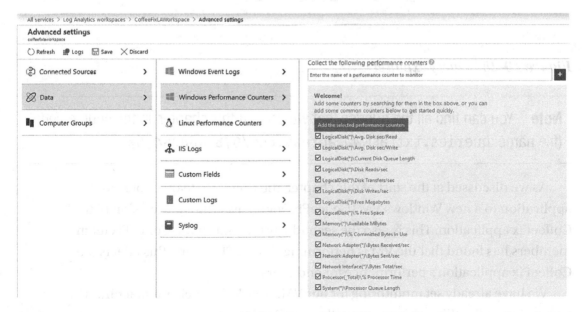

Figure 10-27. *Adding the selected performance counters*

Note   By default, common counters have preset values of 10-second intervals.

Now click Save and save the settings (see preceding Figure 10-26). The preceding setup steps must be followed so that we can collect the data and prepare health reports for our CoffeeFixDev VM.

Getting the log data for our machine is as simple as writing a query to fetch records from a table. Azure provides an editor to write and run these queries (Figure 10-28).

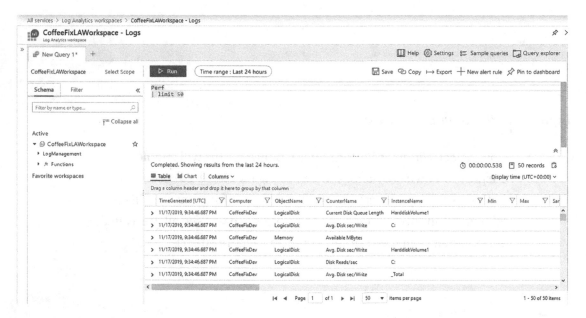

Figure 10-28.   *Query explorer*

Note   You can find all the queries that we used in this chapter, in the source code (file name: `queries.txt`) at `www.apress.com/9781484254363`.

As we discussed at the start of this chapter, the CoffeeFix team deployed its application to a new Windows VM (CoffeeFixDev). This is the new version of the CoffeeFix application. This is also the second day that one of the CoffeeFix team members has found that the VM is performing slowly. Therefore, this affects our CoffeeFix application's performance for end users.

We have already set monitoring for our VM. Now let's check our machine's performance. For this, we must query the logs (Listing 10-1).

Listing 10-1. Querying the Perf Table

```
Perf
| limit 50
```

The preceding query produces a result that allows us to analyze the data (Figure 10-29).

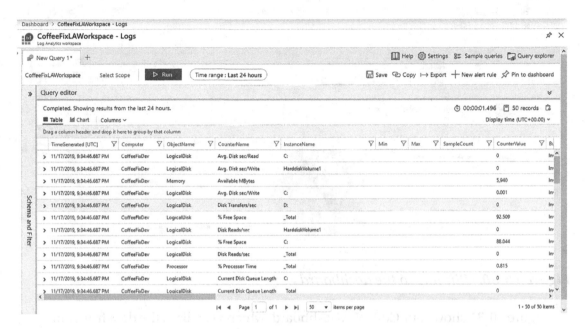

Figure 10-29. *Query result*

Let's narrow down the records and summarize them by column, to get a count (Listing 10-2).

Listing 10-2. Querying by `ObjectName` to Get a Count

```
Perf
| limit 10
| summarize count() by ObjectName
```

We can also visualize the report. Let's query the Event (Listing 10-3). From the available chart options, we pinned (Figure 10-30) the result to our CoffeeFixDashboard.

Listing 10-3. Query Event Table

```
Event
| where EventLevelName == "Information" or EventLevelName == "Error"
| summarize count() by Source
```

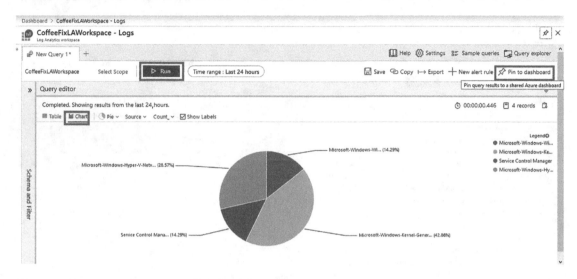

Figure 10-30. *Pinning to the dashboard*

Figure 10-31 shows our CoffeeFixDashboard, which visualizes the data from our CoffeeFixDev VM.

Figure 10-31. *CoffeeFixDashboard*

As we must check performance, we can get the relevant report data by using the code in Listing 10-4.

Listing 10-4. Query to Get the Processor Time

```
Perf
| where TimeGenerated > ago(1h)
| where (CounterName == "% Processor Time" and InstanceName == "_Total") or
  CounterName == "% Used Memory"
| project TimeGenerated, CounterName, CounterValue
| summarize avg(CounterValue) by CounterName, bin(TimeGenerated, 1m)
| render timechart
```

Figure 10-32 shows the data retrieved from Listing 10-4 in graph form.

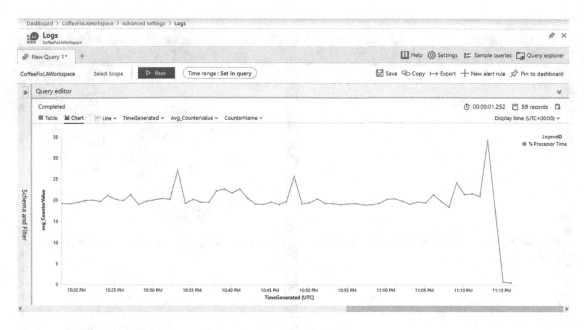

Figure 10-32. *Line chart—processor time of CoffeeFixDev VM*

Note   For a more detailed analysis, we must enable Insights. Note that this feature is currently in preview.

For a more detailed analysis, go to CoffeeFixDev ➤ Insights (preview). Figure 10-33 shows the logical disk performance data of the CoffeeFixDev VM for the preceding hour.

DISK	CURRE...	CURRE...	P95 I...	P95 I...	P95 I...	P95 ...	P95 ...	P95 M...	P95 LATE...	P95 LATEN...	P95 LATEN...
C:	126.51	12%	5.28	14.3	14.69	0.45	0.57	1.02	0.67	1.1	1.33
D:	100	2%	0	0	0	0	0	0	0	0	0
HarddiskVolume1	0.49	7%	0	0	0	0	0	0	0	0	0
Total	226.99	8%	5.28	14.3	14.69	0.45	0.57	1.02	0.67	1.1	1.33

Figure 10-33. *Logical disk performance data—CoffeeFix VM*

The CPU usage and memory usage of the CoffeeFixDev VM can also affect the performance. Figure 10-34 shows a graph of the CPU usage and the available memory of our VM.

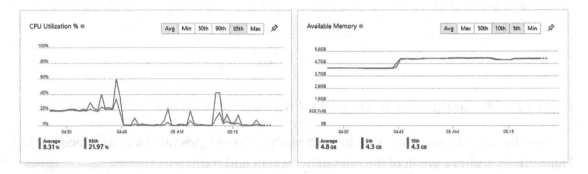

Figure 10-34. *CPU utilization and available memory charts*

If disk usage reaches 100%, we should be alarmed and determine what is eating our disk size. The chart of disk usage is very helpful in identifying the disk usage and the critical time when such usage is highest (Figure 10-35).

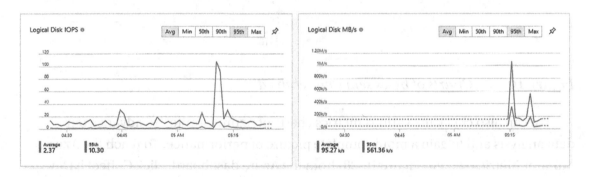

Figure 10-35. *Logical disk IOPS and MB/s charts*

Disk latency is also important for analysis that is related to checking the performance of the CoffeeFixDev VM (Figure 10-36).

Note   In simple terms, disk latency is the time delay from the disk input/output (I/O) request creation to completion. It indicates how quickly a system completes I/O requests.

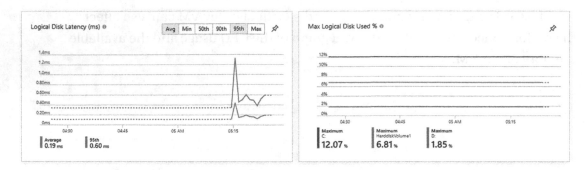

Figure 10-36. *Logical disk latency and disks used (%) charts*

Another performance measure for data analysis is the bytes rate (sent and received). Figure 10-37 shows a graph of the rates of bytes sent and received.

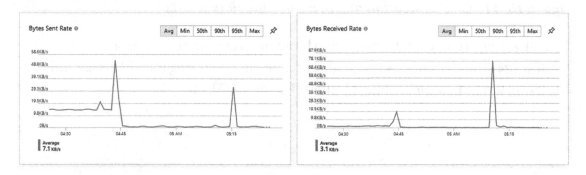

Figure 10-37. *Charts of bytes sent and received*

We can also check the various metrics charts of Azure Monitor, to advance our data analysis and to gain a more complete picture of performance. To reach the Azure Monitor Metrics screen (Figure 10-38) from the Azure dashboard, click CoffeeFixDev and then Metrics (from the left-hand navigation).

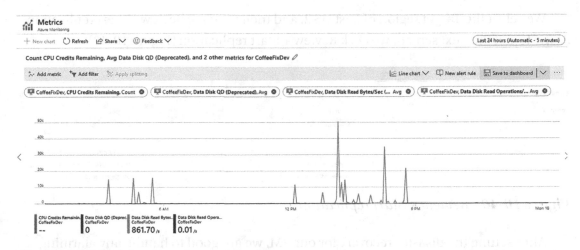

Figure 10-38. *Metrics—Azure Monitor*

Disaster Recovery for CoffeeFixDev

The CoffeeFix team has reported that we should be making some disaster recovery plans for our VM, so that we can handle and recover our system and resources in an emergency. To overcome disasters and provide solutions to the team, we have configured disaster recovery for the CoffeeFixDev Windows VM. From the Azure portal, we select Virtual machine CoffeeFixDev, and then we select Disaster recovery (Figure 10-39).

Figure 10-39. *Disaster recovery*

We select the Target region of East US 2, and then we click Review + Start replication. At the top of the next screen, we click Review + Start replication (Figure 10-40).

Figure 10-40. *Review + Start replication*

After setting the disaster recovery for our VM, we are good to handle any alarming situation. Our VM is replicating in two regions, East US and East US 2.

Monitoring the CoffeeFixWeb Application

The CoffeeFix team had received a complaint from stakeholders that they were not receiving reports of their stores. After the initial investigation of this issue, the production support team reported that the application was working fine, and they had been able to make requests and receive store reports.

Now we must analyze the log data received from Application Insights. (This was set up for our CoffeeFixWeb app in Chapter 4.) To do this, we make a request to generate a simple report. To generate a report, we will use an on-premises console application. First, we analyze the dependencies table (Listing 10-5).

Listing 10-5. Query Dependencies

```
dependencies
| limit 10
```

Listing 10-6 queries the dependencies table for unsuccessful API calls from on-premises applications to the CoffeeFixWeb application.

Listing 10-6. Unsuccessful API Calls

```
dependencies
| where success == false
| limit 10
```

Let's check the data and analyze it, to see whether calls are successful (Figure 10-41).

	timestamp [UTC]	id	target	type	name	data	success	resultCode
>	11/18/2019, 4:26:03.227 AM	J99b8665aa86d6a49959102810a6ca5f7.b90076f804c67448.	localhost	HTTP	POST /api/telemetry	https://localhost:5001/api/telemetry	False	500
>	11/18/2019, 4:19:02.633 AM	Jbdd21a4027239642b0c3746f37db449a.3ab8a23204b398...	localhost	HTTP	POST /api/telemetry	https://localhost:44371/api/telemetry	False	500
>	11/18/2019, 4:16:47.554 AM	Jd62c298fe22f2345a7a1813b7db43452.e290bde1fd82c648.	localhost	HTTP	POST /api/telemetry	https://localhost:44371/api/telemetry	False	500
>	11/18/2019, 4:17:21.816 AM	Jfc1a0a13d8774444b31e3721c6dd55b3.ad89bfb7734a61...	localhost	HTTP	POST /api/telemetry	https://localhost:44371/api/telemetry	False	500
>	11/18/2019, 3:55:47.743 AM	J2177c3271945bf4fa42d2c94cb2e13a5.02590c886363d248.	localhost	HTTP	POST /api/telemetry	https://localhost:44371/api/telemetry	False	500

Figure 10-41. Dependencies records

We found that all the calls have failed. So, we know that the request to CoffeeFixWeb is unsuccessful. Further analysis of data provided us with a reason for this issue (Figure 10-42). The issue was that a connection to Entity Framework wasn't established.

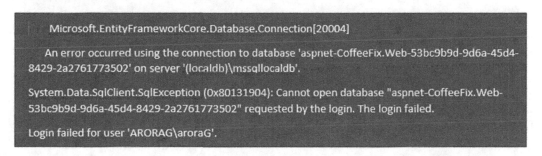

Figure 10-42. Error—Entity Framework Core connection failure

This section described the power of data analysis and of monitoring an application. These activities help ensure our application's health.

Summary

This chapter explored different ways of analyzing log data to monitor our VM and applications. This data also helps us to report and tackle any unexpected problems.

Index

A

Access tiers, 206
API management (APIM) services
    components, 92
    products, 93–98
    resource, creating, 92
    Tag, 99, 100
Application insights
    APM, 151
    Azure monitor, 159
    blade, 134
    CoffeeFix application
        control, 107
        DisableTelemetry property, 120
        Initialize() method, 112, 113
        ITelemetryProcessor instances, 119
        NuGet package, 106
        Package Manager Console, 105
        search, 108
        TelemetryClient, 106
        test suite, 121, 122
        tracking dependencies, 114, 116
        tracking failures, 116–118
    instrumentation key, 105
    live metrics, 160, 161
    monitor, 152
    performance, 161, 162
    portal
        application map, 123–125
        measuring failures, 128, 129

search, 130, 131, 134
    services, 104
    telemetry, 159
    TrackEvent method, 109–111
Application Performance Management
    (APM) service, 103, 151
Application telemetry, 19
App Service Environment (ASE), 150
App service plans
    alerts, 164
        action group, 167
        condition configuration, 166
        creation, 165
    metrics, 163, 164
    quotas, 162
Atomicity, consistency, isolation,
    durability (ACID), 178
Automatic tuning, 198
Azure Active Directory (Azure AD), 5
    activity reports, 232
    adding users and groups, 219–223
    audit logs, 232
    B2B, 217, 218
    B2C, 218, 219
    CoffeeFix web app
        authentication, 224, 226, 227
        registration, 227, 229–231
    MFA, 215
    Microsoft Graph, 217
    monitoring, 233

© Jeffrey Chilberto, Sjoukje Zaal, Gaurav Aroraa and Ed Price 2020
J. Chilberto et al., *Cloud Debugging and Profiling in Microsoft Azure*,
https://doi.org/10.1007/978-1-4842-5437-0

Printed in the United States
by Bookmasters

Printed in the United States
By Bookmasters